Advance Praise for *Sus*

"*Sushi Tuesdays* is an achingly beautiful memoir that I want to put in the hands of every person I know who has experienced grief. Actually, I want everyone who is human to read this marvel of a love story. Charlotte Maya unflinchingly brings light and hope to things most people are afraid to talk about. We need her voice. This book will stay with you long after the last page."

—Jennifer Pastiloff, National Bestselling
author of *On Being Human*

"*Sushi Tuesdays* is a story of hope and healing in the face of unspeakable sadness. With her exquisite writing, unflinching candor, and at times wry humor, Charlotte Maya shares her family's struggle with the abject sorrow of her husband's suicide and the winding path to recovery. It's a beautiful and poignant reminder that even in life's darkest times, daylight is within reach."

—Sam Farmer, *Los Angeles Times*

"*Sushi Tuesdays*, a stunningly honest and beautifully written memoir by Charlotte Maya, does the impossible: answers the question of how you survive after a loved one dies by suicide. One ordinary October Saturday, the author's husband of fifteen years jumped off a building while she and her young sons were at a soccer game, leaving her shocked, furious, and widowed. In an instant. Her account of the minutes, hours, days, months, and years after the suicide is unflinching, opening a window into the most intimate stages of grief that most of us would be too timid to ask about. There are lessons here for all of us, for those who have wondered about what it must be like absorb that kind of loss and for those of us who have experienced suicide in our own lives. As we learn from

Maya, moving forward involves anger, love, patience, therapy, friends, running, faith, and yes, sushi on Tuesdays."

—Lian Dolan, Author of *The Sweeney Sisters*
and Creator of the *Satellite Sisters* podcast

"'*Why?*' asks Charlotte Maya in this eloquent and heart-wrenching memoir of the aftermath of her forty-one year old husband's suicide. Left with two young sons to raise she also asks, '*What now?*' As she navigates the days, weeks, months, and years afterward, the *why* is never fully answered but she moves forward through grief, therapy, dealing with extended family, and caring for her boys to discover an unexpected *what now*. Written with grace, grit, and dark humor, Maya's journey through her own grief offers comfort to anyone whose partner has died. To those who are surviving parents of young children it offers even more—the kids can get through it too. This is a story ultimately of love, hope and gratitude."

—Barbara Abercrombie, Advanced Memoir instructor
in the Writers' Program at UCLA Extension and Author of
sixteen books and the Editor of *The Language of Loss: Poetry
& Prose for Grieving & Celebrating the Love of Your Life*

"A heartbreakingly beautiful story of loss and resurrection of both family and faith, shared with generosity of spirit and heart, and the assurance that the deepest wounds in life can, with work, be healed by love."

—Shannon Huffman Polson, author of
North of Hope: A Daughter's Arctic Journey

"Gripping, beautiful, and inspiring. An absolutely stunning memoir from the first page to the last!!"

—Kim Bergman, PhD, Licensed Psychologist, Senior partner of Growing Generations and author of *Your Future Family: The Essential Guide to Assisted Reproduction, You Began as a Wish,* and the upcoming, *Psychological and Medical Perspectives on Fertility Care and Sexual Health*

"Everyone knows someone who has taken their own life…and everyone knows someone who is thinking about it—whether we know it or not. But we don't talk about it. Ever. And that silence isolates. That silence kills.

I wish I had read *Sushi Tuesdays* twenty years ago when I had to preside at the funeral of a college student who had taken his life. I wish I had read it three years ago when a parishioner of mine jumped off a bridge leaving his wife and young child behind. I wish I had read it and I wish I had had it to give to those who were going through this nightmare because it is simply the best, most honest memoir of suicide I can possibly imagine.

From the very first chapter, Charlotte Maya gently invites us into the brutality of someone you love taking their own life. *Sushi Tuesdays* is vulnerable without being self-indulgent. It is raw without being grisly. She masterfully captures the complexity of the emotions and experiences she held and still holds in tension, resisting the temptation to tie it up in a bow. Her pain and rage is as real as her hope and love. This book changed me…and I am deeply grateful for it and for her.

Sushi Tuesdays should be required reading in every seminary…and really for every person. Because everyone knows someone who has taken their own life. Everyone knows someone who is closer to it than we think."

—The Rev. Mike Kinman, Rector, All Saints Episcopal Church, Pasadena, CA

"*Sushi Tuesdays* captures the beautiful ache of being human. If you're in the depths of loss, wondering how you will open your heart again, this book is for you. Charlotte Maya is a stunning writer who shows us how to hold space for grief with unflinching truth and love."

—Nadine Kenney Johnstone, author, writing
coach, and *Heart of the Story* podcast host

"In *Sushi Tuesdays*, Charlotte Maya offers us a glimpse into the lives of her and her young sons in the devastating aftermath of her husband's suicide. With unflinching honesty and unexpected humor, Maya shares her family's journey from overwhelming grief to surprising new beginnings. It's not a spoiler to say love wins."

—April Dávila, award-winning author of *142 Ostriches*
and co-founder of A Very Important Meeting

SUSHI TUESDAYS

A Memoir *of* Love, Loss, *and* Family Resilience

Charlotte Maya

Post Hill
PRESS

A POST HILL PRESS BOOK
ISBN: 978-1-63758-727-0
ISBN (eBook): 978-1-63758-728-7

Sushi Tuesdays:
A Memoir of Love, Loss, and Family Resilience
© 2023 by Charlotte Maya
All Rights Reserved

Cover design by Tiffani Shea

Post Hill Press
New York • Nashville
posthillpress.com

Published in the United States of America
1 2 3 4 5 6 7 8 9 10

For My One

CONTENTS

If you or someone you know is experiencing suicidal thoughts, please call the Suicide Prevention Lifeline at 988 or text HOME to the Crisis Text Line at 741741. Help is available; please ask.

Tis a Fearful Thing
by Yehuda HaLevi (1075–1141)
translated by Chaim Stern

'Tis a fearful thing
to love what death can touch.

A fearful thing
to love, to hope, to dream, to be—
to be,
And oh, to lose.

A thing for fools, this,
And a holy thing,
a holy thing
to love.

For your life has lived in me,
your laugh once lifted me,
your word was gift to me.

To remember this brings painful joy.

'Tis a human thing, love,
a holy thing, to love
what death has touched.

CHAPTER 1

FALL IN SOUTHERN CALIFORNIA (2007)

It would have been a perfectly ordinary Saturday if only my husband had taken a nap like he said he was going to.

Six-year-old Jason skipped into the family room dressed in the ubiquitous AYSO shirt and shorts, holding his "shin-kickers" and cleats.

"They're shin-*protectors*," said Danny, as authoritative as only an eight-year-old can be. "I can kick you in the shins and it won't even hurt. See?" He lifted one foot and pretended to take aim at his little brother.

"Mommy!"

"All right, gentlemen, let's go." I was a suburban soccer mom with a clipboard and a bob haircut. Juggling snacks, a camera, and the soccer gear, I turned to my husband. "Sure you don't want to join us?"

Sam looked vaguely amused at our shenanigans. But mostly he looked stressed, and his wide brown eyes were rimmed red with exhaustion.

"No," he said. "You go ahead. I'll stay here and take a nap."

Good idea, I thought.

Danny offered to stay home with Daddy, hoping to avoid watching his brother's game. Sam shook his head. Danny resigned himself to an hour's boredom, protesting the sport of soccer in general and wishing he were playing baseball instead.

I ushered the boys toward the door. "We'll meet Daddy at Berge's after," I said, bribing my children with their favorite lunch. "And then we'll all go for a hike."

Danny looked thoughtful. "Can I get a tuna melt?"

They did make great tuna melts—crispy sourdough, the warm cheddar just soft. I could already taste it.

"I want turkey!" Jason hollered, and bounced out of the house.

Sam half smiled his amusement and shook his head. After seventeen years together, I knew what he was thinking. The boys had inherited my obsession with food. I thought about lunch and planned dinner while I was eating breakfast. I loved to eat and to cook. Sam couldn't even begin to think about food until he was actually hungry, which, in my opinion, was entirely too late. The biggest fight we ever had, early in our dating days, was the result of postponing a meal for too long. Ever since, if Sam thought I was being unreasonable, he would gently ask, "When was the last time you ate?" And I would scowl and grab a snack, secretly pleased that he knew me so well.

I turned to my husband to give him a kiss. His normally bright eyes looked muted and far away, as if he was having trouble focusing. It seemed almost as if he was about to cry, except that Sam rarely cried.

"Get some rest," I said. "I'll call you after the game."

"Bye, Daddy!" the boys shouted from the driveway before they climbed into our Ford Expedition "Mommy Edition," stocked with organic granola bars, stick sunscreen, and sand toys. No sooner was I down the block when I remembered there was a UCLA football game that day. The corresponding Rose Bowl traffic would dictate our route. I flipped open my phone and dialed Sam's number without looking. I knew it by heart.

He didn't know where the Bruins were playing or who they were playing against. It surprised me that my Bruin-loving husband didn't know what time the UCLA game was. That's how I knew he was worn out. I decided to avoid the Rose Bowl just in case. I told him to go back to sleep.

"Bye, sweetie, I love you."

"Bye, sweetie, I love you," he mirrored.

We always said our goodbyes the same way. Sam was my constant. Just the week before, I had been cleaning out a drawer of cards he had given me over the years—birthday, anniversary, Mother's Day, no-par-ticular-occasion-I-love-you cards—which had grown into a giant stack. I selected a few favorites to keep and threw the rest away, thinking I had a lifetime ahead of me of handwritten cards from my husband and not nearly enough storage space in my desk to hold them all. I had done the same with his voicemail messages, deleting them almost as soon as I listened to them, not realizing that one day they would stop, that one day I would no longer be able to retrieve his voice.

I didn't know when we ended that call that it would be our last goodbye.

Sam did.

* * *

When we arrived at the soccer field, Jason ricocheted out of the car like a rogue marble and ran to join his team. Danny ambled off to find a friend.

Coach Ben corralled the Green Goblins, a team of six-year-olds buzzing with energy. They played soccer like a hive of fluorescent green and navy-blue bees, swarming the ball in its erratic path up and down the field. Ben had a *laissez-faire* attitude and a British upbringing, which rendered him the obvious choice to coach the young boys' team.

It was a gorgeous fall day: clear blue sky, not too hot but not too cold, a gentle breeze. As most of our daily forecasts go, it was "Mostly sunny, no chance of rain." This is why we paid the Southern California "weather tax." It's a joyous climate. As the Green Goblins started to play, I set up a camp chair on the sidelines. Danny grabbed our soccer ball and went to the far side of the field to kick around.

Ben's wife Linda arrived with their toddler on her hip. A pretty petite blonde, she was nervous about all manner of evil that could befall her children. Ben joked that she would still keep them safely *in utero* if she could.

"Where's Sam?" she asked.

"Taking a nap. He was up late working. The stock market fell three hundred and sixty points yesterday."

Linda shook her head sympathetically. Then she set up her chair next to mine and sat down. "How is your work going?"

"The transition is hard," I admitted. It had been a logical time for me to go back to practicing law part-time. With the boys in first and third grades, they finally had similar schedules at the same school. "I will confess, though, that it is gratifying for the boys to see me in a different light. I'm not just the purveyor of PB&J. I had a court appearance first thing Thursday morning, and when the boys saw me wearing a suit and heels, they were shocked. Danny said, 'Mommy! You really *are* a lawyer!'"

Linda laughed. I felt my throat constrict around what I didn't say: I would have preferred to be home full-time with my boys and a third baby. Sam and I had stopped using birth control, and I was two days late. But even if I was pregnant, not working was no longer an option. Sam had become increasingly concerned about our finances.

Linda's toddler squealed and squirmed to the ground to wobble-walk toward his daddy on the field. She got up and gently guided him back along the sidelines.

I snapped a few pictures on my digital camera of Jason and the Green Goblins, Linda and her little one, and Danny laughing and kicking the ball.

I called Sam after the game. He didn't answer his phone, and I was grateful that he was letting himself rest. I left a voicemail to let him know we were heading to lunch, hoping he would meet us there. The boys hollered in the background so Daddy could hear their munchkin voices: "See you soon, Daddy!" "We won!" "No, you didn't!" "Did too!" "Come have lunch with us!"

All of us ended with "I love you."

The hometown sandwich shop was adjacent to the junior high school I attended when my family first moved to La Cañada, and the proprietress "Queenie" sat at her designated table, doing her accounting and greeting the community. The walls were covered with plaques of AYSO soccer and peewee baseball teams Berge's had sponsored over the years. I was not the only patron who came here as a kid and now brought her own children.

Queenie welcomed us and commented, as people often did, that we had a "hers" and a "his." Danny was blond and blue-eyed, just like me and my Swiss mother. Jason looked uncannily like his Cuban father, with round brown eyes and olive skin. Their coloring was so opposite that a stranger once asked me if my sons had different fathers.

I smiled at Queenie and tousled their hair. "It's true. We've got one vanilla and one chocolate!"

***

When we arrived home with Sam's tuna melt to-go, his car was missing from his normal parking spot in front of the house. *Weird,* I thought. I would have expected him to be home. *Maybe he went to the office?* I called again. Again, no answer. I left another voicemail. "Hey sweetie! Where'd you go? We're going to go hike soon. Hope you can join us!"

Had he forgotten about the hike?

I felt my chest start to tighten. It was unusual that Sam had left without calling me, but I also knew that sometimes he liked to drive and think. His car was a place of solace for him. More than once, he had taken a nap in his car, where he could rest undisturbed.

I waited a bit, delaying our start—but we would lose daylight if we didn't hit the trail soon. I was disappointed that he would miss out on the hike, but I appreciated that he needed time to himself, away from the demands of both work and home.

I left another voicemail, so Sam wouldn't worry about us when he returned to an empty house. "We're heading out for our hike. We've got the dog with us. I love you, sweetie."

I leashed up our black and tan Cavalier King Charles Spaniel, loaded up the kids, and drove to the trailhead.

"I want to hold Parker's leash!" Naturally, our family dog was named after a superhero (Peter Parker, aka Spider-Man).

"No, me!"

"Let's both hold it!"

"Okay!"

I never got tired of the combination of the boys and their dog, all eight of their feet kicking up a dust flurry of joy and mess. If everybody ended the day with grass-stained knees and covered in mud, that was a good day.

A hiker coming off the trail looked at our pandemonium and said something I couldn't quite understand. He approached us, looking serious. "There's a baby rattler up around that corner."

"A rattlesnake?"

"Yeah, right in the middle of the trail. Be sure to hold on to the pup."

We continued on our way, and sure enough, up and around the bend lay the baby snake, only a few shades of brown darker than the dusty trail. Baby rattlers are particularly dangerous because they are quick to strike. Their rattles not yet developed, they sound no warning. Thank goodness the hiker alerted us.

"Mommy!" Danny urged. "Pick up Parker!" Dogs are the most common victims of snakebites, so I grabbed our fifteen-pound designer dog and held him under my arm.

We stood back cautiously and admired the baby rattler. It was beautiful, in a vulnerable and lethal kind of way. That snake—barely the length of a ruler—held venom potent enough to jeopardize a human life. Strangely, a young rattler's bite doesn't swell, so its victim might not realize the danger until it's too late for an antidote. Meanwhile, the victim hemorrhages internally, invisible from the outside.

The rattler relaxed in the warmth of the sun, even as the fall days were shortening. It was not interested in us. Giving it a wide berth, we walked around the snake and continued up the trail. As I guided my sons around the viper, I thought, *Safety Dad is going to kill me!* As protective as he was, Sam might even have turned around at that point on the trail, and I wondered if there was any chance that the boys wouldn't rat me out when we got home.

We continued up the trail until we reached a little pond. I sat on a nearby rock, enjoying the soothing splash of the stream descending from the pond. Parker wagged and sniffed. Danny sat next to me, contemplative. Jason squatted at the edge of the water, his shoes covered in mud, and caught a tiny, greenish-brown frog.

"Mommy! Take a picture of my frog so we can show Daddy!" Jason held his small, soft hands up toward me, and I snapped a photograph.

Danny wondered aloud, "Mommy, do you think it hurts the tadpoles when they turn into frogs? Or do they get excited for the transformation? Do they even know? Maybe they wake up surprised. Like, whoa! Where did my tail go? And then they look into their froggy mirrors in the pond, and they don't know their new names."

I wished I had a pen and paper to write this stuff down so I could tell Sam later. He had a better memory than I did for the funny things our children said.

Jason interrupted. "No, Parker! Don't eat my frog!"

It was time to put the beleaguered frog back in the pond. Jason gently coaxed the frog off his hand and back toward the water. "Bye, froggy! You'll be safe here. We're going now."

With thoughts of dinner and Daddy, we headed back down the trail. As the sun descended, the temperature cooled. We passed where the snake had been, and I was relieved to see the rattler had retreated. *Surely Sam has returned my call by now*, I thought, knowing that the reception in the mountains was so poor I would not have received it while we were hiking. As we got into the parking lot, I checked my phone. Nothing from Sam, although there was a missed call from a number I didn't recognize.

I called again. Still no answer.

Ever since Sam had been seriously injured in a car accident ten years earlier, I could go from zero to abject panic in no time flat. Sam helped me manage my anxiety with frequent calls and emails. We never went a full day without checking in, not usually more than a few hours, and now I hadn't heard from him all day. I didn't want to alarm the boys, but something felt very wrong. I steadied myself with a few deep breaths. I talked myself down. *He's fine*, I reassured myself. *I'm sure he's home.* But I could feel my heart beating faster and the panic rising. I focused on seeing his car in its normal place, parked in front of the house. Once I spotted his sensible used Volvo, I would know that he was safely inside. Danny and Jason were chirping in the backseat, but I heard them only as a distant soundtrack. All I could think about was getting home to Sam.

I turned the corner and looked down my street. Sam's car was missing. Instead, parked in his spot was a police car. Blue and red lights flashed silently. I held my breath. I moved in slow motion. As I drew close enough to see the front of my house, I could see that the chairs on my front porch were empty. *If the police were at my house*, I thought, *they would be sitting in those chairs; and since they're not, then they must be at a different house.* I exhaled. My shoulders relaxed. *Oh thank God. It's one of the neighbors.* Not my most charitable moment, but I was relieved that the emergency belonged to somebody else.

I pulled into the driveway, and there they stood: a policewoman, a policeman, and a priest. When they saw me, the three figures adjusted stiffly, official and expectant.

My mind reeled. *Oh, no no no no. They don't belong here.* For a fleeting second, I considered backing out of the driveway, but it was too late.

I focused on one little square of white in a field of black, something so terribly out of place that I couldn't take my eyes off it. *Where is Sam? What is going on? Why isn't he calling me back?*

I kept staring at that clerical collar. *A priest?!*

I shifted into park and cut the engine. I didn't want the boys to hear what the trio had to say. I didn't want to hear it, either, but I had to protect my sons from whatever this was.

"Boys, stay here." I slammed the car door closed, then hesitated. None of the uniforms were smiling. "My children are in the car."

The female officer took a step forward. "They need to talk to you inside," she said, gesturing toward her partner and the priest. Her tone was cordial but businesslike. "I'll watch the boys," she continued. It was not a request.

How did she know I have boys? What I said was "my children."

The men ushered me into the house, pushing the front door open.

Why was the front door already unlocked?

"Please sit down," the priest said. I looked from the white clerical collar to his face. He had kind eyes.

I didn't move.

I didn't want to sit down. *If I keep standing, maybe they won't tell me,* I thought, as if I could stretch time to a standstill. I didn't want to hear what the white collar had to say.

"Please," the officer said gently, leading me toward the sofa as though I were a guest in his living room. As though he had already planned out how this conversation was going to go. His stiff blue uniform seemed unnaturally free from wrinkles.

I sat. I looked down at the folded hands on my knees. I could see my fingers, but I couldn't feel them. I closed my eyes and exhaled. I opened my eyes and looked up at the gleaming badge.

The officer spoke. "You are Charlotte Maya?"

I nodded.

"I am very sorry to inform you that your husband is dead. He jumped from a parking structure in Pasadena earlier this afternoon."

I held my breath. My legs went numb, as if all the blood in my body was rushing toward my heart and lungs, willing one more beat, another breath.

I shook my head. "No. No. No."

He didn't. Not Sam. He wouldn't.

"I'm sorry, ma'am."

This isn't real. Sam's not dead. It's somebody else.

"Sam Maya?" I confirmed.

The officer looked at me and nodded. "Yes."

"No," I said, still shaking my head.

"I'm sorry, ma'am."

It was as if I physically couldn't hear what the officer said. My brain was willing his words away. I repeated his words back to him, but they didn't make sense.

"Sam killed himself? It wasn't an accident?"

"No, ma'am." He was exceedingly patient.

I tried to pinch one hand with the other but felt nothing. A thought occurred to me, something that would make what was happening even worse. *Had they separated my children from me to remove them from my custody?*

"Maybe I've watched too much *Law & Order*, but am I in trouble?"

He looked as though he wished he could smile but didn't. Still, I was relieved when he assured me that I was not a suspect in my husband's death.

I asked if they needed me to identify the body. He told me it wouldn't be necessary. "I'm sorry to have to ask," he said, "but do you know why he would have taken his own life?"

"He didn't sleep last night. He mentioned something about people losing money." I thought he meant clients. I didn't know whether we had lost money, too.

The officer watched me carefully, the way a person might look while explaining a new concept to a young child, or to someone who spoke a foreign language. Then he continued, "He left a note." He handed me a white piece of paper. "It's a really nice one."

I recognized Sam's handwriting, but I could hardly comprehend what I was reading:

Dear Charlotte,

Loving you and helping bring Danny and Jason into the world has been my greatest joy and accomplishment.

You have been an amazing wife and you are the best mother in the universe. Danny and Jason need you without the burden of me.

Please tell Danny and Jason that I love them with all my heart. And I love you with all my heart.

I'm so sorry.

I LOVE YOU.

Sam

My eyes blurred. I couldn't bear it. I heard myself saying no over and over, shaking my head. *No. No. No.*

"We often see much worse," the officer said. He explained that most suicides don't leave notes, and the ones that do are ugly, blaming others for their own misery and untimely death. This information did nothing to comfort me.

"It's not exactly the love note I would have wanted."

He then informed me that they kept the original note as evidence. The note in my hand was a "cleaned-up photocopy."

I looked up from the paper in my hand. "Can I see him?"

The policeman held my eyes with his gaze, pointedly trying to convey a silent message. Then he shook his head slowly back and forth, indicating no, still keeping eye contact. But the words he said—the words he was required to say—were "You can."

My stomach clenched, comprehending. "It's not pretty, is it?"

"No, ma'am, it's not."

I will never see my husband again. I wanted to throw up.

"How am I going to I tell my children?"

He exhaled slowly, closed his eyes momentarily, and then looked at me. He spoke carefully. "We will tell the boys *that* their father died, but you will have to tell them *how*. And we recommend that you tell them the truth, because you do not want them to find out what happened from somebody else."

I looked at the officer for a long moment. What he said made sense, and yet the fact that he was standing in front of me made no sense at all. "Do you have children?"

"I do."

"I'll bet you hug them extra tight on days like this."

"I do."

"I can't feel my legs."

"That's normal."

"I don't think any part of this evening has been normal."

"I'm sorry," the policeman continued. "This is the worst part of our job."

"It's not much fun from my side, either."

He then advised, "Don't assume that because Sam killed himself that you are not entitled to his life insurance."

My brain couldn't process all the information. It was too much, like a freeway's worth of rush-hour traffic funneled through a single lane. It would take hours to hear what he had said in the last few minutes, and yet it boiled down to three words: Sam was dead.

"Do you have family close by?" he asked.

"My parents live in Ventura, and my sister lives downtown."

"Anyone closer?"

"Dave and Nancy. They live around the corner." They were close friends from church—so close that Danny and Jason called them "Uncle Dave" and "Aunt Nancy." Dave was an attorney who had tried to talk me out of going to law school. Nancy was the elementary school librarian who knew the name, reading level, and favorite book of each child at her school. The officer nodded and wrote down their names and phone number, then helped me to my feet and walked me to my bedroom. "We'll talk to the kids," he said, "and then bring them to you."

I settled into my oversized reading chair and sat there, shocked. I could not wrap my mind around the idea that Sam was dead. *He jumped. He jumped off a parking structure adjacent to his office building.*

Another idea hit me. *Sam lied to me. He never lied to me. He said he was going to take a nap. Whose idea was that—mine or his?* I couldn't remember. It seemed so logical, because he hadn't slept at all the night before. I had taken both boys to the game so he could take a nap. *Was that the opening he was looking for? Why didn't he just take a nap? What if he had gotten some sleep?*

This isn't happening. But it did happen.

I pictured Sam sitting on a barstool at the kitchen island writing the note. *Is that what he was working on last night?* I imagined the white paper, wrinkled from having been stuffed in his pocket, or maybe held tightly in his hand. Then I imagined an officer finding the blood-spattered note on the sidewalk near Sam's body.

Sam mentioned people losing money yesterday. Did they? How much? Was it his fault? What did he do?

My thoughts flitted. *There must be a way to turn back the clock. There is no way Sam would have killed himself. I have to find a way back to this morning. He was here this morning. Just a few hours ago. He was supposed to take a nap, meet us for lunch, and go with us on the hike.*

I thought back to the tears in Sam's eyes and how strange they seemed. Sam was rarely outwardly emotional. He hardly ever cried. The man did not laugh out loud, and he was not prone to tears. I could count on one hand the number of times I had seen my husband cry: 1) After seeing his dying uncle and knowing it would be the last time, 2) During the first dance at our wedding, 3) Upon Danny's birth, 4) And Jason's, and 5) On the day he died. I thought those bloodshot eyes were evidence of how exhausted he was. Only then did I understand he had been crying.

Should I have stayed home to make sure he took a nap? What if I had gone to the game with Jason and left Danny home with him? Would Sam have taken a nap then? Or would he have taken Danny with him? I learned later that when the police couldn't reach me on the phone, they used Sam's house keys, as per protocol, to check his home to make sure it wasn't a murder-suicide. That's why the door was unlocked. They went through my home and saw the piles of laundry, the dog's dish on the floor, the family pictures hanging on the wall. That's how the policewoman knew I had sons. She knew before I did that our lives as we knew them were over.

When she brought my sons to me, I scooped them into my arms. Their confused faces looked to me for answers. I could not fall apart; these little ones were depending on me. I went into Mommy mode. With a child tucked under each arm, I told them what little I knew. I told them the truth. The truth of Sam's life—that he loved them dearly.

And the truth of his death—that he killed himself by jumping from the top of a tall building.

It was the hardest thing I have ever done.

Danny asked, "Did somebody push him?" The idea of suicide was unfathomable.

"No, sweetheart."

The young boy was incredulous. He screwed up his face, trying to understand. "Daddy did that," he paused, the idea so ludicrous it could hardly be articulated, "*to himself?*"

It didn't make any sense.

"Are you *sure* he wasn't pushed?"

That would certainly have made more sense.

Jason asked, "Daddy would rather die than go to my soccer game?"

My heart shattered. How on earth were my children supposed to make sense of their father's suicide?

As I held them, I heard myself say, "Your father's love for you will protect you for your entire life." These words rang true. I hoped we would find comfort in them.

The police and the priest must have welcomed Dave and Nancy into my home, because when I looked up, I saw all five of them standing at the edge of my bedroom, listening to my conversation with the boys. They nodded their approval. There was no pretense of privacy in those terrible moments of our lives, laid bare before our dear friends and complete strangers alike.

The police and the priest had now completed their assignment—taking care of Sam's body, cataloguing his belongings, notifying me, and calling in my crisis support team. It was time for them to go. The policeman gave me his business card, an identification number for the police report, and the telephone number for the County Coroner's office. The priest handed me his business card as well. I took them, tentatively. It would be years before I could look at a gold police badge or a white clerical collar without shaking and bursting into tears.

"You take care of yourself now, ma'am," said the policeman.

They returned to their lives, and I was left with mine.

CHAPTER 2

THE LONGEST NIGHT

It was dark. I had no idea how long we had been home with the police. Our hike felt like a distant memory. We had lost the soccer ball at the field earlier; it had seemed important at the time.

Dave wrapped me in a bear hug. At almost 5'9", I am tall enough to have flirted with a career in modeling. Dave dwarfed me. I was keenly aware of my own powerlessness. Part of me longed to collapse, but I wouldn't allow myself to. I had two sons who needed me.

Dave handed me to Nancy, and she held me for an extended moment. My same height and build, she had been mistaken for my older sister before. The woman radiated tenderness, and it would have been easy to stay in her embrace. Uncharacteristically, she pulled back. Then, with her hands grasping each of my shoulders, she focused her blue eyes on mine and said, "This is going to sound really unfair, but you are going to have to comfort a lot of people."

She was right. It sounded completely unfair.

***

Somebody had to tell Sam's parents that their only son was dead. That somebody should have been me, but I couldn't bear to tell my in-laws that their forty-one-year-old son had killed himself.

I needed Zack.

Technically, Sam and Zack were cousins, but their relationship was more like brothers. Six months apart in age, Sam and Zack were raised together, inseparable friends, sleeping over at each other's houses almost every weekend. They grew up to be each other's closest confidants and best men in each other's weddings. I met Zack practically within minutes of meeting Sam. My first dinner date with Sam was a double date with Zack. He was also a lawyer—bright, insightful, and big-hearted. Zack wanted to save the world, or at least, our corner of the world, or at least his own family (and his definition of family was expansive). I could tell immediately when Sam was on the phone with Zack from the prolonged "Heyyy" that they used to greet each other. It made me smile, their silly call and response, *Heyyy, Heyyy, Heyyy,* each progressively lower.

Somebody called Zack. I'm pretty sure it was Dave.

Somehow, I was holding the phone to my ear. A stunned Zack sputtered on the other end of the line. "What did he say?"

"He said he was going to take a nap."

"I mean, did he say why?"

"No, he just…He left a note. He said he was sorry. And now he's gone." I repeated what I couldn't believe.

I begged Zack to tell Sam's parents.

Sometime later—half an hour, maybe longer—Zack called me back from the landing in front of my in-laws' apartment in the Mid-Wilshire area of Los Angeles. Rabbi Jonathan was with him. "Stay on the line," Zack said. "I'll tell them now."

I heard Zack knock on their door. I heard elderly voices chattering over television dialogue and the scuffling of feet about to be interrupted by impossible news. I imagined that my in-laws took one look at their nephew's face and knew that something was terribly wrong. The rabbi's presence confirmed their worst fears.

I heard Sam's mother Eleana in the background. *"Está muerto?"*

She could not understand what Zack and Rabbi Jonathan were saying. She started shrieking, *"Está muerto?" Is he dead?* It was horrific. *"Se mató?" Did he kill himself?*

I held the phone to my ear, eavesdropping on their hearts breaking. With each blink, my tears spilled recklessly to the floor.

* * *

It was a miracle my own mother didn't get a speeding ticket in the seventy-five miles between her home and mine. She drove the way every mother races to the side of her child in distress. My parents arrived on my doorstep, shaken and speechless, armed with a pair of toothbrushes, a change of clothes, and a Christian Science periodical stuffed into my mother's purse.

* * *

My sons looked so small, so vulnerable. They needed baths and books and bedtime, a familiar and comforting routine. That night, the three of us put on jammies and crawled into Danny's queen-sized bed with a stack of picture books and the dog. Eventually, Danny and Jason fell asleep, their warm bodies curled up next to mine. I listened to their soft, rhythmic breathing. I thanked God for them. I clung to my boys as they held onto me in their sleep. I tried to relax into their breathing patterns, brushing the hair from their warm foreheads, wiping their tear-streaked faces, praying beyond hope that this wasn't happening to them.

I didn't sleep. The shock froze me in place. When I closed my eyes, I imagined Sam falling. I saw tears in his swollen eyes. I opened my eyes to beat back the images of his body broken on the sidewalk.

I watched the boys' chests rising and falling with their breaths in the dark, too young to bear the weight of their daddy's death. I leaned closer and breathed in the baby-shampoo scent of their little heads, assuring myself of their physical presence. *They're here. They're mine. We're here. Sam's gone. He's dead. He cannot be dead. He was just here. He was right here.* My heart quickened. *Maybe the police missed something? Maybe the doctor made a mistake? No. They said no.* I tried to wrap my head around the words, "Your husband is dead."

Really? Dead?

Dead. Really.

Dead can't be right. He was just here this morning. Why didn't he say anything? What could I have said to change his mind? What did *I say?*

I started to pray. "Our Father…" *Really? What kind of father are You? Who lets this happen? My children need their father. I need my husband. Sam needs to be here. His life wasn't supposed to end yet. Nap. Lunch. Hike. That was today's plan.*

I started over. "Our Father, Who art in…" *Where are You, exactly? Where could You possibly be in this?* I stared into the darkness.

Sam never came to bed last night. This fact blinked at me like an obvious clue in a mystery novel. That hadn't happened in all the time we were together, other than when one of us was traveling. We slept like spoons; when one of us turned to the opposite side, the other would follow, and we woke up still curled together. Sam always kissed me before he got out of bed, even if it was early and still dark. A whisper kiss on my cheek or forehead, a gentle gesture that left me feeling warm and safe, strong enough to notice but not so much as to rouse me from a deep sleep. Until he wasn't there. I was jarred by his absence. I had woken up Saturday morning with a start, heart pounding, because he hadn't kissed me. *I must be the first princess ever to be woken out of her sleep by a missing kiss.*

Why didn't he come to bed? Did he not want to sleep? Could he have been so committed to ending it all that he didn't dare risk anything—confiding his fears, asking for help, physical intimacy, actual sleep—that might have interfered with his plan?

What if he had just come to bed? Doesn't every problem look easier to tackle after a good night's sleep? As a mother, I had often said that I could solve most of my kids' problems with food and sleep. Feed them a snack, send them to bed, and we could easily solve any problems remaining after that. If Sam had gotten a few hours of sleep—if not a full night's rest—might things have looked brighter in the morning?

We had gone to see *A Midsummer's Night's Dream* with Nancy and Dave the night before. Their niece was in the production, and Dave thought Sam could use "a bit of cheering up." It was fun. We laughed, we held hands. *Just last night.*

My whole body ached with the missing of him.

We hadn't been intimate in almost two weeks, and I had found his lack of interest in me alarming. He had seemed distant and preoccupied. I wondered whether he was doing something that I didn't know about. I had begun to worry there was another woman in his life.

I had even asked him, "Are you *sure* you're not having an affair?" I waited for his answer, on the verge of tears, my heart threatening to beat out of my chest. An affair was the worst thing I could think of.

I remembered his downcast eyes. Sam shook his head. "Oh, Charlotte. No." Then my warm, gentle man wrapped me in a hug. *How could I have doubted him?* The very question seemed ridiculous in the safety of his arms. It wasn't someone else, just my overactive imagination. And work—both his and mine. We were simply exhausted. Things were going to get better. *Weren't they?*

Now I wondered anew if *she* was the reason he left. It would take years to admit to myself that the lover whose touch Sam longed for was death.

I reached further back into my memory. Six weeks earlier, Sam had stayed home from work to walk with me and the boys to their classrooms for the first day of school. Our house was just a few blocks from Paradise Canyon Elementary School, and he and I walked home together holding hands. Even though I loved being home with my kids, I had been looking forward to having a few quiet hours of my own choosing, maybe to take a second yoga class, or to start a writing project, or just to go to the grocery store alone.

Once we got back home, Sam had said, "We need to talk"—the standard introduction to a conversation that nobody wants to have. My stomach sank.

As we stood in the living room, he told me he was worried about our financial situation. "We're going to be fine for four years, and then we're going to have a problem."

I stood frozen. Without elaborating on the problem further, he confidently proposed a solution. "We can sell our house and move to Surprise, Arizona. You can stay home with the boys."

My face must have betrayed my consternation.

He kept talking. "I talked to José. He thinks it's a good idea."

It was one thing to have that husband and wife heart-to-heart about income and expenses, cash flow and net worth. It was another to find out that my husband had been having the heart-to-heart with his stockbroker cousin on the opposite coast, and the two of them had cooked up a plan. I wasn't happy. "Hold on. Your cousin in Miami thinks it's a good idea for us to pick up and move our family to Surprise, Arizona?"

Sam had reached for his laptop and pulled up photographs of a pretty gated community in the early phases of construction. I was stuck on what "good for four years" might mean when he said that he had already talked to a real estate agent about a specific floor plan. She estimated that the cost of the new home would be a fraction of what our house in Southern California could sell for. And then he told me that I could start picking out tile and granite and paint colors.

I was incredulous. "You talked to a real estate agent before talking to your *wife*?! Are you going to ask me what *I* think is a good plan?"

I was outraged. He had discussed the personal details of our finances with his cousin and a complete stranger before talking to me? I was incensed that he had made a decision and was presenting it to me as a *fait accompli*. We had never make decisions like a patriarchal 1950s sitcom. We reviewed the possibilities together.

"Did you even consider the fact that I have lived in this city for twenty-five years?" I had grown up in this house. Sam and I had bought this house from my parents after we graduated from law school. We had brought our babies home to this house. And he was asking me to pick up and move? I loved being an at-home mom, but if I had had to make a snap decision, I would rather have stayed put and worked part-time than pick up and move to godforsaken Surprise, Arizona. Not to mention that I wilted in temperatures over eighty degrees. I chalk that up to my Swiss heritage. We didn't know a single soul in Surprise, Arizona, unless you counted the real estate agent. Which I didn't.

That night neither of us slept.

I told Sam I would consider moving as a last-ditch effort, but not as the first attempt at making a change. He said that he had been thinking about it for months and moving was the only solution. I dug in my heels, determined to find another way. Ultimately, we agreed that I would go back to work, and we would stay where we were. We implemented our own austerity measures: eating at home, shopping only for the kids' necessities, and giving up the summer pool membership. In a display of optimism, we kept our reservation for the following summer's vacation.

I dusted off my license to practice law. I called Uncle Dave, and he gave me the names of two colleagues who practiced Trusts and Estates. Within a week I had reactivated my status with the California Bar and landed a part-time gig. Problem solved.

I started feeling more optimistic almost immediately, even with the belt-tightening and demands of work. I remembered aspects of working that I had missed: the part where clients appreciated what I did; the part where I got paid; the part where I managed to complete full sentences and thoughts; and finally, the part where nobody banged on the bathroom door.

I also prayed. I had grown up in a devout Christian Science family. We attended services without fail twice a week, on Sundays and Wednesdays. Religiously, as it were. Like every other spiritual denomination I was familiar with, Christian Scientists approached life's challenges through the lens of prayer. Most people know Christian Scientists as those people who do not seek any medical care, and while that is not the entirety of the religious tenets, it is mostly true. I never took an aspirin until I went to college, and I never had a vaccination until after I gave birth to my first child. It was also true that growing up, the problems I encountered physically and intellectually were resolved through prayer. Everything except the tubal pregnancy, but that came later. Sam and I were married by then, and my Jewish husband insisted—thank goodness—that I be rushed to the obstetrician's office. In the operating room, as I counted backwards from one hundred, I felt as though a presence was guiding me, and I was surprised (and relieved) to feel that the divine had not, in fact, been banished from the hospital grounds. I had relied on prayer my entire life, and as we faced our financial challenges, I resolved to devote extra time to it daily.

I started going to the Christian Science Reading Room weekly to pray about this Surprise situation. The Bible readings one week included the story of Moses guiding the children of Israel out of Egypt and toward freedom. I had a soft spot for the reluctant Moses, who wanted nothing more than to tend to his sheep and stay home with his stutter. He found himself the commander of a band of refugees and arrived at an impasse. The Israelites were crabby, tired, and hungry. They regretted having followed their unlikely leader, and the Egyptians were hot on their heels. As Moses stood at the brink of the Red Sea contemplating the impossible—the waters, the children, the rapidly approaching chariots—did he even notice the breeze blowing against his face?

I imagined Sam felt much as the Jewish prophet Moses might have, shouldering the responsibility for our little family, standing in front of a seemingly insurmountable obstacle, hearing hoofbeats in the distance and knowing that they did not bear good news. I sat in the quiet Reading Room and closed my eyes. I felt a growing confidence that the winds of change would be a partner for our journey forward. I prayed that Sam would feel the presence of an ally, that even in the midst of not knowing how we would pull through, he could trust in a power bigger than himself.

I started to gain confidence. I thought Sam had, too. He never mentioned Surprise again.

Now, as I lay awake in the dark, I thought again of Moses, how desperate his circumstances must have felt. Moses didn't jump. He prayed. He trusted. Sam wasn't supposed to jump. *Why did he jump? Couldn't he hear me encouraging him? Didn't he trust—even a little bit—in the Yahweh of his youth? What made him so afraid? What could have been so bad that he would end his life to avoid it?*

On the soccer field earlier that day, I had told Linda that things were going well—indeed, I thought they were. Or at least, that they would be. Little did I know how wrong I had been.

The minute hand taunted me with its measured waltz around the face of the clock. It danced infuriatingly forward despite my desire to will it backwards toward morning, the last time I saw him, a chance to change my future. To change his. To give the children back the father they had lost.

I pleaded with the divine and bargained with the clock.

Go back, go back, go back.

I spent the night adrift, awash in unanswered questions. I closed my eyes and inhaled the exhales of my sleeping children.

At some point I wondered whether anyone remembered to feed my children dinner. A few days later it occurred to me that I never did feed the dog.

CHAPTER 3

THE FIRST DAY OF THE
REST OF OUR LIVES

When you multiply a family of four by one suicide, the ensuing calculus of grandparents, siblings, aunts, uncles, cousins, and in-laws requires an abacus, a consanguinity chart, and several religious texts. Add friends, neighbors, colleagues, community connections, and well-intentioned onlookers, and then it becomes downright unruly.

It was amazing to me how people I didn't know well—or at all—stepped up to help. Some had a unique skill or special access. Others had shared experiences, useful perspectives, or simply a broken heart. Every one possessed their own quality of light that they shined in my world. These lovely people made cameo appearances and long-term commitments to the well-being of my sons and me in ways I could never have imagined. I am profoundly grateful. I won't name each individually—not because they aren't desperately dear to me—but because there were so many. In the interest of clarity, therefore, I will call them collectively the Janes.

I would not have known just how many modest and simple acts can have a significant impact in the healing journey had I not been aided and abetted by the Janes. Entrepreneur Jane sent a crew from her housecleaning business to my home for weeks. Sister Jane, an actual nun, prayed for me years before I met her in person. Jane the Artist painted with Danny and Jason in her art studio, giving them a safe place to explore their grief with palette and brushes, and Jane with her Mountain Home introduced the boys to skiing. I do not forget their kindnesses. But I get ahead of myself.

* * *

I didn't even know where to begin that next morning. It was Sunday and too early for phone calls.

I recalled that on a recent walk, Jane the Journalist mentioned that her father had killed himself on an Easter Sunday when she was young. I couldn't remember how the subject of suicide came up. She was so gentle and grounded that this bit of her personal history surprised me; now it seemed a sad serendipity.

I sat down at the computer to tap out the first of many emails. The Green Goblins soccer game seemed forever ago.

> *Subject: call me*
>
> *Hi Ben and Linda ~*
>
> *Please call me.*
>
> *~ Charlotte*

When the phone rang shortly thereafter, it was Linda. "Is everything OK?"

Of course, she suspected that it wasn't. There would be no easy way to say what had to be said.

I took a deep breath. "Sam died yesterday."

"What? What happened?"

I did not employ the euphemism "passed away." Such expressions attempted to soften the blow of death, but they confused the children, as though their father had absentmindedly toddled off someplace.

I told Linda that Sam had killed himself.

She was dumbfounded.

I told the truth. *Suicide*.

It was so hard to say the word out loud that I paused and took a slight breath before uttering it. "Sam died by suicide. He jumped from the top of a parking structure across the street from his office. I don't know why. I took the boys on a hike, and when I got home there were two policemen and a priest in my driveway."

As I flipped through my address book, thinking of people I needed to call—classmates of Sam, the boys' teachers, their pediatrician, Sam's assistant—I realized that it was not too early to call Rob and Caroline on the East Coast. They were friends of Sam's from high school who then lived in Virginia. Caroline answered on the first ring.

I repeated what little I knew, in snippets and phrases, not believing the words I heard myself say, "Sam died yesterday."

Gentle and earthy, Caroline calmed me even from across the country. She and Rob immediately made plans to fly out with their three children, even though we hadn't set a date for the funeral.

* * *

La Cañada is a suburban city of about twenty thousand people; it's part of the greater Los Angeles metropolitan area, about twelve miles north of downtown. I had lived here for most of my life. I had attended a local church and graduated from the public high school. I left to go to college and returned after I was married. I couldn't go to the post office or the park without seeing someone I knew. People had seen the police car parked in front of my house for hours. I couldn't have kept my husband's suicide a secret if I had tried.

We didn't send group emojis then. Texting was cumbersome and required tapping the numbers on the keypad—once, twice, even four times—to get to the corresponding letter of the alphabet. Instead, we called and emailed and whispered in grocery market aisles, "Did you hear?"

I made more phone calls: "I can't believe it, either. It doesn't make any sense. We're heartbroken. Feel free to tell anyone you think might want to know."

Women appeared on my doorstep—first Linda, then a neighbor, and a few Janes. I handed Linda my address book, and she started making phone calls. She called my college roommate, who contacted all my other college friends, and so it went, like a PTA-orchestrated phone tree disseminating emergency instructions. One Jane showed up with her hair still dripping from the shower. She was stunned, grief-stricken, and I was grateful to see my own shock reflected in her eyes, raising the same question…. *Sam?*

A blur of people gathered in my home, some in tears, others stoic. They dropped everything to rush to my side. I sat on the floor of my living room, surrounded by people. So many people showed up that I stopped closing the front door. It didn't occur to me to turn anyone away. My pain was too raw to hide, as was theirs. We found solace in each other.

I cannot remember where the boys were or what they were doing. I remember a series of hugs. I remember numbness in my hands and legs. People showed up with cookies, coffee cakes, sandwiches, and bright fresh apples. The mere sight of food made me physically ill. I was too nauseated to eat, but the children would need to be fed and my visitors might need snacks.

The Janes began to mobilize, ready to roll up their sleeves and get to work. But in that moment, there was nothing to be done. It was Sunday, so next steps would wait. I secretly hoped that there was a way, somehow, to turn back the clock.

In the meantime, we sat together.

* * *

At some point, somebody wondered aloud whether I had a therapist. I did. Dr. Newland was a registered nurse and local therapist who specialized in children on the autism spectrum. Sam and I had consulted with her to help us navigate parenting Danny. We didn't understand why a kid who was obviously bright hated school so vehemently; he managed through the school day but then exploded at home. She encouraged us to have him tested for learning differences and to implement an

Individualized Education Plan (IEP) at school, which seemed to help. We had stopped seeing her as part of our cost-cutting measures.

Naturally, she didn't answer her phone on the weekend. Her prerecorded greeting instructed callers to hang up and dial 911 in the case of an emergency, but nobody could fix my emergency. I left a message. I would not remember what I had said, but Dr. Newland told me she would never forget: "Please call me. Something terrible has happened."

* * *

Night was black as heavy silk. I was exhausted, and still sleep would not relieve the monotony of wishing that Sam had not done what he had done. The day was filled with death's aftershocks and life's child-rearing; as the solitary hours pressed on, I had time to think. Sam had survived so much: debilitating back pain from the time he was a young teenager, his parents' bankruptcy, his own mid-career direction change. I lay in bed, flanked by my young sons, watching their little chests expand with each gentle breath. I thought about the young princes William and Harry trudging behind Princess Diana's casket. Danny and Jason were half their ages.

Even when I closed my eyes, I didn't drift into sleep. I was stuck in perpetuity, longing for what I couldn't have.

At some point, I gave up and extricated myself slowly from the bed, careful not to disturb my children. They needed sleep more than I did, and I was grateful that they were resting. I didn't know what time it was. It didn't matter. I had always liked walking around my own house at night with the lights off. It was comforting to me, quietly navigating the contours of my home in the safety of the dark, like those sweet and secret moments mid-pregnancy when I felt my baby moving and stretching safely, a quiet awareness that something special was happening. But the darkness that followed my husband's death was cold, and the silence alarming; it was not a place I wanted to inhabit, or even step into alone.

I headed to my desktop computer, where there was an email message from my college roommate Bess encouraging me to call her any time. *Seriously*, she wrote. *Nothing is ever too late or too early.*

I closed my eyes and rested my head against my hand. Knowing she was there was hugely comforting, but I didn't call. Not yet. I didn't want to risk waking anybody up—not the boys, not my parents sleeping on a borrowed air mattress in the living room, and not even Parker, whose softly thumping tail betrayed the fact that he was keeping track of my movements.

CHAPTER 4

DAY TWO

Monday morning arrived entirely without my consent. They say that children in grief need some sense of consistency. I certainly hadn't studied this. Maybe I knew intuitively, or maybe it didn't occur to me not to take them to school.

I squatted down to look Danny and Jason in the eye and told them, "Just do your best, and whenever you're ready to come home, ask your teacher to call me." And then we walked to school.

Paradise Canyon Elementary had an open-air campus with three asphalt playgrounds and a grass baseball field. We walked past the administrative offices and down a gently sloping ramp toward the single-story buildings where the classrooms for the younger grades were.

Most of the parents ignored me, giving the boys and me a wide berth. Several avoided eye contact and kept their distance; some glanced in our direction and looked quickly away. Suicide's stigma already separated us from them. The friends in my home the day before were heartbroken along with me, but out in public, I had no reason to expect understanding, let alone empathy. I would be ostracized because of how Sam died.

I took Danny to his classroom first, where his teacher waited for him. Young and normally vibrant, her pale face looked like it would crack. She glanced down at my children, about as tall as my elbow. I wondered whether they offered a seminar in How-to-Keep-it-Together-When-a-Child's-World-Falls-Apart in her Master's in Education program. At that moment, reading, writing, and arithmetic seemed to be an almost wholly irrelevant but very welcome distraction for my third grader. I worried that my intensely shy boy might resist, but he disappeared into the classroom.

Jason's first grade teacher happened to be one of my friends from junior high school. Julie is that rare friend who can be both a homecoming princess and a down-to-earth confidante. She was equally as comfortable in an evening gown and lashes as she was in sweatpants with no mascara. Not only was she a trusted friend, but she was a gifted teacher. In our first parent-teacher conference, she had said, "It's not that Jason thinks outside the box; he doesn't realize that there is one." She understood my imaginative, exuberant, and social child. He would be safe with her.

I gave Jason a hug and turned away quickly, before either one of us could cry. I half-expected that I would get a phone call from one teacher or the other before I left the campus. I braced myself for the short walk home.

I crossed the front lawn, where a few parents milled around, the daily post drop-off social gathering. I looked down toward the grass, not wanting to lose my composure or meet the judgment in their gazes. A mom I hardly knew caught up to me, touching my arm to get my attention, and then embraced me tightly. As she released me, she said words I would hear over and over again: "I am praying for you and your children. Please let me know if there's anything I can do." She had barely let me go when the next pair of arms reached in to hold me close. I was met with a wave of mothers, so many that I could barely move.

Susan, a friend and the PTA president, held me for a long moment. With tears in her chestnut brown eyes, she told me, "I will never, ever show up on your doorstep unannounced. I wasn't raised that way. But Charlotte, if you need anything, just say the word, and I'll be there in a flash. Anything at all."

One of the Janes, a district attorney and deeply passionate student advocate, rushed up to me. I didn't know her particularly well, but her youngest child and Danny were in the same class. "I know exactly how you feel!" She welled up with tears. "When my mother died, it was just like this."

Her mother? What was she talking about? My mother was in my house fretting over me. At first I thought the rumor mill had confused the facts. I wasn't sure how to respond, but District Attorney Jane kept talking. I caught a few words—"cancer," "faith," "focus." *Was she one of the people Aunt Nancy predicted I would have to comfort?* I nodded. On the periphery, I could hear the principal whisper conspiratorially, "Somebody— get her out of here." I gave D.A. Jane a hug, or maybe she gave me one, still talking. "The County Coroner is a personal friend. Call me with the case number." Next thing I knew, I was swept up in another hug, and D.A. Jane hurried off.

The only dad on the front lawn, an Irishman, looked at me with both tears and a twinkle in his eye. "She doesn't have a fucking clue, does she, love?"

"I'm afraid I don't have a fucking clue, either."

"Suicide is a bitch."

"Seriously. I came home to find two policemen and a priest in my driveway—a fucking priest—and I'm staring at that white collar and I keep thinking: this can't be right...Sam is *Jewish*!"

He laughed.

"Holy shit. I'm going to hell, aren't I?"

"Darlin'," he said, with a smile and sad eyes, "I think you might already be there."

It felt both cathartic and irreverent to laugh aloud when I could still count in hours—forty-three, for the record—how long my husband had been dead.

He promised to teach me a few Irish curse words over a pint, and another mom swooped in for a hug. The whole thing felt surreal. I could have stood on the front lawn hugging people all morning, but I had a phone call to make.

I dreaded making the call to Sam's office. I was panicked that we had lost everything, and I was afraid to find out what nasty surprises might await me in our account. Sam would normally have arrived at his office before the 6:30 a.m. stock market open. I didn't know if they thought he was late or already knew he was dead, but I waited to call until after my children were safely out of earshot.

"Charlotte." His assistant Olivia picked up without introduction. She was thoughtful and maternal, always remembered the boys' birthdays. Her voice caught with emotion. "I can't believe it." They knew.

"Me neither. It doesn't make any sense. Olivia, can you see our account?"

"Of course. Oh, Charlotte. How are Danny and Jason?" I heard her typing. "Hmmm…"

"Do you have Sam's password?" I asked.

She responded to a muted voice in the background and said, "Let me call you right back." When she called me back a few minutes later, she told me she couldn't give me access to our personal account. "I'm so sorry. You'll have to talk to the branch manager, but he's in a meeting."

I hung up the phone, discouraged and afraid. *Had we lost everything? Was Sam investing in high-risk assets? Or churning accounts?* I thought he had been conservative in his investment approach. *What was he really doing? Should I have paid more attention to his work, or to our personal accounts?*

But I didn't have time to deal with Sam's office. I had an appointment with my therapist.

* * *

What I would learn about Dr. Newland years later, after we had concluded our work together, is that she herself had consulted with two therapists and a chaplain on the day I called. She suffered her own devastation, heartbreak, and feelings of professional failure at not having seen any signs of Sam's struggle, and she had wanted to show up on my doorstep herself. Instead, she created her own support team and was then able to provide a refuge for me to process my grief.

Dr. Newland's expertise was not grief, but she offered me something that no other therapist could. She had known Sam. She knew Sam as a kind and conscientious father and a loyal husband. Like everybody else, she missed the clues that might have pointed toward his suicide. We were all looking in a different direction.

In the safety of her office, I talked and wept. It would take weeks and months for me to sift through the pieces of the story. Dr. Newland didn't ask a lot of questions. Her first order of business was to make sure I was eating and sleeping, which I was not.

I looked at the tissue in my hand, holding the last vestiges of the eye makeup I had applied that morning. "What a waste of perfectly good mascara."

Dr. Newland chuckled.

"If I lose my sense of humor, call 911. That's when you'll know I'm on my way out."

I couldn't afford to fall apart—not completely, not yet.

"I can't get into my accounts. I can't set a date for the funeral. I can't bear this. I can't." The powerlessness numbed me. The list of the things I didn't know was long, and a therapist's fifty-minute hour was short.

Remarkably, neither teacher had called, and it was almost time for school to release and me to switch back to Mommy mode.

* * *

The boys and I walked home together, just like every other Monday, except that it was nothing like any Monday we'd had before. They plunked down at the table, and I dished up carrots with ranch. I sat with my sons and watched them eat. The ordinariness of it was extraordinary. *How can anything possibly be normal in the midst of such upheaval?*

My parents watched the boys while I made phone calls. My conversations were peppered with words incongruous to my life: suicide, coroner's report, autopsy, and then the predictably dreadful question from the insurance company: "Are you the widow?"

Widow. The word left an acrid taste in my mouth. I wished I could shed the term, which felt like an itchy, ill-fitting suit, but when I caught my reflection, I noticed that I had dressed entirely in black.

"Yes," I said, still looking in the mirror to confirm that it was me. "I am."

* * *

When I crawled into bed that night, exhausted, the sheets smelled fresh. My Swiss mother had put clean linens on my bed, a thoughtful gesture that under normal circumstances comforted me. Except what she didn't know—and I hadn't anticipated—was that in washing away the scent of Sam, she destroyed something I couldn't get back.

I was losing him. With each passing hour, I felt Sam slipping further from reach, the distance between us growing. I lay in bed, a boy on each side and Parker in the mix, wagging his tail.

"Parker's tail never stops wagging," Danny mused as he stroked the dog's ears gently. True to his breeding, that dog's tail wagged from the moment he woke up until the moment he wiggled under the covers down at our feet in bed. It always amused me that this little spaniel who couldn't be sweeter shared the same markings as a Rottweiler, with his black coat, brown eyebrows, and brown muzzle. Small white patches on his chin and chest rendered him endearingly imperfect; "pet quality," the breeder called him. "He is love in a dog shape," Danny said.

Jason added sleepily, "Daddy is love in a Sam shape."

In that moment, I knew my boys would heal. And it broke my heart that they needed to.

The boys eventually succumbed to the pressure of heavy eyelids. Yet sleep eluded me. My own body was thick with the weight of grief, and the only thing I wanted was relief from the exhaustion. For a moment I drifted toward sleep, and Sam's presence felt closer than it had in three days. I strained to hear his voice. I wanted to hear him say he was sorry, that he loved us, that he made a mistake. But when he spoke, he said: "Kill the kids and yourself and come with me."

Suddenly alert, I shouted, "*NO!* You left us, and now you are going to have to wait!" Both boys startled from their sleep.

"Shhhh…" I patted them gently. I hoped they couldn't see my tears in the dark, hoped to hide the fear pounding in my chest. Parker's tail thumped rhythmically at the bottom of the bed.

Maybe it was really him; maybe it was my own sleep-deprived delusion. Either way, I never heard Sam's voice again.

CHAPTER 5

THE MOST EXPENSIVE REAL ESTATE IN LOS ANGELES

On Tuesday, I started counting the time since Sam's death in days instead of hours. I also chose a burial plot for my husband. Neither of these seemed possible.

When I have breathed my last, I don't care whether my remains are buried or cremated. Give whatever parts or pieces to someone who can use them and then dispose of the rest with my blessing. But Sam didn't want to be cremated; he wanted to be buried in a Jewish cemetery.

Thus began the first family disagreement: his family wanted him to be buried at a cemetery near Los Angeles International Airport, where his grandfather, an uncle, and a cousin were buried. That was too far away. People on their first visit to Los Angeles are surprised by how vast the city is; the view at night of the sprawling city lights from a plane descending into LAX is spectacular, but the miles on the ground can be prohibitive. I wanted Sam closer to me and our boys. In our estate planning documents, Sam had granted me full discretion to do what I wanted with his remains. I decided to bury him in a Jewish cemetery on Forest Lawn Drive, about ten miles from my house.

Zack picked me up for the appointment. It would be weeks before I drove myself. I felt safe confiding in Zack; I knew he understood. His heart had been torn apart, too. We drew comfort from each other's presence, the wife and the brother/cousin being the next closest thing to Sam. We two loved him fiercely, protectively; and the two of us felt deeply betrayed by his suicide.

When the funeral director ushered us into a private room, we found that Sam's cousin José had just arrived, straight from Miami. José has big brown eyes like Sam's, rimmed with pain that day, but stoic and intense. I trusted that he cared about Sam and me and the boys, even though I disagreed with his judgment on the Surprise move. Anyway, I didn't blame José for that. I blamed Sam.

I took a seat at the table, and another cousin arrived with her husband. Moments later, Sam's sister Miranda and her husband showed up. I wasn't sure why all of them felt the need to attend the meeting, but I wasn't opposed to the support.

The funeral director looked at the form in front of him and then addressed me. "I have a few questions. Place of birth?"

"Los Angeles, California."

"Place of death?"

"Pasadena, California." Sam hadn't traveled far. Never even had a passport.

He continued down the form. I was grateful that he didn't ask the cause of death. I thought I remembered that suicides weren't permitted to be buried in a Jewish cemetery.

"Date of funeral?"

I hesitated. Tradition required a burial within twenty-four to forty-eight hours, but the county coroner hadn't yet released Sam's body. There was no doubt over the cause of death, but for some infuriating reason they had to conduct an autopsy.

I heard laughter from across the room and looked up. Sam's sister was trying to find their grandmother in the cemetery directory, but *abuela* had been widowed and remarried so many times that Miranda couldn't remember her latest last name. It might have struck me as funny, too, if I hadn't just been widowed myself. Instead, her laugher grated on me. I didn't think about how Miranda might have felt, having been blindsided by the suicide of her younger brother, her only sibling. I didn't note whether her laughter seemed nervous. It struck me that even in the presence of all these people who loved Sam and who loved me, nobody got it. Everyone there, including the funeral director, had a spouse. A living spouse. I had a dead one.

"Open casket or closed?"

José perked up and interrupted, "Closed, of course." It irritated me that he answered my question. *Was he afraid I might give the wrong answer?*

The funeral director looked to me for confirmation, and I nodded. Then he continued as casually as if he were taking the order for espresso shots in my morning latte. "Single plot or double?" The question hit me like a sucker punch. Sam wanted a plot. I did not. Not then. Not ever. But especially not then. I didn't want to live the rest of my life thinking of that place as my ultimate destination. I didn't want to be that grieving widow who lived her lonely life longing to be reunited with her late husband. I didn't want to see a half-completed plaque with empty space reserved for my date of death whenever I visited Sam at the cemetery. And I really didn't want my sons to be haunted by that image. I knew instinctively that my mourning process wouldn't end where it began. I did not get to choose Sam's death. I was left to choose my life.

"Single."

"Let me see what's available." He excused himself.

I stared out the window.

Zack put his hand on mine. It felt like he was my only ally.

The funeral director came back with completed paperwork and three potential sites for Sam's body. Zack, José, and my brother-in-law reviewed the papers briefly and then slid them across the table for my signature. He pointed to the bottom of the page. "Sign here." Too many years of practicing law, I guess, but I scanned the form before signing.

My brain was mushy, but one stark detail remained clear: My husband died on Saturday, October 20, 2007. The form in front of me, however, showed the date of death as October 19. *Seriously? An attorney, a stockbroker, and an accountant reviewed this form, and none of them noticed?* My eyes were so swollen I had stopped wearing contact lenses, but I saw the error. I pushed the paperwork away from me. "The date is wrong."

I felt edgy. I suspected these in-laws were not here to support me but to make sure the *shiksa* honored Sam appropriately. It bugged me that they thought they knew Sam better than I did. If I couldn't trust the date on the form to be accurate, what else might be wrong? So much paperwork. So many details. I had to get a grip. I could only rely on myself. In a room full of grieving family who desperately loved Sam, I felt profoundly alone—the sole, solitary gentile.

Zack noticed that I'd withdrawn, and he came to my side without a word. He accompanied me in the funeral director's van to look at the first plot. It was the least expensive option, on a steeply sloping hillside near the busy street. It reeked of exhaust and horseshit.

"This is nice," someone said.

It was nothing remotely resembling nice.

Sam didn't deserve this, I thought. I looked at Zack. "Sam would never have done this to me." I turned and walked back to the van.

Zack looked at the funeral director and shook his head. He turned to the cousins. "Not this one."

I can't remember what I hated about the second plot, other than the fact of it.

The third plot was higher up the hillside, enough removed that I could no longer hear the cars racing below, with a view of the San Fernando Valley where Sam had spent most of his life. It was a newer section of the cemetery, the landscaping young and accessible by a cement path. I thought of Sam's parents visiting their son here. His mother could access this spot without fear of falling herself. I pictured the boys scrambling up the grassy knoll to visit; it was a place they could be proud of. It would be Sam's final earthly resting place—beautiful, as these things go—but it would not be mine.

That little ground space in the Hollywood Hills was exorbitantly expensive, almost eight hundred dollars per square foot, as they say in the parlance. I would never purchase such overpriced real estate again. The upside was that it was entirely my decision. The downside: it was my bill to pay. I didn't care. I handed the funeral director my credit card and hoped that Visa hadn't caught wind of Sam's death.

* * *

A Jane wrote Sam's obituary for the local newspapers. "Sam Maya died suddenly…. He was forty-one." The word "suddenly" served, as it commonly does, as a euphemism, replacing one S-word with another. It was hard enough to say "suicide" within my circle, and I objected to its use in a published format; it felt important to protect Sam's memory. Jane formulated the broad strokes. I filled in the biographical details, graduation dates, the suggestion for *in lieu of flowers*.

She also set up a Caringbridge.org website where she posted funeral information. There were so many details to coordinate, and most of them couldn't be finalized until I had a date certain for the funeral. District Attorney Jane had requested an expedited release from the coroner's office, but for the time being we were in limbo.

* * *

The boys managed another entire day at school, and Danny even went to a friend's house afterward. By the time we sat down to dinner, I was looking forward to something that felt normal, even though I wasn't hungry and my father occupied Sam's chair.

"Let's play Best and Worst," I suggested, looking around the table at Danny, Jason, my parents, my sister, and my brother-in-law.

Sam and I often started our family dinner conversations with a round of Best and Worst; each of us shared the "best" thing that had happened that day, and the "worst." We wanted to encourage the kids to think about what they were happy about, but also develop the confidence to talk about their struggles in a safe place. I had been raised at a table that only allowed sunshine and roses; I wanted my children to feel comfortable bringing their whole thorny selves to the conversation.

Happiness is not a zero-sum game. Life includes the range from joy to devastation, and there was room for all of it at our table.

Danny started. "My best was my playdate with Kevin," he said, smiling. Kevin who, after his older brother died, used to pretend to play board games with him. Kevin would take turns, first moving his own piece and then switching to the other side of the table and moving his brother's pieces for him. By the age of eight, Kevin was already a more comfortable companion through grief than many adults, and the ideal friend for Danny to hang out with that afternoon.

Danny continued, "And my worst was that Daddy died." All the gratitude in the world would not negate this fact.

"Yes." I encouraged him for naming the worst thing. "That might be your worst for a long time."

Next was my father's turn. He looked like a cross between an absent-minded professor and Santa Claus, slightly disheveled, snow-white hair and beard, and his smiling cheeks blushed pink. "My best was meeting so many of Charlotte's friends." My dad is gifted at finding the best in every situation. "And my worst..." His voice caught. I knew he would struggle with the "worst" part of the conversation; the man practically had rose-colored corneas.

"My worst..." he began again, and his eyes welled up with tears. He could not speak the worst. My father had a PhD. in nuclear physics, but he was chronically incapable of acknowledging negative emotions. As a child, I sometimes felt invisible; he lavished his attention when I was happy or successful and all but ignored me when I was angry. When I was emotional, I was told to go to my room. "Come out when you feel better," my father would say. I was terrified of being abandoned for revealing the intensity of my feelings. For years, I had tried to stuff them. No doubt, the Best and Worst conversations with my kids were in direct response to this piece of my upbringing. It had been profoundly healing when I learned to acknowledge the hurt. I waited for my father's response, daring him to say his worst out loud. He didn't. He could not tolerate the pain. He took a breath, his voice hitched on what was too horrifying to say, and then he blurted, "...but they were tears of joy."

Tears of joy? You've got to be kidding me.

The doorbell rang right at that moment, probably saving my father's life. I left the table to answer the door. On my front porch stood two people: Steve, a friend and financial advisor, holding account transfer forms for my signature; and Jane, M.D., with Xanax in hand.

By the time I returned, the dining table had been cleared, Best and Worst had been abandoned, and my dad was sitting on the sofa chatting with my sister.

I was still seething. "Tears of *joy?*" I said incredulously.

My dad stopped talking and turned to look at me.

I stared down at him. "Are you insane?!" I yelled. "Dad, those are not tears of joy. Those are tears of pain! We are not joyful. We are *suffering*! I am a *widow* and my little boys have lost their father!"

My physicist father looked like he was trying to meld into the sofa.

"Honestly, tears of joy? Fuck you!" How insensitive it felt that my own father conflated tears over Sam's suicide with joy of any kind. How wildly inaccurate it seemed to confuse the shock and sadness over Sam's death with anything remotely related to joy.

Fueled by exhaustion and rage, I continued my tirade. "Tears of joy are for births and graduations and weddings. Tears of joy are about love or relief or pride. Nobody is happy about Sam's suicide, Dad. And I am telling you to go fuck yourself because I know you are going to love me anyway!"

And then I stormed out of the room.

I had never told my dad to fuck himself. Not even as a teenager. I had been biting my tongue (mostly) my whole life, hiding the intensity of my feelings from my father, who couldn't abide them, but I refused to soft-pedal how much pain we were in, even if it reduced my dad to tears. Maybe tears would be good for him; people survive tears.

One of the reasons I married Sam was that I could share the full range of my feelings with him. Mister Rogers was the first one to tell me that my feelings were okay, but Sam Maya was the first one to allow me to experience my feelings bodily, without banishing me from the room. When we argued, Sam would hold my hand gently but firmly. It infuriated me. I was terrified that he would leave me, the unspoken word *divorce* rising like a specter and creating a conscious dread. I felt like my body might implode in the confusion of holding both emotions—anger and tenderness—at the same time, but Sam remained sturdy in this space. He was confident enough to let me rage, tears of frustration spilling down my face. I didn't wipe them off, because I didn't want to let go of his hand.

"Sweetheart, we are on the same team," he would say.

I retreated to my bedroom, sadness washing over me. I held my own hand and imagined the warmth of Sam's.

A voicemail blinked for my attention.

"I have some good news for you." The voice belonged to D.A. Jane. "I talked to the county coroner. You will have Sam back by Thursday." My whole body exhaled. On a day full of worsts, this might have been my best.

I took the Xanax that Jane, M.D. brought over and slept for the first time since Sam's death. I woke up at 2 a.m., but still…it was progress.

CHAPTER 6

FUNERAL AND OTHER ARRANGEMENTS

What was great about Rabbi Jonathan was that he was not some random rent-a-rabbi. He and Sam were friends. They had attended UCLA together, had argued points of theology and politics, laughed together, and shared a Shabbat dinner or two. He was as surprised as the rest of us by Sam's suicide.

Although I had attended multiple Jewish funerals, I had never planned one, and I wanted to honor Sam in the process. I had ideas about the eulogies, and I leaned on Rabbi Jonathan for his insight. I believed he would officiate Sam's funeral with care, but it was a schlep for me to get to his temple, close to where Sam's parents lived on the West Side of Los Angeles. Depending on traffic, the thirty-mile drive could take an hour and a half or longer.

Zack drove me to Wednesday's meeting. En route, he answered a call. "Hey." A single, short *Hey*, not the signature Sam *Heyyy* with the call and response *Heyyy, Heyyy, Heyyy*. I didn't know who it was, and I was trying not to eavesdrop, mindful that he had his law practice to keep running and might be speaking with a client, but we were sitting together in a small car.

"Okay. Sure. We're on our way, but we might be a little late." *It's Rabbi Jonathan*, I thought.

"There's more traffic than we expected." *Typical Los Angeles.*

"Sure. That's fine. Go ahead and start the meeting without us." *Wait. What?*

"See you soon. Bye, Miranda." *Miranda? Why is she there? What is going on?* Zack glanced over at me. "Miranda is already there with her parents."

My relationship with my sister-in-law was one I struggled with. Before meeting me, Sam's sister had tried to talk him out of marrying me because I wasn't Jewish. The term *shiksa*, I learned, was not a term of endearment. I was twenty-three. When we later met in person at my bachelorette dinner days before my wedding, Miranda extolled the virtues of Sam's high school sweetheart. It wasn't an auspicious start.

I started shaking. "What? This is *my* meeting. It's not her place. How did she even know about it?" I was outraged that Miranda had horned in on my meeting with the rabbi. The news knocked the wind out of me. I couldn't draw my next inhale.

Zack saw me struggling to breathe and panicked. "I'm sorry! I'm so sorry. It's okay. I'm so sorry."

Nothing about this episode was conducive to freeway driving. A car pulled up next to us. The driver blew his horn and flipped Zack off. I caught a breath, rolled down the window, and yelled, "I am thirty-nine years old, and I am a widow. DON'T. FUCK. WITH. ME."

Zack rolled up the window without saying a word.

I fumed for a mile and then made a decision. I delivered my next words in a controlled rage. "I am Sam's wife and his widow, and I know what my husband wanted. I have been respectful of his family, but they are completely discounting me and I won't stand for it. Call Miranda back. You tell her that if they want to talk to the rabbi, now's their chance. But the *second* I walk into that office—and I mean *that exact second*—I want them *out*. I know I'm not Jewish, but guess what? The *shiksa* is in charge. This is about Sam and me and Danny and Jason, and everybody else comes after that. I will do what's right, but this is my show. I am the widow, Zack."

He called them back and relayed the message, edited for the sake of family harmony, then reached over and put his hand on mine like an apology. We spent the rest of the drive in silence.

When we arrived at the temple, Miranda scuttled out of Rabbi Jonathan's office with my in-laws, and I walked in alone. He closed the door. I sat down, still seething. I could see the heartbreak in his eyes over the death of his friend, and I softened. We talked about the Sam we knew: the friend, the intellectual, the husband, the father.

I asked whether someone who died by suicide was allowed to be buried in a Jewish cemetery. Rabbi Jonathan regarded me over wire-rimmed glasses. "I don't want you to worry about that." He never mentioned it again.

We discussed logistics—the format of the service, the burial, and the meal following. He explained that the meal following a funeral service was called the *Seudat Havra'ah*, a condolence meal.

"I don't think I've eaten since Sam died," I said.

He nodded his understanding, and then emphasized that this was a healing meal provided by the community to demonstrate their care for the ones who are living. At that point, Rabbi Jonathan invited everyone, including Zack, back into his office and shared the details we had worked out for the service.

"Oh!" Rabbi Jonathan had remembered something. "One more question. There are three chapels at Mt. Sinai. They seat one hundred, two hundred, or three hundred. Which one would you like?"

For the record, the rabbi asked *me*, but before I even opened my mouth, both Sam's sister and his father answered, simultaneously and with the same dismissive wave of the hand, "There won't be more than one hundred people."

I couldn't believe it.

Rabbi Jonathan looked to me for confirmation. I gave a quick shake no. They didn't know. Nine years older than Sam, Miranda often referred to him as her "first baby" instead of her brother; when he failed the bar exam, she told him he'd be nothing if he didn't pass it the next time. Sam's father didn't know him as a competent professional and a well-regarded community member. I refused to dignify their shame of Sam's suicide by choosing the smallest chapel.

"Give me the chapel for three hundred."

* * *

On the car ride home, Zack said, "I'd like you to think about something. You don't have to decide now."

I didn't want to hear what he had to say next. It wasn't even noon. I didn't know how much more I could take.

"I want you to consider moving closer to us."

Does he think I can't do this myself?

I had no intention of moving to the West Side. I knew Zack wanted to help. I understood he felt an obligation to Sam, but it wasn't his job to rescue me or take care of my sons.

I didn't answer. I just looked out the window as we drove past Los Angeles landmarks: the J. Paul Getty Museum, Universal Studios, Griffith Park (home to the Hollywood sign), and the cemetery where Sam would soon be.

Could we slow down? Sam had only been gone a few days. It felt like a lifetime.

The minute Zack dropped me off at home, I sent an SOS email to my inner circle: "So, among the many strange things that are happening, Zack asked me to move to the West Side. Keep your game faces on, girls. I need you."

* * *

In the afternoon, I took my young sons to buy suits for their father's funeral. That Wednesday still consistently appears in the top five on my personal list of bad days.

My mother drove us to a Talbots Children on Lake Avenue in Pasadena. We were standing on the sidewalk in front of the store when

I saw a couple walking toward us, smiling and waving. In a moment of serendipity, Rob and Caroline had arrived from Virginia. Even on my most miserable of days, life threw me a bone.

We found navy blazers for the boys and gray slacks, white dress shirts, and ties in shades of red and blue. How endearing it was to watch Rob, a devoted father himself and dear friend of Sam's, helping Danny and Jason fit their suit coats and showing them how to fix their clip-on ties. And how utterly wrong that the boys needed to prepare for such an occasion at all. They would soon grow out of these suits and I would find new ones for cotillion, bar mitzvahs, and homecoming—suits that did not contain the whiff of death in their seams.

Sam never let me pick his clothes, like some wives do, but I did choose what he would be buried in. I stood in our closet picturing my husband. He had broken his nose in a fistfight as a teenager, leaving a bump that bent slightly to one side. Even so, I thought Sam looked handsome with his dark hair, broad forehead, and narrow chin. I pulled out a dark green suit with a green-and-gray patterned tie. Something about Sam in that combination—his olive skin against the white shirt— made me fall in love with him all over again. I sighed, looking at the suit and tie for the last time, and then handed the combination to my friend. In a Jane-like display of grace, she took Sam's clothes to the mortician. When I thought about Sam settled peacefully within the casket, resting on the padded lining, I imagined my husband wearing my favorite of his ties.

Caroline helped me choose my dress. I had one black suit I wore to court and a little black dress for cocktail parties, neither of which was appropriate for Sam's funeral. After shopping for the boys, I didn't have the energy to shop for me. The Janes sent around an email requesting the loan of a size eight black dress. Next thing I knew there were half a dozen options on my doorstep.

Caroline sat on the bed while I tried them on. The dresses fit easily—I had lost five pounds in four days. It was surreal, like trying on wedding gowns with my maid of honor, only without the bubbly anticipation and the trifold of full-length mirrors. One dress was too matronly, baggy and shapeless, another too short, more suited to salsa dancing. Caroline said nothing but shook her head.

With a sinking feeling in my center, I tried on another dress. This funeral was really going to happen.

Jane, M.D. had sent over a simple, sleeveless sheath dress. The hem fell at the knee and the V-neck right below the collarbone, modest but still young. The black dress came with a coordinated black coat almost the length of the dress, with a traditional collar and full-length sleeves. I pulled up the zipper on the dress, put the coat on and turned to Caroline.

She smiled and nodded. "It's beautiful."

And then the two of us started to cry.

CHAPTER 7

ESTATE SETTLEMENT 101

The fact of another sunrise was infuriating. How could the world possibly keep spinning without Sam? It was already Thursday.

Jason seemed to like seeing his friends enough to get through another day of first grade, but as the week dragged on, Danny's reluctance to go to school grew. I walked both boys to school thinking that Danny would very likely return home with me. I would not have forced him to go, but with funeral plans ongoing and the constant phone calls, I was relieved when, at the last minute, he decided to stay "just until lunchtime."

Later that afternoon, my team of family advisors—Zack, José, and Caroline—gathered around the dining room table. Their agenda: to figure out how much, if anything, was left in my personal accounts. I still didn't know the password, and I was dreading that we might find a drop in the value of our retirement funds or a transfer to someone I didn't know. I was too nervous to sit. I kept walking out of the room. Caroline kept retrieving me.

Zack had Sam's laptop open, and he asked what passwords Sam might have used. Jason handed Zack a piece of notebook paper on which he had diligently written a series of letters in random order, scrawled in his adorable first-grade handwriting, hoping it would be helpful.

"Thanks, buddy," Zack said, ruffling his nephew's hair.

Zack tried a few variations on passwords I guessed.

"We're in!" Zack called out.

I looked over his shoulder with both interest and trepidation. The accounts I thought we had—his and her retirement plans plus one savings account—were all shown. No unusual activity. No significant losses. No big withdrawals. I was relieved but confused. If we had lost money, then Sam's death might have made more sense, but we hadn't. *What could have been worth losing his life for?*

I was at a loss. Zack, José, and Caroline were equally dumbfounded.

What surprised me was the outstanding balance on our mortgage. We paid $400,000 for the house in 1996, and it doubled in value over the next ten years. I hadn't paid close attention when Sam and I later refinanced the house, and frankly, as dumb as it sounds, I hadn't realized quite how much we owed. Or maybe $800,000 just sounded like a much bigger sum when I suddenly became the only one responsible for paying it back.

In good-ish news, the life insurance company confirmed that they would pay, even though Sam's death was a suicide. Most insurance policies include a "suicide waiver," meaning that the insurance company will deny coverage if the death is ruled a suicide, but this waiver is only valid for two years in California. We had purchased the policy when Danny was a baby.

In light of the outpouring of support that arrived daily in the form of food, hugs, encouragement, and presence, it was a relief to know I could afford to stay in my home. Sam had previously urged me to pay off the mortgage if anything ever happened to him so that I would always have a place to live. But all my advisors told me to keep the mortgage, deduct the interest on my tax return, and invest the proceeds in the market instead. Immediately following his death, I didn't trust Sam's judgment. Later, I would wish I had listened to him.

The life insurance proceeds would take some of the pressure off. I wouldn't have to rush downtown to get a high-paying job in a fancy law firm. Initially, I could take a three-month leave of absence from work. When I did start working again, it could be part-time, while Danny and Jason were in school. I didn't want the boys to feel that when they lost their father, they lost me, too. As José described my financial picture, "It's not that bad. It's actually a pretty picture." That is, if you ignored the dead body.

***

As I was settling the boys into bed Thursday night, Jason said, "Daddy's brain got completely discombobulated, and I hate that." The father he knew was loving and kind and held his children above all else. My little boy was already coming to terms with something important: Sam had not been in his right mind.

Danny, who loved to get lost in a story, turned to a favorite book to find insight. In the world of Harry Potter, the basilisk is a snake of enormous size and of a power so evil that if it looked someone directly in the eye, the look alone would kill them. "Mommy," he asked, "are you *sure* that a basilisk didn't kill Daddy?" It was easier for Danny to believe in the magical world of Harry Potter than to believe that his daddy could have left him.

CHAPTER 8

SHABBAT WITHOUT SHALOM

Friday arrived, and it felt too soon to say goodbye. We were dressed for the funeral, but we weren't ready to let go.

Jason refused to leave the house. He looked so handsome in his little coat and tie, but no amount of begging, reasoning, or bribing would motivate him toward the limousine at the curb. He sat on the bathroom floor, not budging. Whereas normally I might have been patient, or creative, or cultivated a sense of humor to coax him along, I had nothing. It was all I could do to get myself dressed and out the door with my eulogy and Xanax in hand.

With her signature warmth and patience, Caroline sent me out to the black limousine waiting at the curb while she joined Jason on the cold tile. Meanwhile, to my surprise, Danny gamely got dressed and into the limo. I suspected he just wanted to ride around in the limo, or maybe he was relieved not to go to school. After a few minutes, Caroline and Jason emerged from the house, hand in hand.

The chapel at the cemetery had a family alcove, to the side of the stage and hidden from the view of the congregation, and there was a private bricked-in garden patio right outside, perfect for children to run around in safely. Danny and Jason vacillated between dashing around in a game of tag with Zack's twins and curling up miserably in the lap of a grandparent or an aunt.

I noticed I was holding my breath. I took half a Xanax.

There was no formal procession. Rabbi Jonathan began the service promptly twenty minutes late with a welcome and a prayer. He then gestured to the family alcove, indicating that it was time to deliver the eulogy. I had wanted to speak, because I wanted my children to see that their mother was strong enough to do this. And I chose to speak first in order to set the tone. I wanted the assembled congregation to know that, notwithstanding the horrible pain his suicide caused, Sam had my compassion. Even in my rage and confusion, I wanted to honor him. I stood, and as I made my way to the podium, I heard a collective gasp. They had not expected the widow to speak.

My legs trembled beneath me as I walked across the stage. I couldn't see Team Jane from the family alcove, but they were seated front and center. Their presence sustained me. They were everyone I needed. Once at the podium, I turned to face the congregation. I saw a crowd of mournful faces who had come to offer their support. The chapel was standing-room only. People spilled outside onto the sidewalk. The largest chapel wasn't big enough.

My first thought was gratitude. *Thank you all for coming.* My second, less charitable thought, was *I told you so. I knew there would be hundreds.* Sam and I had come together from two different backgrounds—Jewish and Christian—but we saw eye to eye on the transcendent nature of love, treasuring our children, and rooting for the UCLA Bruins. It was a testament to his life that the chapel was filled with Bruins, Bears, Cardinals, Owls, Sagehens, and lots of Trojans.

I began. "Our sons Danny and Jason are so blessed to have had this wonderful father, and the loss of him is very painful. Jason told me, 'Mommy, it would take a whole year to say all the good things about Daddy.' I promise I won't talk that long. We only have the chapel for an hour."

I didn't offer any answers. I didn't have any. I had to believe his suicide was a mistake. The only thing I knew for sure was that Sam loved me and I loved him. His life was his gift to us. "This is my gift to him," I concluded. "I know who he was, and I know who he is, and I love him still. I love you, sweetie."

I hadn't planned to blow him a kiss at the end. It was just so ingrained in how we said our goodbyes, so natural to express our affection in this way, that I instinctively brought my hand to my lips and blew toward the heavens. All afternoon, and for weeks later, when people commented on the eulogy I delivered, what they most remembered was the kiss.

When the service concluded, my parents whisked the boys to the reception, while the rest of us made our way over to the gravesite for the burial. I took the other half of the Xanax. I was walking behind the casket, crying softly, longing to hold onto Sam's arm for support, imagining his presence. I sniffled sharply and suddenly felt an altogether too tangible presence. I had inhaled a fly. The fly wiggling in my sinus cavity made me snort. And I laughed at the absurdity of it. I could practically hear Sam mischievously humming the tune to the children's song *I Know an Old Lady Who Swallowed a Fly...*

Both Caroline and José turned to glare me into submission. *If looks could kill the widow*, I thought, which made me laugh harder.

I grabbed a tissue to cover my face, hoping to give the impression that I was crying, but every time I thought about the fly, it struck me as funny all over again. Sam would have thought it hilarious, me trapped in a fit of the giggles while his friends and family gave me the side-eye.

Once graveside, we assembled for the ritual goodbyes. The metal crank ground and clacked, lowering the casket holding my husband's body into the earth. Then followed a hollow silence when the casket came to rest. This excruciating moment was the reason I sent Danny and Jason (and my parents) straight to the reception.

Rabbi Jonathan intoned the requisite prayers and then explained the tradition of scooping dirt into the grave. I had always considered this a tender practice, loved ones using their own hands to cover the deceased with a blanket of earth, like tucking a child into bed. The rabbi handed me a single long-stemmed red rose. As the widow, it was my job to release the rose, to let it fall onto the casket below, and then to shovel the first three scoops of dirt. As I stood graveside, inches from the edge, I understood Laertes' Shakespearean urge to jump into Ophelia's grave. What I would have given to hold Sam one more time. I did not want to let that rose go. I held on, as if I could stop the whole process by refusing to relinquish the red flower. I felt the heat of hundreds of eyes on my back, and the reality of Sam's death pressed me forward.

I drew a long breath, catching a hint of the rose's fragrance, and let it go with my exhale. I can still hear the hollow thump of the rose against the wooden casket, like the chime of a grandfather clock, marking the change between one hour and the next. I reached for the shovel.

After the burial, as I was making my way toward the waiting limousine, an elderly woman I had never met approached me. I was confused. *Who is she? Why the urgency?* She told me she was a client of Sam's and that she had a gift for me. Then this tiny wrinkled woman held up a little wicker cage with a small bird inside. She explained that when I got home, I was to release the bird, and the bird would carry my troubles away. She handed me the birdcage and disappeared into the crowd.

I went to the reception, bird in hand. One of the Janes hosted the reception at her house, and several other Janes pulled together a beautiful meal. Not an entirely kosher one, but one prepared with much love. The rabbi was right about the *Seudat Havra'ah* being a healing meal. It was the first time I had felt hunger in a week, and I finished the bagel Jane set in front of me.

After several hours of hugs and shared stories, we arrived back home with the bird. The boys wanted to keep it. *Not a chance*, I thought. This widow could not take responsibility for one more life. I had burdens enough already, and this sorrow sparrow was here to lighten my load. We sat together on the front porch, expectantly—dare I say, optimistically, for the first time in a week—and reverently said our thank yous and farewells to our partner in flight. We opened the cage door to set her free.

That fucking bird did not budge.

At first I thought she was dead, too. She blinked, and I was flooded with relief that I had not killed her. She blinked again. I grew irritated. She had work to do, and if she didn't start flapping, I would have to wring her feathered neck. But Danny and Jason were watching, so the four of us—two little boys, a disheartened mom, and a flightless bird—sat. The boys soon lost interest and went into the house. The still bird sat there, torturing me with her misguided promise. I sat stubbornly on the front porch.

I felt guilty. The bird might be dehydrated. I put some water out. It was the least I could do for her since she was about to fly off into the sunset with the weight of my world on her avian shoulders. After a long while she hopped out of the cage and onto the grass. Eventually she opened her wings, and flew, lifting my heart up with her momentarily, until she settled on my crepe myrtle, only eight feet from my front door. She perched there for an hour. I sat, still watching. Damned if I was going to let that stupid bird take up residence on my own porch. Her job was to take my troubles away. As the sun set, it grew cold, and I grew tired of waiting. This business of flying off with my problems would be slow going.

The first week after Sam's death felt like racing through a long checklist. Notify God and everyone. Check. Brush teeth. Check. Count children. One, two, check. Feed dog. Oops. Death certificates, ordered. Obituary, published. Life insurance, confirmed. Passwords, found. Funeral and reception, orchestrated. Wear black. Check. Inhale, exhale, repeat as necessary.

Time to think was not on the list.

I had hoped—in the style of magical thinking—that the little bird would solve my problems in tidy checklist form. Bird meet troubles. Troubles be gone. Check. Then I could return to a life I recognized at some level.

But after the funeral, after cousins returned home and the hordes redirected their focus, the grieving began in earnest. It would be a sustained effort, and it would take time. They say that time heals all wounds, but I don't think so. Time by itself does nothing other than tick. What time offers is the opportunity to do the healing work; time gives the space to come to terms with the extent of the loss and the chance to trust again. There are no shortcuts. The little bird was simply corporeal hope that healing was possible. This would be the teaching of the little bird, although I would not understand until much later.

I retreated into the house.

I imagine that the little bird spent the night in my yard gathering her strength for our mourning. Come daylight, the little bird was gone.

CHAPTER 9

STILL OCTOBER

G rief time has a cadence all its own. Every day without Sam was interminable, imbued with a pungency like stale coffee. After seven lonely and miserable nights, it was Saturday morning again.

Rabbi Jonathan had given me a memorial candle, symbolizing the light of the soul, with the instructions to let it burn continuously for the next week. I never lit it. I was afraid that the flame would ignite the house and burn it to the ground. Irrational, perhaps, but crazier things had happened—my husband falling out of the clear blue sky, for one. We had lost so much that I could not bear the thought of losing anything more.

The rabbi had also pinned a black button with a cloth tail to my lapel, as well as to the lapels of Sam's parents and his sister, and then he ripped each one. This tearing of cloth symbolizes the pain and anger of grief. We were supposed to wear those buttons for seven days. Mine didn't last one.

At home, Danny pointed to it, shouting, "Mommy, take that off!"

I tried to reason with him, explaining that it was a tangible and public expression of anger and grief in the face of death. Then I realized my son wanted no more reminders that his father was gone, and respecting my son was more important to me than honoring thousands of years of tradition. I took off the button and tossed it into the garbage.

I did not host an official shiva. We had had our fill of grief rituals.

* * *

Life as a newly widowed single parent was overrated.

The phone calls were constant, in addition to the voicemails, condolence cards, and emails that accumulated in virtual and actual piles. All were expressions of love and community, and I was grateful. I wanted each caller and every writer to know how much I appreciated the support, yet somehow my lack of time to respond developed into a sense of obligation, which morphed into resentment. I felt pressure to answer all the notes and messages, but I didn't have the energy to pick up the phone, and I certainly didn't have the energy to write. Only when I couldn't sleep did I find myself tapping out emails in the middle of the night. My friend Maris was going through chemo and also not sleeping, so we often found ourselves exchanging long emails in the dark. It was a quiet, sacred, vulnerable time. We were both scrambling for our lives.

I found comfort in chatting with friends on the phone, laughing together and hearing their voices soften and break. Yet it was hard to carve out time for conversation between the demands of tending two boys solo and managing the post-death logistics.

The bills seemed to arrive at an alarming rate, along with a veritable army of dust bunnies. I had to figure out online bill pay, a relatively new feature of banking at the time, but my checking account was shut down almost immediately because Sam was the primary. I reverted to using the credit union account my parents had set up for me when I was in high school.

When I called Visa, I learned that I was only an "authorized user" on the credit card. They informed me that Sam himself would need to make any changes, and, in the event of his death, the entire account would be shut down, so I said *thankyouverymuch* and hung up. I continued to use the credit card and paid it off as though Sam were alive. Meanwhile, I called the credit union, but they wouldn't raise the five-hundred-dollar limit on my credit card without a recent income history or my husband's signature as a guarantor. I didn't have either, so I said *okaythanksIwillaskhimandcallyouback.*

I called the utility companies to remove Sam's name, but they all had listed Sam as the primary or the sole person on the account, even though I was the one who set up the services in the first place. One of the utilities—gas? electric? water?—made me shut off the service to the house and restart it a day later. And they required an extra deposit, which sucked.

Sam's death came up at every turn.

I got a call from Penguin's Frozen Yogurt to let Sam know that his favorite flavor—peanut butter fudge—was available that week. I didn't have the heart to let the youthful voice know that he was dead. I just said, "I'll tell him." I canceled our subscription to the *LA Times.* I didn't have the focus to read a headline, or a byline, or even look at the photos. I just threw the paper right in the recycling bin; that is, if I bothered picking it up at all. Every day, mail arrived with Sam's name on it. There were companies to notify and forms to complete. There were questions to answer and questions I could not answer. The bill for the ambulance ride was something like $10,000. The emergency room was more. I didn't know whether our health insurance would cover those costs. For that much money, it seemed like someone could have at least gotten an explanation out of him.

People asked me "How are you?" and I wanted to scream, *How the hell do you think I am?*

There was so much to do, and yet no fix.

Grief brain is real. I spent a lot of time staring vacantly. I used to be intelligent, efficient, and occasionally even funny, but I couldn't hold an idea long enough to form a coherent thought. I was sluggish and unmotivated. I felt blank, like an erased white board; whatever had been noteworthy was reduced to inky flakes at my edges. I rested my chin in one hand, looking toward who knows what—the window? the hardwood floor? a teacup? a pressing task I'd already forgotten?—and felt the warmth of my hand. My eyelids drooped with the weight of exhaustion, and my body fell into its rhythmic inhale and exhale. If it had been intentional, I might have called it meditation, but it wasn't. It was the lungs and heart doing what they do, and while I did not possess the awareness to be in awe of my body's simplicity and power, still, each breath pulled me through to the next moment.

I easily could have been seduced by the inertia. Grief's pressure held me in place. But with two little kids and a dog, shit needed to get done.

* * *

My poor mother. She had been trying to protect me and support me but was generally at a loss as to what to do or say. Or not say. She quietly and thanklessly scuttled around my house noticing and taking care of things. My parents served as the go-to adults for providing snacks, entertainment, and homework assistance to Danny and Jason. They often picked the boys up from school. My father read to the boys for hours on end and picked up the "puppy prizes" off the lawn. If I started a grocery list, my mother would finish it and run to Trader Joe's. If I mentioned a loose button, my mother would sew it in place and iron the item of clothing as well. My mother ran errands and prepared meals and brainstormed with the Janes on what they could do to help.

As helpful as it was to have my parents living with me, it was also a lot of bodies and feelings under one roof. The boys and I slept in one queen-sized bed together with Parker, and my parents slept in the living room. They deflated the air mattress every morning and folded the sheets and blankets in a corner because it bugged me to have the mess of it front and center in the house. I often took phone calls outside so I could retain my privacy. When my parents invited me to read the Bible with them, I declined. I wasn't feeling much love for God. I bristled when I heard my parents say "passed on." They cringed every time they heard me say "died" or "suicide." The pungency of my father's cologne rendered me even more irritable than I was as a teenager, and though I longed for a few hours alone in my own home, I knew I could not handle my life on my own. Not yet.

Susan and Maris knocked on my door. It might have been a Tuesday; I don't know. The days blurred together. They handed me a carefully wrapped box with a pretty bow and a simple card. Inside was a pair of soft flannel pajamas, chocolate brown with cheerful pink and yellow daisies. A simple, thoughtful gesture. Every time I put them on, they felt like a warm hug. Cozy incarnate. I wished Sam had allowed someone to take such care of him.

Another afternoon, I heard what sounded like an argument on my front lawn. I looked at my mom curiously. She had this inscrutable look on her face. I couldn't tell if she was about to laugh or cry, or whether she wanted me to see what was happening or to protect me from it. I moved to the living room, where I had a better view.

Susan was standing on my front lawn with Linda. Neither of them was bigger than a minute, as they say, and the two appeared to be having an argument. There was a large basket between them. If they had been Silky Terriers, you could have lifted them up by the scruffs of their little necks and held one in each hand while they barked themselves into submission. The two of them were engaging in a sort of tug-of-war over what I then realized was several loads worth of my towels and linens. We were witnessing a standoff between two broken hearts aching to heal mine when the only thing possible was to wash, dry, and fold.

One glance at my mother, and the two of us started giggling. When you have friends who fight over your dirty laundry, everything is going to be okay.

* * *

At night my mind went spinning—too restless to sleep, too jittery to pray. I extricated myself carefully from my sleeping boys, and I went outside to the front porch, shivering in the dark and cold.

Christian Science practitioners pray for others according to the teachings of the church, and I had reached out to these healing ministers my whole life for everything from headaches to heartaches to career direction. Deborah answered on the first ring. She exuded confidence and was faithful to the point of force, like the archangel Michael with his flaming sword. The last time we talked, I had asked her to pray regarding the Surprise situation. But this night was about loss. She was so gentle, all Gabriel, the kind and gentle harbinger of the message, "Fear not." I wanted to believe what she was saying about hope, about love's presence, about goodness being the only real power, but the words felt hollow in light of Sam's suicide. It seemed that I had been praying all my life, and it had come to this tragic end anyway. I didn't have the heart to pray anymore.

I could not accept the religious perspective that death was simply an illusion and that the reality was life eternal. I did believe that life was eternal, but to call death an illusion when we felt so alone and sad without Sam bordered on callous. Deborah asserted that Father-Mother God was the source of all fathering, but it wasn't like Jesus was packing the kids' lunches or driving them to soccer practice. My boys missed their daddy, and while I acknowledged an abundance of father-ish figures in their lives—my father, my brother-in-law, an army of uncles, and even me—this theology ignored the traumas my sons experienced daily because their daddy was gone.

When I hung up the phone, it felt like I had said goodbye to a beloved aunt before embarking on a trip to a foreign country, not knowing whether I would return or if I would ever see her again. Or maybe I felt more like Moses himself at the end of his life when, after he did his imperfect best, he was denied entrance to the promised land.

I lingered on the cold porch, thinking. I had me, a bevy of Janes, and a nearly full bottle of Xanax. We were all I needed.

God could go fuck Himself.

*　*　*

It makes me tense when people say things like, "It can't get any worse." That's not true. Things can *always* get worse.

A few Janes were talking quietly near my front door. They didn't realize I was there at first, but when Linda saw me, she stopped talking and looked vaguely guilty. They were shielding me from something.

"What is it?" I asked.

Linda hesitated. I knew she didn't want to increase the emotional load I was shouldering, but she respected me enough to tell me the truth. "Jane has colon cancer."

There seemed to be no end of calamities. The news landed on me like rain on a swimming pool. I was already so full that sorrow spilled off my edges.

Even so, I preferred knowing to not knowing. The not knowing in my own life was killing me. I didn't want to be insulated from my friend's suffering, and it was not a bad thing, actually, to be jolted out of my own self-absorption. I was not in a space to prepare meals or drive carpool. True, nobody wanted me handling sharp knives or sitting behind the steering wheel, but what I could do was get out of my own head and think about somebody else with compassion in my heart. I was on the receiving end of hundreds of well-wishes. So many people cared, and it seemed to be making a difference.

*　*　*

Eventually—a week after Sam's death, maybe two?—I went to the Pasadena Police Department to pick up Sam's few remaining belongings, not knowing what the police had kept. I was hoping for a clue to what he had been thinking. They had Sam's phone, money clip, and glasses. The frames of his rounded black glasses were bent at a vicious angle and one lens had popped out, a reminder of how violent the fall had been. The money clip had a few dollars in it. I wondered why he thought he needed cash at all.

His phone showed a few missed calls on the day he died, all from me, and none after. I was almost disappointed not to find a mistress's number. If there had been an anonymous female voicemail, I could have hated him, and somehow that seemed simpler.

Sam's phone was one of the very first iPhones, still brand new. I scrolled down the list of contacts: Apple Store (pre-programmed), Baja Fresh (our favorite Mexican takeout), California Pizza Kitchen, me, a high school friend, José, Sam's mother, Sam's assistant, Supercuts, and Zack. A tech giant, six people, two restaurants, and a haircut. Ten contacts total. This discovery made me incredibly sad, imagining how isolated he might have felt. Anyone on that short list would have helped him if he had called. Did he not realize he could have easily added dozens to his list? It occurred to me that *all* phones should come pre-programmed with the National Suicide Prevention Lifeline (1-800-273-8255).

Even so, Sam could have had a hundred numbers programmed into his phone, but it only would have made a difference if he had called one. Just one.

* * *

There were scenes I kept revisiting in my mind, like rewinding a movie so I could see the clues I missed the first time, moments that looked very different in retrospect. Only after the initial tumult settled could I start to piece together why Sam had killed himself. I had thought he was stressed, but it never entered my mind that he was suicidal. I thought he needed time off, maybe a guys' night out or a weekend away.

I remembered a night shortly before Sam's suicide. This was after several things: after the Surprise conversation, after I had returned to work, after the boys had drifted off to sleep, and after the dishes were done. Sam and I were exhausted, but we sat together relaxing in the living room. I was telling him about the parts of working that I had forgotten I liked, like an elderly client who appreciated my help, or laughing with a colleague over something only an estate planning lawyer would find amusing. Sam said, "I'm so sorry I failed you."

I was shocked. "Failed me?! What part of this is failure? We have two kids, a ridiculously cute dog, and a white picket fence! So what if I have to go back to work? That's the easy part."

Sam didn't argue or explain how he thought he had failed. He just pulled me into a hug. Eventually, we tumbled into bed. I curled around him like a comma and drifted to sleep.

Thinking about it later, I realized we weren't speaking the same language. Or maybe I wasn't listening attentively enough to what had gone unsaid. I didn't know then that an apology was a warning sign for suicide.

Our lives had seemed so normal—predictably suburban. We had had dinner with Linda and Ben a week before Sam died. We ordered takeout from our favorite Indian restaurant and put together something child-friendly for the boys, probably Linda's crowd-favorite home-made mac and cheese. The children bounced around the backyard with a soccer ball, while we parents chatted over saag paneer and chicken tikka masala.

Ben had asked Sam if he kept his license to practice law. It was a reasonable question; Sam and I had met in law school. He would have made a great litigator. He prepared his arguments thoroughly and argued his position articulately. The mock court judges admired his calm demeanor which, when combined with his tenacity, made him an effective advocate. But Sam had never been licensed. He failed the California Bar Exam the first time he took it, but his position in the tax department of an accounting firm didn't require that he pass it. For a while, this failure troubled him, but soon he transitioned to a brokerage house as a stockbroker, which he much preferred to the practice of law. He decided not to take the Bar Exam again. Sam often said that failing the Bar was a good thing, because it pointed him toward another career.

He looked at me, his mouth full of samosa, so I answered with his usual words: "Sam failed the Bar and then found something better than practicing law." Linda and Ben laughed, but Sam—uncharacteristically—shot me a dirty look.

We had had a nice evening with our friends, but Sam was still pissy when we got in the car to go home. *What nerve had I struck? Why was he suddenly embarrassed? And so hostile?* That episode hadn't bothered him in ages.

I wondered whether I was imagining his reaction or just being hypersensitive, but Linda would later confide that she, too, was struck by the intensity of Sam's response to the Bar Exam comment. It was so unlike him.

In searching Sam's dresser drawer for clues later, I had discovered, with a sinking feeling, my diamond heart necklace. He had given me the necklace for our fifteenth wedding anniversary, just two months before his death. It was pretty, an asymmetrical heart inlaid with little diamonds on a simple silver chain. Following the Surprise conversation, we had agreed that he would return it as one of our expense-reducing measures. When I discovered it tucked away, I wondered why he hadn't returned it. Did he forget? Was he simply too busy with work and the usual family fare? Was he disappointed that I was willing to return it? Did he expect our financial picture to turn around? Was he too ashamed to walk into the jeweler's with it? Why had he purchased it in the first place if he thought we were in such dire financial straits?

I was still wearing my wedding ring on my left hand as well as Sam's on my right index finger; they made me feel closer to him. The necklace, on the other hand, made me feel disconnected, as though I hadn't really known my husband. It reeked with the lingering scent of one more thing that sent him over the edge. I would not wear it again; I shoved it back in the drawer.

There was also the night before Sam died. I had noticed our estate planning documents sitting on the kitchen counter. They were hard to miss; they filled a fat three-ring binder. I didn't even ask why Sam had had them out, because I had been meaning to look at them. I had intended to update our documents myself since I had gone back to work. We had, as many parents do, drawn up our Will after we had had our first baby in order to name guardians for Danny. In the unlikely event of our untimely demise, all our worldly assets would have gone to "Danny and any other children we might have." I wanted to include Jason by name.

I had commented, "Oh, hey! I've been thinking about revising those."

Sam said nothing.

As a Trusts and Estates attorney, I routinely reviewed these types of documents. Maybe if I had been a litigator or a civil rights lawyer, I would have known to be alarmed. I later learned that people contemplating suicide often review their Will to make sure it adequately expresses their wishes. He must have been reading his—not with an eye toward updating the estate plan, but to make sure that it was good enough as is.

Sushi Tuesdays

Some days my only comfort was that our therapist also missed the signs. Dr. Newland spoke the language of emotional distress, and she hadn't see Sam's. I spilled the pieces in her office. It was like dumping a thousand-piece puzzle on the floor, picking up a piece here or there, trying to figure out how it fit into the whole, sorting the pieces into sky and landscape, and looking for corner pieces to frame the picture. Ending the session felt like collecting all the disparate pieces, tossing them back into a box, and tucking the sordid mess away in a closet.

CHAPTER 10

IF YOU LOVE IN THIS WORLD YOUR HEART WILL BREAK

When the realities of Sam's death became too much, I fantasized about expatriating to Switzerland. I imagined renewing my expired passport, cashing out, and finding a little cabin in a remote mountain town.

If I live a simple enough life, I thought, *maybe I wouldn't need to find a job, or learn to speak German, or talk to anyone. I could get a Bernese Mountain Dog and hike alone in the mountains every day, stopping in the local bakery for fresh bread. I wouldn't say a word. I would simply point at the loaf. I wouldn't tell anyone my story. I would be the tall, sad American who walked and walked all alone.*

There were, however, two reasons I could not just up and leave, two reasons for me to get up every morning, and I was their mother. My sons needed me. And I needed them. I was going to have to find my way.

* * *

Danny grew increasingly angry, his blue eyes flashing darkly. He refused to say the words "Dad" or "dead." I started referring to these as "the D words" instead.

Jason, on the other hand, talked to me about everything. He was insightful and articulate about his feelings. If, in our conversations, we uttered a "D" word, Danny yelled at us, which made it impossible to tend to both of them at once. *This is the reason that children come with two parents in a set*, I thought bitterly.

Bedtime became our sanctuary. The three of us snuggled in bed with a book, and the dog curled up at our feet. We were making our way through the Harry Potter books. Sam had been reluctant to share the series with our children—not because he didn't like the story or was categorically opposed to witchcraft—but because he thought the themes of violence, child neglect, and dead parents were too painful to introduce to children so young. "Life is hard enough," he'd say. Boy, how I would have loved to revisit *that* conversation.

What Sam missed, of course, was that the Harry Potter series also outlined resources for kids: love, friendship, uniqueness, insight, creativity, a wanton disregard for certain rules. These are the tools kids use to survive losses and thrive. After all, Harry Potter is "The Boy Who Lived."

Jason drifted off midway through a chapter, but Danny remained wide awake, his imagination stirred by characters to whom he related living in a magical world to which he aspired.

"Mommy, what if Parker was a phoenix and he just burst into flames and then turned into a puppy again?"

The dog cocked his ears and thumped his tail without comment.

"Mommy, what's a mortgage?"

I wondered if his question was inspired by the fictional Uncle Vernon, who found no end of agitation in Harry's shenanigans and costly mishaps. "It's what they pay the bank every month to live in their house."

"The bank owns the house?"

"Kind of. The bank mostly owns it." I found his curiosity endearing but was too tired to engage my eight-year-old in a conversation about principal, equity, and compound interest. I just wanted to read the book.

"Don't we already own our house?"

"Well, the bank mostly owns our house, too."

"How much does our mortgage cost?"

"A lot." I didn't tell him it was $5,000 a month.

"More than a car?"

"Lots more."

"Mommy, how do you pay the electric bill?"

I closed the book and looked at my boy questioningly, now rec-ognizing that this conversation was not about mortgage finance or online banking.

"They told me that now I'm the man of the house and it's my job to take care of you," he said.

It hurt my heart that I couldn't protect my son from the well-inten-tioned but wholly misguided things people said. It was easy for them to forget how young Danny was. He was a head taller than most of the kids in his third-grade class. But the man of the house?

"Oh, sweetheart," I said, holding his little face in my hands so I could look into his eyes. "You are not the man of the house. You are the eight-year-old of this house. Your job is homework and playdates and baseball."

His tears welled.

"Are you afraid?" I asked gently.

He nodded.

"I promise, I can take care of the mortgage and the electric bill and you and your brother. And if it ever gets to be too much, if I can't do it, I will ask for help. I've got people. I will ask PopPop and Uncle Zack and Uncle José and Uncle Dave. I'll ask Grandma and Aunt Nancy and all my friends. Okay?"

He braved a smile.

"Your job is third grade, and my job is everything else."

"Okay, Mommy," he said, relaxing next to me. "Keep reading."

* * *

A word about the Janes: several of these angels were people I didn't know personally, people who heard gossip over coffee, or in the announcements at church. Some were friends of friends. One woman responded to the published obituary, writing me a long letter of encouragement, which included intimate details of her own brush with suicide. These gifts were part of the legacy of flinging my door wide open early on.

But it was not without consequence. Truth can be controversial.

I heard snippets and rumors, from a Jane or from my own children, that some people found the truth so unpalatable that they made up wildly inaccurate stories about Sam's death. That he was bipolar. That a disgruntled client or girlfriend or a "bad guy" pushed/shot/fill-in-the-blanked him. A drug deal gone south might have made sense were it not for the fact that Sam wouldn't even take the Vicodin his doctor prescribed for his back, but of course, the children would not have been privy to this detail. My consolation was that Danny and Jason came to me to vet these scenarios, because my sons knew I would give them honest answers.

One of the Janes reported to me that she saw Danny sitting at the edge of the playground during recess. He wasn't interacting with any of the other kids. I assumed he wanted to distance himself from the chatter about his father's death. Maybe Danny wanted to be alone with his sadness. Jane added that one of the more tender-hearted students sat down next to him. While the rest of the kids played handball and freeze tag, the two third graders said not a word. They sat together on the curb at the edge of the blacktop until the bell rang. It is the rare and precious soul who can offer her presence in silence and simply share the weight of an unbearable grief.

* * *

People said I was brave, but the truth is that it was easier for them to manage their own discomfort if I didn't cry in public. My grief was more palatable if I didn't say something sharply sarcastic to them, or about Sam. It was hard enough to deal with my own feelings, let alone theirs, so I bit my tongue. I shouted in private. I wasn't brave. I wasn't strong. I was exhausted. If I had been strong, I would have fallen apart and not cared who was made uncomfortable by my grief. I would have let them judge me, let them stand aghast at the horror of raw grief, and let them marinate in the reality that nothing was okay. I was not okay. My kids were not okay. Sam was not okay.

I was not brave. I was afraid: afraid that they would think I couldn't handle raising my boys, afraid that they would think I was going to follow Sam off the ledge, afraid that they would think, "No wonder Sam jumped."

* * *

Halloween was my least favorite holiday in the best of years. But 2007 was the worst.

Jason dressed as Harry Potter and looked the part with his naturally unruly brown hair. He, too, was a boy who lived.

Danny, by contrast, donned a costume of his own creation—a pirate phantom. His face and entire body stayed hidden under a white sheet, with two roughly cut eyeholes so he could peer out from his isolation. Atop his head, a pirate hat displayed a grim skull and crossbones, and he waved his sword angrily. I wondered if he knew how uncomfortable his ghost made the adults around him. He was, quite obviously, the boy whose father died.

Not two weeks prior, we had been an unremarkable suburban family of four. But now our lives had drastically changed. Halloween night, we wandered the dark streets, alight with ghouls and teenagers passing as skeletons or wearing gruesome masks, kids playing at death. It was a game and a joke to them, a farce. The next day they would wake up, sneak M&Ms for breakfast, and laugh about the previous night's adventures. Their father might even drive them to school.

The next morning, my sons would wake up and their father would still be dead.

* * *

Sam had been a generous and gentle spirit. He was protective of kids and his mother. He was not the kind of man you'd expect to jump, whatever that means. He was the kind of man you trusted to give you good advice when you were lingering too close to the edge.

Ben had turned to Sam for advice when he was experiencing his own financial upheaval. As had Zack. One of Sam's clients who struggled with depression had called Sam twice when she was contemplating suicide. Sam had calmed her, helped her see the situation differently, and with hope. Consistently, Sam had served as a listening ear and a trusted friend.

His childhood friend Alex came to the house one evening—ostensibly to comfort us—and he was beside himself. "Of all people, he couldn't tell *me*?" Alex, too, had confided in Sam that he struggled with suicidal feelings. The copy of *Darkness Visible* by William Styron, a memoir of depression and near-suicide that Alex had given to Sam, was sitting on the bookshelf in the living room near where we were sitting. No sooner had Alex plopped down on the sofa then he let his rage fly. "That *fucking* cocksucker! Son of a bitch! *Goddamn* motherfucker! *Jesus H. Christ*!"

No book could have prepared this widow for that scene. I wished I had said something in response to his tirade. Something direct, like, *Thanks for coming, but you have to leave now*; or clever: *What does the H stand for?*

I said nothing. I played the graceful widow. I reminded myself to be understanding, compassionate, and comforting. The poor man had suffered from suicidal ideation for years, and Sam's death wounded him deeply. He had lost a lifelong friend.

But it bugged me. Why should I be the one to bridle her rage? Something about suicide seemed to give Alex *carte blanche* to berate its victim.

* * *

A lot of stars have to align for someone to accomplish a suicide. It's like driving on a busy road with no traffic and every single light turning green. *How many green lights did Sam zip through that day? How many did I miss?*

When Sam had come home from work on October 19, 2007, I could see he was upset. He said, "People lost money today." And then commented, "I can't do this anymore, and I'm too old to learn to do anything else."

He said those words on Friday, but it was as though I didn't actually hear them until later. I had taken his words as hyperbole, disappointment, or an expression of irritation after a long work week. *Isn't that the stuff of life?*

Only too late did I understand that he meant precisely what he had said: "I can't do this anymore."

He jumped from a building the day after big losses in the stock market. It conjured images of stockbrokers and investors jumping from high-rises in New York after the Great Crash in October, 1929. This image has very little basis in fact; financial loss by itself rarely inspires a person to take his own life. The national folklore of the classic stockbroker's death is attributed to Will Rogers, who wrote, "When *Wall Street* took that tailspin, you had to stand in line to get a window to jump out of." Nevertheless, the visual was powerful.

Sam jumped, just like our friend Jeff had.

That same Friday night, Sam had also said, "Jeff Wall was a smart guy." His words sounded ominous after the fact, rumbling like dark thunderheads before a lightning strike.

Jeff was, in fact, a very smart guy. Sam and I graduated from law school with him, but Jeff had gone to medical school first. He was already licensed as a physician when he started law school. If he hadn't been such a nice guy, too, we would have been contractually obligated to hate him, because he ruined the curve in every class he took.

Jeff had killed himself six years earlier by jumping off a parking structure adjacent to the high-rise where he practiced patent law. For days afterward, we and our law school classmates harbored the belief that the police would find evidence that Jeff had been pushed. A multifaceted scheme forming the basis for an espionage novel would have made infinitely more sense.

"Jeff Wall was a smart guy," Sam had said, and I had answered immediately and viscerally, "Jeff was an idiot! He left his wife and two daughters!"

I didn't understand why Sam had said this. His comment seemed to come out of nowhere, and I dismissed it. Jeff had left us all in a state of disbelief. Sam had attended his funeral, but I stayed home that day with an infant Jason. As I inhaled the top of my baby's head—you can still catch a whiff of heaven on a child that young—I found it impossible to imagine what could have driven Jeff away from his little girls.

What Sam meant, I figured out too late, was that Jeff knew how to get the job done. It never occurred to me that Sam was planning his own death. Was he trying to tell me that he was desperate, that he understood why Jeff had jumped? Would he have admitted that he was suicidal if I had understood what he was hinting at? Did he want me to stop him? Or did he intentionally stop short of letting me know exactly what he was thinking, so that by the time I figured it out, it would have been too late?

Would it have killed him to ask for help?

* * *

Each new morning warranted a victory lap, evidence of having survived the darkness. Each successive sunrise offended me. I resented that every day took me farther away from my life as it had been, distanced me from the man I loved, the man I thought I knew.

It had always cracked me up that Sam couldn't dance and didn't like coffee. He was Cuban, for crying out loud. But people can be incomprehensible.

I used to begin my mornings with a cup of black tea. I enjoyed the ritual of preparing my English Breakfast in the early quiet, warming both hands around the sides of my favorite mug, usually after Sam had left for the office and before the boys were awake. A still, meditative, cozy moment to sit, breathing in the steam and welcoming a new day.

After Sam's death, however, my morning tea was no longer…well, my cup of tea. It felt empty. It wasn't cozy; it was supremely lonely.

Nothing about my cup of tea lifted my spirits. Often it sat, untouched, growing cold while I stared out the window, not comprehending the path before me.

I hadn't scrutinized Sam's Will and Trust in the immediate aftermath of his death. I already knew what his planning documents said. By the time I sat down to peruse Sam's legal paperwork, the funeral song had been sung and the body buried. Reviewing his instructions was largely a *pro forma* exercise. Or so I had thought. Sam, it turned out, had prepared a detailed list of everything he had wanted me to do, giving specific instructions on his burial, potential organ donation, whom to notify and the funeral itself.

My heart sank.

I had checked the box that gave Sam full discretion to do with my remains whatever he chose. I thought Sam had done the same for me. He had not.

I was horrified. Sick to my stomach that his family might accuse me of subverting his wishes—or worse, the thought that I had neglected something Sam himself had asked of me—I carefully reviewed the list.

No organ donation. Check.

No cremation. Check.

Jewish funeral service. Check.

Burial. Check.

Check.

Check.

Check.

I had done it all. Every last item on Sam's list.

At a time when I was full of doubt, bursting with questions that couldn't be answered, afraid that I did not, in fact, know my husband at all, this sterile legal form gave me comfort. It was, oddly, a form of proof to me that I did know Sam. I knew exactly what he wanted, and that's what I had done. Not because I had consulted an attorney or heeded the advice of well-intended family. I did it simply because I knew and loved my husband.

* * *

One of the collateral casualties of Sam's death was my lost interest in reading. Apparently, this inability to focus is common among those who have recently suffered a significant loss. Normally, I kept a stack of books within arm's reach—fiction, nonfiction, literary and otherwise— along with a persistent longing to curl up with a book in my chair-and- a-half-sized reading chair, overstuffed comfort in a pale mint tweed. But I barely had the attention span to read the back of a cereal box. My finishing an entire novel was unlikely at best.

With all good intentions, Uncle Dave brought me a legal treatise on retirement plans and spousal rollovers. Even without the grief-induced brain trauma, my eyes rolled up in the face of phrases like "defined con- tribution plan" and "minimum required distributions." I was astonished that Dave still had faith in my capacity to focus and comprehend, but I would need a more compelling reason to curl up with the Internal Revenue Code. I just wanted him to tell me which box to check for Sam's IRA. I checked a box and kept moving.

One of the Janes recommended the book *The Year of Magical Thinking* by Joan Didion, which chronicled the year following her husband's fatal heart attack. As I recall, it was the only book I actu- ally finished in the months following Sam's suicide. Jane thought the story would resonate with me, that I would appreciate the perspective of a fellow widow navigating a new world by herself. But I resented it. Throughout the book, I kept thinking, *The man had a pacemaker, for crying out loud. How surprised could she have been? My husband wasn't diagnosed, medicated, or even in therapy. Her daughter had graduated from college. My youngest son was in first grade!*

I couldn't handle her fragility. I was entirely fragile myself.

The boys had some friends over to play one afternoon, and one of the kids was pretending to host a game show he called *"What's Your Tragedy?"* He stood on the bed, pretending it was a stage, and spoke ani- matedly into his curled fist as though it were a microphone: "Hellllloooo Cincinnati, you're on live with Widows and Orphans. Tell us: What's your tragedy?" He then extended the "mic" to the contestants, who shared their wretched histories in an effort to win the prize for having the worst life.

I would have laughed out loud if it hadn't been so pathetic.

It occurred to me that some people lived their real lives this way, and I didn't want it to be us. To play this game was to lose.

It's a natural impulse, to compare and contrast tribulations: heart attack or homicide, sudden death compared to drawn-out illness, death of a spouse against death of a child, young woman versus old man. Unless this analysis forms the basis of a graduate thesis, however, it is largely futile. Loss, while universal, is also individual. There is really only one story, and they are all different.

I wish I could say I didn't get sucked into playing my own version of "*What's Your Tragedy?*" but I did, at least for a while. Marinating in the misery of a painful loss can be a vital part of the healing process. It can be helpful to visit that place, but I didn't want to take up permanent residence there. It's the competitive practice of suffering that is counterproductive. I didn't like the way I felt when I was trying to convince myself (or somebody else) how much worse my own life was. There is no room for gratitude in that space.

Even though suicide is messy, I didn't want to get stuck in the mess of Sam's death. I didn't want to identify myself primarily or exclusively as a widow. But I didn't know how to avoid it.

***

Sadly, I wasn't the only young widowed mother of both a first grader and a third grader at the elementary school that year. There were two others—one whose husband died from cancer and the other from a sudden heart attack. "It's the club you don't want to be in," the Widowed Janes said, welcoming me with open arms, broken hearts, and pomegranate martinis. There is no good way to widow.

These Janes invited me to attend a family grief group they found helpful at a local family welfare organization whose grief and loss program was well respected. I liked the idea of finding a community of healing and hope. I imagined a tribe who weren't afraid to talk about the awful reality of loss, but who had also found a way past the misery. I thought it would be good for Danny and Jason.

The Widowed Janes picked us up, and all nine of us piled into two Mommy-Mobiles. When we arrived, my boys reluctantly joined the children's group with the other kids. Meanwhile, the head of the program met me privately, so she could fill out paperwork and get a feel for the dynamic of our family in crisis. She seemed competent, efficient, and kind, but neither warm nor fuzzy. The word "suicide" grabbed her attention.

"Are you suicidal?" she asked.

"No."

"What about the children?"

"No!"

"Gun in the home?"

"No."

"It's just you and your sons living in the home?"

"My parents are living with us right now."

"Have them lock up all your knives—anything sharp."

Seriously? I thought. *How will I feed my children without a chef's knife?*

"Also lock up all medications."

This would be awkward, asking my parents who didn't approve of medicine in the first place to safeguard my Xanax. I was thirty-nine, for crying out loud, but she seemed to know what she was talking about, so I dutifully transcribed her instructions.

I joined the adult group midsession, where my Janes had saved me a seat. There were about ten women in the circle and just two men. One of these widowers let his friendly gaze linger uncomfortably in my direction. The female moderator welcomed me into the group. I can't remember what she looked like, only that I felt warmth in her gentle smile. I shared my name and the fact that my husband had suicided the previous month, and then she continued the discussion on grieving rituals for children in different developmental stages. She encouraged us to use clear language in discussing death with children and teenagers, avoiding euphemisms like "we lost him." *Okay*, I thought, *I've done that right*. Toward the end of the session, the widower asked the moderator when he could start looking for a "replacement wife," a comment I found so repugnant that I wished I had introduced myself with a pseudonym.

We attended the next week or two, but Danny detested speaking of his father's death. We stopped going. I never did lock up the knives, and after a week or two, my dad just handed me the key to the small, metal toolbox in which he had kept the medication.

Dr. Newland then suggested that I try a suicide survivors' group at a local hospital. I found this term *suicide survivor* misleading. By definition, there is no survivor of a suicide. *Suicide survivor* sounds like someone who tried (and failed) to complete a suicide, but that person is referred to as a *suicide-attempt survivor*. By contrast, I am a *suicide survivor*, meaning that I have survived my husband's suicide. Journalist Jane was also a *suicide survivor*, as her father took his life when she was twelve. She picked me up, and we went together to the group session.

People were kind and welcoming, almost apologetic. As the evening progressed, everyone told their stories. One or two had lost a parent to suicide. Most had lost a child. I was the only widow. Each speaker, still raw with emotion, painted vivid details of lives lost. One petite woman described finding her daughter's limp body hanging from a noose in the garage and desperately cutting the rope to release the teenager. She rocked slightly as she spoke, her soft hands slightly open, pleading. These were the hands that welcomed her newborn, and the same hands that held the young girl as all warmth left her body.

I sat, transfixed. I could not imagine how I would ever come to terms with so great a loss. The statistics on children who have suffered the death of a parent (for any reason) are terrifying. Many struggle with academics, addiction, and an increased risk of suicide. Hence the advice to lock away the knives. Children as young as mine had accomplished their own suicides, as horrifyingly implausible as that sounded. I had to help my sons. I could not let my sweet and shy Danny or my sweet and social Jason become statistics. The loss of a child in addition to the death of my husband was beyond overwhelming for me to contemplate.

How would I get out of bed in the morning? Why bother? Indeed, every soul in the room seemed mired in their grief, even decades after the fact. They talked about hope, but not one emanated hope. I saw no evidence of healing. If they lived lives beyond the loss, they did not share them.

Jane and I walked in silence to her car, avoiding eye contact. Once buckled in, we turned toward each other. I was relieved to see that she, too, was appalled by the wreckage we had witnessed.

I had no intention of joining what, through the lens of my own raw and tender distress, appeared to be a suicide-sanctioned pity party. It pointed in a direction I did not want to go. I needed a balance between facing the loss and healing from the loss, but there was none to be found in the suicide survivors' group that night. I never gave it a second chance.

I turned to Dr. Newland for support. She understood me. She saw the confused and wounded little girl, tucked tight in a ball. She saw my grizzly bear instincts, rising to protect her cubs, and my mother bird nature, gently folding a soft chick under each wing. And she saw my inner princess warrior with a poem in one hand and a sword in the other. Without judgment, and with recognition, she saw all of me.

I curled up on her sofa and wept.

* * *

I didn't want Sam's death to define our kids, even though his death was clearly a watershed moment in our lives. I didn't want my kids to be the "boys whose father jumped off a building when they were little"—a constant reminder of tragedy. I wanted Danny and Jason to write or play guitar or baseball or do whatever cool things they would do, *even though* their father died when they were little. I wanted them to be the kind of people who rose from the ashes. I didn't quite know how to get them there, but I knew that ignoring the loss would not work. I had grown up in a culture of denominationally issued rose-colored glasses, and I understood all too well that you cannot fix a problem you do not acknowledge. Faith and gratitude were well and good, but they didn't countermand Sam's suicide.

The only ritual I kept after Sam's death was this: every morning I filled a bowl with water, and every evening, I poured it out. I adapted this practice from one Rachel Naomi Remen described in her book, *My Grandfather's Blessings*. I stood at the kitchen sink, and as the bowl filled with water, I reflected on everything in my life: my health, my family and friends, my talents and strengths, my fears and failures, my home and dreams and regrets. I accepted my whole life, not just the pretty bits, but all of it, and then placed the bowl on the counter, where I would see it frequently and be reminded to bring my whole self to whatever the day presented. This daily practice grounded me in one day at a time. Last thing before bed, I tipped the bowl, released its contents, let the day go, and rested. Danny and Jason called this part "dumping Mommy's worries down the drain." If things were going especially poorly, they had been known to dump Mommy's worries mid-afternoon and call it a day.

I had found this practice of acceptance and letting go profoundly healing. I had suffered from recurring nightmares from the time I was a young child, but when I started this practice in my thirties, the nightmares stopped.

To hold the stream of life's offerings in one unifying bowl had been novel to me. I had been adept at holding on to the good and ignoring the bad. My gratitude lists had not included anything negative unless that "challenge" had been overcome. And releasing both the gifts and the glitches had also been a new idea. I did not want to let go of the smart and sunshiny parts. Nevertheless, those joys splashed down the drain along with my worries. The idea in filling the bowl was to accept the whole beautiful, crazy, mixed-up mess and to use everything in the service of life. And then to release it all.

This open stance toward the whole of life signaled a paradigm shift that would become foundational for my healing after Sam's death. In my religious upbringing, certain emotions were acceptable and pleasing unto God, worthy of God's perfect child. Others were not. Moving toward gratitude in the wake of Sam's suicide seemed Pollyannaish when his death cast such a dark shadow over our lives. I was not grateful for

Sam's death. I did not feel his absence as a blessing. My parents were afraid of what my rage might do, but how the hell was I supposed to feel?

As I stood in front of the sink, hands holding the bowl, arms stretched toward the flowing water, I felt the power in accepting Sam's suicide along with the recognition of the light still present in our lives— parents who rushed to my side, friends by the dozens bearing gifts, my dog's ridiculously incessant tail, and always, my two sons. None of this gratitude canceled out how bereft I felt. Grief and gratitude did not create a neutral canvas. They both existed in full Technicolor. The darkness lent perspective on the beauty of the points of light. Even on my darkest days, I had something to be grateful for.

I wondered whether those old nightmares were simply stuffed emotions—fear, anger, envy—that had nowhere else to go, so they came out in bad dreams. Perhaps once they had been acknowledged and honored, they could be released. They had served their purpose, and I let them go. The strong emotions were no longer a threat, and I was left to sleep in peace.

Healing would require me to explore the contours of my own emotional landscape. My life partner would not be able to help me, and my parents couldn't do it for me. Neither could my Janes. Or even my therapist, although she was already helping me become the expert in my own brand of grief.

I would tend to my own heart.

CHAPTER 11

HEAVY LIFTING

I was relieved when, after six weeks or so, my parents moved back home. When I found myself more annoyed that my father would not bring the trash cans to where they belonged behind the gate than grateful that he had pulled them up the driveway, it was clearly time for me to put my own damn trash cans away.

We needed space from each other and a semblance of normality. They wanted—desperately—for me to be fixed, and I was exhausted putting up a good front. They didn't seem to understand why I was so overwhelmed, emotional and distractible. At times they acted as if I was overreacting. After all, they loved Sam, and they were grief-stricken, too. But they still had each other; I had lost my partner. They raised their children together; I would have to raise mine alone. They could temporarily forget the tragedy; everything in my life had been tainted by Sam's death.

I was reminded of the Northridge earthquake that struck in the early hours on a January morning in 1994. My parents' experience and mine had been so different, it was hard to believe that we had lived through the same seismic event. Sam and I had just bought our first home, and the quake shook our little house to its foundation, causing tens of thousands of dollars of damage, bursting pipes, cracking the chimney, and shattering everything shatterable—wedding china, stemware, framed photos, the television. The noise was deafening, the destruction overwhelming. The terror of the vicious shaking lasted much longer than the eleven eternal seconds of the initial quake. Sam and I were as rattled as the contents of our home and retraumatized with every aftershock. Nothing in our home went unscathed. We had lost nearly everything, and we clung to each other.

Meanwhile, only twenty miles away, my parents' house sat securely on bedrock. One glass fell off a shelf but didn't break. My father rolled over and went back to sleep.

Suicide was cataclysmic. I kept reaching for Sam to stabilize me through the violent aftershocks, and he was gone.

* * *

One afternoon, probably early November, Danny came home from school brooding. Braden's dad had brought a prototype Mars rover for science class. Danny would normally have been excited about space exploration, but the fact of a father in the classroom highlighted that his own was missing. His grief simmered, quiet and hot.

Another day, Jason came home sad because Jake's father did an art presentation on Picasso. Jason loved art (and Jake and Jake's dad), but again, the dad's presence was a painful reminder of what he had lost. He sat in my lap and cried while I stroked his head and wished I could save my boys from rocket scientists and art docents and dads who came home on any given day.

I couldn't protect them from the anguish of this life without Daddy. I could only be with them in their pain. It didn't seem like enough.

I called my college friend Kirk for guidance. He recognized my voice immediately. "I heard. I am so sorry."

I didn't have to explain. He understood all too well. His own father had killed himself when Kirk and his brother were young. Kirk had not merely survived his father's suicide but matured into a successful adult with a career and family of his own. I needed to know how he did that.

We talked for an hour. Kirk didn't sugarcoat. "I saw my father in the coffin. Still for years, I had a nagging suspicion it was all fake. I would look for him in crowds and at airports." He had suffered. He had made some regrettable decisions. But along the way he had also gained perspective, compassion, and grit.

I found his voice of experience comforting. "You'll be amazed at what you and your boys can accomplish," he said.

Toward the end of our conversation, he said something that has stayed with me ever since. "Grief is like a heavy sandbag at your feet," he told me. "And if you do not pick it up, it will trip you for the rest of your life. But when you do pick it up, you will notice there's a little tiny hole in the bag. That's where the grains of sand start to fall out."

Kirk showed me what was possible for my boys. His was the encouragement I needed to hear.

He didn't pretend that healing would happen quickly, but he assured me that each grain of sand falling, however imperceptibly, inevitably lightened the bag. "When you do pick it up, two things will start to happen," he continued. "The sandbag will get lighter, and you will get stronger."

* * *

Jason's tears fell naturally, releasing grains from his grief sandbag. Danny, however, would neither express nor articulate his grief, and I imagined his sandbag sitting stubbornly at his feet. It terrified me to think what might happen if Danny's anger flared. Sam had hidden his emotions, and they killed him. I had safe outlets for my feelings: middle-of-the-night emails, conversations with friends like Kirk, and the safety of Dr. Newland's office. There was something sacred about being heard.

I decided it was time to find Danny a therapist. He agreed to the appointment, but when we arrived at Dr. Kimberly's office, he refused to get out of the car. The ever-flexible and creative therapist was not deterred. She cheerfully came out to conduct her session with Danny in my car.

I handed Dr. Kimberly my keys and waited anxiously in her office for the hour.

For his next session, Danny got out of the car but refused to go into Dr. Kimberly's office. The obstinately good-humored Dr. Kimberly brought out giant hedge trimmers, and Danny whacked away at the bushes in front of her office for the hour. Meanwhile, I sat in her lobby with a book in my lap. I didn't read it. I just carried one around like a prop. Anyone watching closely would have noticed that the only thing that held my attention for any length of time was a yellow butterfly flitting around the courtyard. I could not imagine moving with such joy, or really moving at all. I was so very tired, living in a fugue state of fatigue.

* * *

I thought a lot about Kirk's sandbag. It is hard to explain the constant weight—not just the holidays and the Hallmark days, but the every days. We moved from tantrum to tantrum. In our hearts, the pounding. In our lungs, the gasping. In our ears, the howling. Deep in our bones, the understanding that the words *It's going to be okay* were hollow and meaningless. It might never be okay again. And even if it were okay for a moment in time, it would not last for long. We would never be fixed. We could not be. We would always carry with us the knowledge of what it's like to lose everything that matters.

One afternoon, Danny's third grade teacher unwittingly sabotaged me with a field trip permission slip. I had been composed, reading the form letter addressed "To the Parents of" until I reached the bottom of the page, where the directions read: "Both parents must sign unless a single parent has sole legal custody."

Both parents…single parent.

Those words landed on my heart with a thud. I didn't feel like a single parent. I constantly thought about asking Sam his opinion. I picked up the phone to call him before realizing he was not call-able. I continued the conversations in my imagination.

Sole legal custody.

More heavy words I could not ignore but was not ready to embrace. The practical, legal ramifications of one parent's death introduced a new vocabulary to my daily life. Each unspeakable word uttered aloud was a grain slipping through the tiny hole in the sandbag.

Like many parents of young children, Sam and I had been circumspect about the words we used, especially when the boys were within earshot. In the aftermath of Sam's death, the boys heard a lexicon that was previously unfamiliar to them. Uncle José, for example, liberally seasoned his commentary about Sam's death with a variety of expletives: *That little dickhead, what a dumb shit, he couldn't fucking call me? Goddammit!* To their innocent ears, these new words sounded intriguing and naughty.

The night of his father's funeral, Jason had said, "Mommy, remember when Aunt Fanny said that Daddy flipped off cars? Wasn't that so funny?"

It was.

He giggled and then asked, "What does it mean, flipping off cars? Did he climb on the roof of the car and jump high in the air and do a flip and then land?"

That was the night I demonstrated for my six-and-eight-year-old sons the hand gesture for the universal symbol of ill will. I told my innocent ones the actual word: fuck. And because they asked what it meant, I explained that fuck was an ugly word for a beautiful act between two adults who cared for each other. Then we practiced the gesture, flipping off Daddy with our right hands, flipping off homework with our left hands, flipping off the world with both hands.

As the head of my family of three, I became much more lax about the use of certain so-called four-letter words, which we then referred to as "Uncle José's Colorful Words."

"Sometimes we use strong words to express strong feelings, but there is to be no brother-bashing with four-letter words," I explained. I established clear parameters for their at-home use. "That having been said," I warned the boys, "even God Himself cannot save you from the principal if you drop an F-bomb at school."

When hurtful and ignorant words were spoken on the school playground, I intentionally and with considerable restraint did not ask the offending child's name so that my sons would not have to visit their sole surviving parent in the penitentiary. But my children were allowed to hurl those words around at home to vent their fury. Words can be a powerful tool for self-expression.

Dr. Newland helped me develop the perspective that my anger was a signal toward something that needed attention, rather than a character flaw that I needed to ignore or keep under wraps for fear that I might ruin everything. I would not get to the other side of my feelings without actually *feeling* them first: the stuffy nose, the headache from the building pressure of uncried tears, the empty ache in my heart. The lump in the back of my throat would not yield to the words I wanted to say—that knot would strangle my voice into something high pitched and barely intelligible—until after the tears had had their way with me. Perhaps this was the meaning of cleansing tears…that I would not go back to being the same person I had been.

Dr. Newland encouraged me to be a container for the boys' anger and not to be afraid of it. She helped me see that there was a place for my sons' anger and that strong emotions need not overwhelm us. Some days I felt like I needed a cosmic pause button so I could call a professional first or read the right book and then resume my parenting responsibly. Sometimes I felt like Sam would be much better at this than I was.

One night Jason shredded "Softie," his favorite yellow baby blanket, in a fit of rage and confusion. I let him, thinking I could replace it. Once he had calmed down, however, the little one burst into tears, because Softie was his transitional love object, and now he couldn't sleep. He was inconsolable. "Mommy, you should have stopped me!" I felt guilty and sad. It was impossibly hard to know the right thing to do.

One day when Jason was in a particularly foul mood, he went outside to break big rocks into little rocks. I was chopping carrots in the kitchen but checked on him from time to time. He kept telling me to go away, so I retreated back to food prep. Eventually, he flung open the back door. "Mommy!" he demanded with both hands on his hips.

"What's for fucking dinner?" His invective launched, he stood there defiantly, glaring at me.

I turned my head slowly in his direction, raising my eyebrows questioningly. There was something incongruous about my innocent, adorable boy baiting me with an F-bomb. I suppressed the urge to laugh out loud, because I didn't want him to think I was dismissing his anger. I imagined the look of shock on my mother's face if I had dared such impudence as a child and the knee-jerk reaction of my father, which almost certainly would have featured a bar of soap. I considered briefly how Sam might have responded under the circumstances but dismissed his viewpoint, because his absence had created this situation. I was on my own. I was free to forge the path forward that I thought most promoted my son's healing. To focus on the "fuck" would have missed the point entirely. Sometimes those four-letter words are simply effective attention-getters.

I looked my little one straight in the eye, took a deep breath, and smiled. In the kindest voice I could muster, I told him what I was serving: "Fucking mac and cheese."

Mother of the Year.

He smiled.

In that moment, my boy needed me to see how much pain he was in. He needed me to acknowledge him, to turn toward his suffering, to speak his language, in which "Fucking mac and cheese" translated to: *I hear your pain. I'm with you, baby. Let's eat.*

CHAPTER 12

CHARLOTTE SHABBAT

I originally started going to Roger's Tuesday yoga class when Jason was in preschool because it fit into my mommy schedule. I dropped him off, went to yoga, and returned in time for preschool pickup. *Shavasana*, the final resting pose, was a moment of bliss that carried over into the rest of my day. Life with kids and dog and carpool and soccer and play-dates at the park was full and crazy fun, but my heart also needed still-ness and silence, even as the rest of me stretched and strengthened.

After Sam's death, Roger's yoga class became a lifeline. The mind-fulness, the peacefulness, the coordination of movement with the breath provided a gentle hour in the midst of an otherwise chaotic existence. Roger embodied nonjudgmental presence. If all I could manage was to sit on the mat and cry, it was enough. "It's like this," Roger would say, with a kindness and an acceptance that I could not quite imagine possessing myself.

The only hiccup was that *Shavasana*, also known as the "corpse" pose, brought morbid images of Sam, sometimes with his body splayed on the sidewalk, sometimes settled peacefully in the coffin, but in both cases equally dead. It was exceedingly difficult to inhabit my own body in those moments. I moved to an upright seated position. It was easier to breathe that way.

Meanwhile, Dr. Newland offered me a recurring Tuesday time slot in her schedule. I could have time for both yoga and therapy and then an hour or two to myself before picking up the boys from school. One Tuesday, I walked the horse trail. Another Tuesday, I took myself out for a bite at a quiet sushi bar in town. Table for one.

It happened gradually, over the course of several weeks, that Tuesdays become an oasis in the grief shitstorm. What started coincidentally became intentional. I stopped making any other appointments on Tuesdays, not even coffee with a friend. I didn't want the pressure of showing up on time, or choosing a meeting place, or getting dressed, or having to cancel last minute because I couldn't stop crying and didn't want my swollen, mascara-less eyes to be seen in public. I began to protect the day with an almost religious fervor. Yoga and therapy were the staples, and I reserved the rest of the day for whatever I needed for my own healing and well-being. If I was tired, I napped. I might just sit and listen. I might take myself shopping. I might treat myself to a pedicure, my colored toes a lasting reminder that I had taken time for me. I focused on what my heart needed. I didn't do chores or catch up on emails. I kept my Tuesdays sacred. I didn't make appointments: absolutely no MDs, CPAs, JDs, or BFDs. Before long I started looking forward to Tuesdays more than Fridays or Saturdays.

When my closest friends stopped calling me on Tuesdays, not because they didn't care but precisely because they were cocooning me in my time for myself, it became official: Tuesdays were my Charlotte Shabbat.

* * *

In typical Tuesday form, I didn't turn on the radio en route between Roger's studio and Dr. Newland's office. No music, no bad news, just me and my own laughter. Jason had said the funniest thing.

He had this little stuffed dog he named "Baby Piggy." Nobody knew why he named it Baby Piggy; it was soft and yellow and had Labrador ears. Baby Piggy went with Jason everywhere. I kissed them both goodnight. That morning, he had been holding Baby Piggy and looking thoughtful. After a few moments, he said, "Mommy, I'm going to change Baby Piggy's name."

I assumed my baby had realized that Baby Piggy was, in fact, a dog, and he was ready to change his name to "Baby Doggy." The moment was bittersweet, like the day he started writing his Js properly, with the tail curving to the left instead of to the right, which I found especially charming, because it was the first letter of his own name. I missed those innocent backward Js.

"Mommy," he had said in all seriousness, "I'm changing Baby Piggy's name to *Big Boy* Piggy!"

Big Boy Piggy. It was all I could do to keep a straight face.

"Good morning, Big Boy Piggy! What would *you* like for breakfast?"

Thinking about the conversation, I burst out laughing, the kind of laughter that shook me until my abs ached and tears formed in my eyes, the kind of laughter that was meant to be shared. Big Boy Piggy. *HE WAS A DOG!*

I reached for the phone. Not until I heard Sam's voice answer on the fourth ring did I realize what I had done.

I pulled to the curb and called his cell phone again so I could hear him say, "Leave me a message, and I'll call you back." I was almost glad I hadn't gotten around to disconnecting his phone, another of the myriad tasks on death's to-do list. I realized that this might be the only recording I had of Sam's voice. And no matter what it said, Sam wouldn't be calling me back.

If I had been telling Sam the Baby Piggy story, I wouldn't have had to explain that Baby Piggy was a dog, describe that his ears were pink and floppy and rounded, that his tail was too long and straight to be a pig's. I would have simply said, "Jason is changing Baby Piggy's name to…wait for it…*Big Boy* Piggy!" We both would have dissolved into peals of laughter. We spoke in that shorthand adopted by partners with decades of shared experience—a language for two.

And now I spoke a language no one else understood.

By the time I walked into to Dr. Newland's office, I was a mess. I kicked off my flip-flops, curled up in the corner of the sofa, wrapped my arms around a pillow, and cried. Her presence was steady and kind. When I looked at her gentle, brown eyes, everything spilled out in tears and gasping ragged breaths. Her office held children's toys and board books, many designed to help autistic kids learn about a range of feelings. Who knew these tools would be so useful for grieving widows as well? She didn't send me away to my room. She stayed near, allowing me to feel the black ache, the gaping hole in my center. She bore witness to my pain. She wasn't afraid, didn't shush me or rush me, or even push the box of tissues toward me.

I told her about the stuffed animal formerly known as Baby Piggy. Then I told her about the last time I went to Starbucks. As I was walking out with my café au lait, I had heard someone behind me say *sotto voce*, "She's the one whose husband killed himself."

Dr. Newland's eyes reflected my sadness.

"I don't *want* to be the one whose husband killed himself. And couldn't that bitch have waited until I was out of earshot to start gossiping?"

She let me rant. She seemed to appreciate that her office was the only place I could safely rage.

"I cannot believe Sam did this! I am so fucking pissed. It's like he took all his pain and dumped it on us. He didn't ask, didn't warn me, just up and left. Fuck him! He could have told me, but he didn't say a word. He said he wanted to move to fucking Surprise, Arizona. He didn't have to hold in his emotion. Not like he didn't have people to talk to. Or other options. Hey! I have an idea. Why don't you talk to your wife? Or your cousin? Or your fucking therapist? Oh no, I think I'll just jump off this nice building instead. Are you kidding me?"

I wasn't done.

"And if you don't care about your wife, fine. But your kids? If he needed to leave me, fine. I'm a big girl. I can take it. But don't fuck with my kids. And don't you *dare* give them the message that suicide is okay. I don't know what problems he thinks he solved."

Another idea occurred to me. "Do you think Sam could have been schizophrenic?"

Dr. Newland turned the question back to me. "What makes you think about that?"

Sam had had a first cousin who was diagnosed with schizophrenia as a young woman. I didn't know the details. She was in her fifties, lived on the East Coast, took her medication, and hadn't had an episode in decades. If Sam had had the same affliction, it seemed he would have exhibited some kind of aberrant behavior before he was forty-one. He didn't experience the extreme highs and lows I'd heard about for people who live with bipolar disorder. And it seemed unlikely that he suffered from alcoholism or addiction. Occasionally, we would share a bottle of wine on an anniversary, but otherwise we didn't keep alcohol in the house.

Dr. Newland threw a question my direction. "Do you think Sam was depressed?"

I shook my head. "He didn't act depressed. Not sad or moping around. I mean, he was stressed. Especially about work. But who isn't? If you have a job, you have job stress. If you don't have a job, then you *really* have job stress."

Sam depressed? It didn't make any sense. He had never once told me he was depressed. I was the one who called her gynecologist in a shaky, tearful voice begging for a different birth control method after a few short weeks on the pill because I was terrified of the depression I was sinking into. A week later, I was back to myself, but the episode scared the lights out of both me and Sam.

I didn't seriously consider the idea that depression could have played a role. It seemed to me that his suicide would have been related to something else, something bigger. Everybody is affected by the garden variety blues at one time or another, but that doesn't mean they kill themselves.

"You know what he used to say to me?"

Dr. Newland shook her head.

"If I said I was having a bad day, he'd say, 'You're not having a bad day, you're having a bad minute.'" I rolled my eyes. "Was *he* having a bad minute?" I paused. "I'd like to tell him just how many bad minutes I'm having now."

By the end of our session, I was wrung out, like a washcloth twisted tight to squeeze out the last drops of water—and then twisted again.

CHAPTER 13

NAMES WILL BE TAKEN IN VAIN

In the weeks after Sam died, Susan politely described my faith as having been "challenged." The truth is that I had told God to take Her own flying leap at least a dozen times.

I felt abandoned by God. Clearly God abandoned Sam and my sons. This was part of God's plan? To push a loving, devoted father and husband off a building? To deprive my boys of their favorite baseball coach? I wasn't interested in this kind of plan. Or that kind of God.

One of the Janes (whose faith was still intact) gave me a book of 365 quotes. Some were truly inspirational, and others went like this: "God can take tragedy and turn it into triumph. He routinely does this for those who love Him." For those who love Him? What about those of us who were enraged by Him? Now that would be a God I could respect. But this God who conditioned His care upon my love for Him? This was why I had a dog.

Danny had thrown a major fit one night because I wouldn't let him watch television before completing his homework. Why he flew into a rage about this, I wasn't entirely sure, because the family rule had always been "homework first, then TV."

But as I stepped back, I realized I knew exactly why he was mad. It wasn't about the homework. He was hurt and furious because his daddy jumped to his death, leaving my son without a loving father, without faith in the strongest man he knew, without a catcher to pitch to, without his personal morning alarm clock.

So I let him rage. He hit and kicked; he shredded the geometry homework he had worked on for three days; he destroyed his brother's art project; he turned the hose on me. I stayed with him as best I could, protecting him, Jason and me, recognizing and understanding his anger, but also terrified of it. When I called the therapist in a panic, Danny followed me around the house, first like a crazed stalker and eventually like a puppy dog. By the end of the thirty-minute telephone conversation, this grief-stricken boy wrapped his arms around me in a hug. By the end of the evening, both boys were fed, baths had been drawn, and books read. The homework was even completed. I had called Linda and asked her to read all the geometry vocabulary from her son's homework; then my blue-eyed boy looked up all the definitions again. He dictated, I typed, and it was done. Lastly, I sent an email to his teacher explaining that Danny had to do the entire page of geometry definitions all over again because Parker had shredded the page.

My dog provided unconditional love and a plausible alibi. I didn't need a God who was less compassionate than I was. I *had* loved God, and tragedy happened anyway.

Now a God who would let me rant and rage…and still love me? That would be a God I could respect. But not the One who needed me to love Her first.

* * *

Prayer Warrior Jane showed up one cloudless afternoon. She explained that she would be going to her temple the next day, and she wanted to pray for me there.

"That sounds great," I told her, "because—I don't know if you've heard—I'm not really on speaking terms with God at the moment."

She put a hand on my shoulder and looked into my eyes. "Okay, tell me what specific prayers you need." Her authenticity was disarming.

"What I need more than anything right now is rest." She made a note. "Also strength. And focus." I could have gone on.

"Now," she continued earnestly, "tell me what to pray for for Danny."

I was so touched by her acknowledgment that each one of us had different needs that I started to cry. "Danny is so angry. And kids are so mean." She wrote that down.

"And Jason?"

"He is so sad. It's so unfair."

She hugged me again and, like a prayer emissary, tucked my hopes into her bag.

CHAPTER 14

LESSONS IN LEGO

Healing did not travel in a straight line. And time was sludgy. It must have been mid-November-ish. The arrival of my first post-funeral menstrual period set off a fresh wave of grief, as though I had stepped on an unexploded ordnance. It reignited the grief of my earlier tubal pregnancy and two miscarriages and reinforced the permanence of Sam's death.

And when the tremors of my own losses subsided, I wondered whether Sam had been overwhelmed by the potential of having a third child. He hadn't wanted another baby. "We already have two healthy children," he said. And then, "You don't know what you're like when you're pregnant."

As if I could forget how debilitating the nausea was, not only in the morning, but all day long, and not just the first trimester, but for five unrelenting months. Not to mention the bone-crushing exhaustion and the inability to draw a full breath or tolerate a half-full bladder. The gnawing hunger persisted with no cure other than to wait out the nine months, and then the baby himself was so demanding with his own pain and cold and fear and hunger and exhaustion that my time to myself was measured by the two-minute microwave countdown to heat a frozen burrito. And when the baby cried relentlessly, I threw my half-eaten burrito into the sink, wishing I had pitched the plate along with it, imagining the satisfying crash of the ceramic shrapnel. Instead, I picked up my suffering little one, settled into a chair, and let him suck the life out of me.

I dared not say such things out loud, for fear that Sam would suggest I go back to work and hire a professional to care for our son. How could I have explained that I felt this depth of despair while at the same time my lungs burst with joy at the whiff of his baby head, and my heart swelled beyond beating at the love I felt for this tiny human? I didn't know. I didn't know it was possible to love someone so much and to feel so much anguish at the same time. I would have given my very life for my child. The love for my next child was no less all-consuming. And I would have done it again. I would absolutely have endured the emotional storms of pregnancy and nursing one more time, but Sam was hoping not to. It wasn't as much the third baby he didn't want as it was my perinatal depression.

* * *

Just when I thought we might have survived another grief-steeped day, Jason picked up a Lego spaceship that he had carefully crafted from one of those Star Wars kits with a seventeen-page instruction manual. It had taken days to complete. He then further modified it to suit his imagination, investing his time, creativity, and heart. He looked at the spaceship thoughtfully. Then his brown eyes grew darker. When he had put it together, his father was still alive, had helped him scour the illustrated pages of the instructions, and even found certain pieces to put in place. Jason's bottom lip quivered. The spaceship was in his hands, but Daddy was gone.

He hurled the entire ship against the hardwood floor. A wing flew off and skidded across the living room.

"Sweetie pie!" If I distracted him, I thought he might stop. The body was mostly intact. I could grab the renegade wing and fix the ship before he went to bed. I picked up the dismembered wing.

In the grip of rage and confusion, he snatched the body of the spaceship and hurled it against the floor. Fragments scattered.

I moved toward him, hoping to calm him and prevent further damage to the ship. He pushed me away, shouting "No, Mommy!" He grabbed chunks and threw again, thoroughly dismantling any remaining clusters of bricks. Seven hundred tiny pieces went flying.

One of the challenges as a grieving parent was to recognize my sons' needs, which were not only distinct from each other, but also different from my own. My initial instinct had been to stop him, to preserve the work of his diligence and imagination, but at that moment what he needed most was a safe place for his mad. I went through my mental checklist: He wasn't hurting himself, his brother or me, and the spaceship could be replaced. The best I could offer him was my presence as the tsunami of emotional turmoil washed over him, leaving a detritus of Lego bricks in its wake. Like Humpty Dumpty after falling to the ground, the spaceship was beyond repair. All the kings' horses and all the kings' men couldn't do a damn thing.

When the rubble of his former spaceship covered the floor, he looked up at me, red-faced and out of breath, still enraged, tears streaming down his face. "Mommy!" he shouted. "You have to *FIX IT!*"

Indeed.

It wasn't lost upon me that the shrapnel from the Lego spaceship bore an alarming similarity to the state of our lives, sharp fragments rendering each step dangerous and painful. A daunting task to put the pieces together again. No obvious beginning point or organizing principle. Chaotic. Loud. Shattered.

He sat at the edge of the sofa, watching me defiantly, tears brimming in his eyes.

How was I ever going to fix this?

It was late. Past bedtime, again. One of the many aspects of our lives that had fallen apart was a regular bedtime. It was dark. It seemed like it was always dark. We were exhausted; that, at least, was consistent.

I retrieved a large Tupperware container from the kitchen to hold the remains of his devastated ship. I dropped to my hands and knees.

Pieces scattered to the corners of the living room and under the furniture. *Sam could not have wanted this pain, this rage, this jagged mess,* I thought as I collected Legos.

Through my own tears, I told my son, "These pieces are like the broken pieces of our lives, and they are broken. But we will gather them all, and we will build our life again. It will take time. And we will do it together."

According to my physicist father, the Humpty Dumpty nursery rhyme illustrated the second law of thermodynamics, which translated approximately as "Things that fall apart into more and more little pieces are less and less likely to go back together." While this might be true in physics, I didn't want my life to be governed by a principle where disorder prevailed.

In the midst of this devastation, all I knew for sure was that the boys and I were not done writing the story of our lives. And I would not believe that our lives were beyond repair. Even though they completely sucked.

The next morning, Jason cheerfully asked for the Tupperware containing the Lego remnants of his spaceship. He sat on the hardwood floor, feet splayed to his sides, absorbed in his project.

"Can I help you, sugar?"

"Nope." He got to work. I started a load of laundry.

I wandered back through the living room and asked, "How's it going, buddy?"

"Good." He was so focused he didn't even look up. I fed the dog.

I circled back to him. "Need anything?"

"No, thanks. I'm okay."

I poured a cup of coffee and sat down to answer emails.

After a while, Jason came to me with his reconstructed spaceship, and he held it out toward me in his soft little hands. He was excited. It looked nothing like the original. This version was entirely his creation. He showed me the features of his spaceship—the laser blasters, the rocket boosters, an escape pod. Then he said, "Look, Mommy, it's better than it was before!"

Better than it was before.

CHAPTER 15

HOLE-HEARTED

"**M**ommy, I need you to get married again, because I need a step-father, because I'm too little to be the man of the house."

Again with the man of the house?

It's not uncommon for the firstborn to feel pressure to take care of the surviving parent, whether the survivor is mother or father, and whether the firstborn is a son or a daughter. I wanted to relieve Danny of this burden and help him understand that I was capable of leading the way forward. I patted the space next to me, and he cozied up with me in my reading chair. I set aside the volume of Harry Potter that we had been about to read and put my arms around him.

People had often mistaken Danny for being older than he was and expected more from him as a result. Years ago when we were in the grocery store, he had asked me what a magazine cover said. The woman behind me in line interrupted, "Why can't he read?" I turned to her, incredulous that a stranger could be so rude. "Because he's three," I said. She offered nothing further.

"Please, Mommy?" Danny's eyes were searching, brimming.

My heart ached for him. "You are the eight-year-old of the house. Your job is making your bed and brushing your teeth."

He was stuck on a stepfather, but getting married again was the furthest thing from my mind. It must have been late November; Sam had barely been gone seven weeks. I still wore my wedding ring on one hand and Sam's on the other. When I folded my hands together, I could almost imagine that I was whole. I rubbed my right thumb against his gold band, a talisman of sorts, when I didn't know what to say.

I was getting used to thinking of myself as the widow, my very identity wrapped around my husband's death, but I wasn't quite accustomed to Sam's pernicious absenteeism. I still tripped over his shoes. I picked up his mail and answered his phone calls. The term *widow* is so intertwined with marriage that I didn't think about the fact that a widow is also, by definition, single. I didn't think of myself as single. I didn't think of my future, I thought of my past. I wanted my husband back. *Go on a date?* No, thanks. *Find a stepfather for my sons?* Not interested.

Jason padded in in his jammies, his hair damp from the bath, and offered his thoughts. "I don't want a stepfather, because nobody will be as good as Daddy!" The truism that two siblings will have at least that many opinions on any given subject might have struck me as amusing if the youngsters hadn't been discussing my marital future. If I added their ages together, they weren't old enough to drive a car.

I lifted Jason into the mint green chair with Danny and me, the same oversized chair the three of us sat in together when I told them of their father's suicide. The little one continued, "If you get married, I'll kill that guy. And then I'll kill his ghost. And then I'll kill his ghost's ghost!"

The child was emphatic.

I took a deep breath and told them what little I knew for certain. "I don't know what is going to happen, and I don't know if I will get married again, but here's the thing: there is a Daddy-shaped space in your heart that will be there forever. Nobody will ever take over that spot, because nobody else fits. But the thing about love is that it grows, and if somebody special comes into our lives, then our hearts will grow. He won't take over the Daddy spot. He'll have a new space, just for him."

* * *

The boys were not the only ones thinking about adding a man to my life. Well-meaning friends mentioned to me that the boys needed a father.

As if.

Danny and Jason already had a father. He was a good man, a smart man, a handsome man, and, sadly, a dead man. They had two grandfathers and enough uncles to stage a community production of *12 Angry Men*. They had positive male role models without my having to add a stepdad. I honored the Sam-shaped space in my heart, but I wasn't looking to expand my own heart's real estate to accommodate another man. I didn't need the trouble of upended toilet seats, the ring of stubble in the sink, sweat stains on shirt collars, birth control, or the constant ESPN soundtrack. I started to note a certain simplicity to my widowed life. I no longer picked up his dry-cleaning when the cleaners were fifteen minutes from closing and Sam was still half an hour's drive away and wearing his last clean shirt. I didn't have to coordinate with his schedule or accommodate his preference for peas over broccoli.

Sam had loved watching television, especially when he could switch back and forth between two simultaneous baseball broadcasts. I never watched much television, but occasionally, Sam would choose a show for us to watch together. Early in our marriage, we had watched *Mad About You*. The newlyweds' struggles around transitions, work, and infertility mirrored our own. I enjoyed sharing the time and resulting conversations with Sam.

More recently, we had watched the premier season of *Mad Men*, and the season finale had aired just days before Sam died. It concluded with typical suspense: Was Don Draper going to have an affair? Leave his wife? I never saw another episode. I didn't want to watch without Sam. There was also this: the opening sequence of the show featured a two-dimensional shape of a man falling from the top of a New York high-rise. I couldn't tolerate that visual; it made me sick to my stomach imagining Sam himself falling from a parking structure. I stopped watching television altogether.

I could not, however, avoid my closet. Every time I walked into it, I was surrounded by Sam's clothing. Suits hung neatly in a row, ties filled the designated rack, and his shoes took up several shelves. Without Sam to cheer on his favorite team, his Angels baseball cap hung forlornly from a hook. I buried my face in a shirt and inhaled, but it no longer carried his scent. It smelled like cedar. I crumbled on the closet floor and dissolved into tears. After half an hour, his shirt was soaked, and I couldn't remember why I had gone into the closet in the first place.

I mentioned to Susan that I had taken to holding up my hands like horse blinders so I wouldn't be sabotaged by Sam's belongings. Within days, Susan arrived with several large, empty plastic boxes and a Jane. She sent Jane and me to lunch while she addressed Sam's half of the closet, saying, "I promise not to get rid of anything without asking you first."

By the time Jane and I returned from lunch, Susan had sorted all Sam's clothes and keepsakes into labeled boxes and stored them neatly in the garage. "Everything is here, so you can deal with it whenever you're ready," she told me, holding up a black plastic garbage bag. "Socks and underwear. Okay for me to toss these?"

Then she led me back to my closet. There was no gaping void where Sam's stuff used to be. She had reorganized everything. It was a closet to be envied, shoes lined up on shelves, organized by type—sandals, pumps, boots, tennis shoes. My tops were hanging neatly in rainbow order, jackets and sweaters grouped by season, handbags easily accessible.

Susan handed me a small brown box. "These are Sam's watches. I thought you might want to keep these in your dresser."

Sam owned two watches, one casual and one he wore to work. We had treated ourselves to watches early in our careers. He had received a year-end bonus, and we squirreled most of it away for a down payment on a house, but first, we purchased his and her watches. We liked the idea of focusing on our "time" together. I wore mine every day. Danny and Jason didn't yet know how to tell time on an analog watch, and their wrists were too small to wear Sam's watches. But I thought that someday they might find comfort or connection in wearing their father's watches.

As I tucked them away in the back of the drawer, a white jewelry box caught my attention.

I pulled out the diamond heart necklace and showed it to Susan. "What do you think I should do with this?"

She looked at me curiously. "I've never seen you wear this."

"Sam gave it to me three months ago," I explained, "for our fifteenth wedding anniversary." Fifteen years had seemed like a good running start at the time, but it turned out to be the finish line.

"It's so pretty," she said. "Won't you wear it?"

I shook my head. "It makes me too sad." I had tried putting it on a couple times since Sam's death, but I took it right off. I didn't feel loved when I put it on, I felt guilty. And it was tempting to wonder whether he had really loved me after all.

"Okay, I'll see if the jeweler will take it back," she said, anxious to relieve my load, but obviously haunted by the weight of it. I handed her the necklace with the original receipt.

A few days later, she returned with the necklace in hand. The jeweler had remembered Sam and was shocked and saddened to hear of his death. He himself had designed the necklace, with its asymmetrical heart. He offered to issue a store credit but not a refund. Susan asked me, "Have you thought about donating it to the education foundation for the gala and taking the tax deduction?"

I tried to imagine how the necklace might be described in the auction program, this hardly-ever-worn diamond heart necklace. *A quarter carat's worth of remorse? The last fling before the fall? The widow's regret on an 18" white gold chain?* It seemed like bad karma. What if nobody bid on it?

I stuck the necklace back in the drawer.

* * *

The single parent shtick sucked. It was the Mommy Channel 24/7. Danny and Jason were sick of my voice. I was sick of my voice. I was tired of wearing all the hats: chef, chauffeur, chief financial officer, counselor, reader of bedtime stories, disciplinarian, cheerleader, head coach, entertainer, laundress. Anything that got done around the house got done by me. All the parenting. All the errands. All the dogshit. All the time. Even my divorced friends had every other weekend off.

On the plus side, I never negotiated with an ex. I didn't have to coordinate vacations or alternate holidays. I didn't need his permission for field trips or vaccines. I didn't nag him for child support or pay him alimony. In that respect, being widowed was simpler than divorce.

But it wasn't simple for the kids. "I wish *Daddy* was here instead of *you*," Jason said, his voice dripping with disdain, as we sat in a home-work deadlock at the kitchen table. I wasn't entirely shocked. He and his brother never got a break from me. They couldn't argue their case to another parent. They grew weary of my decision-making, my sense of humor, my taste in music. I understood that he didn't wish me dead. I was a safe landing place for his pain. Still, it hurt me less when he threw Legos. I was doing my best, and my best didn't feel good enough.

I wished Daddy was there, too. I felt lonely in ways I had never imagined, even when I was surrounded by people who loved me.

Time eked on ploddingly, a never-ending November.

* * *

Linda watched me with the concern of a mother whose underweight child was failing to thrive. I still wasn't hungry, and my weight continued to drop. One afternoon, she appeared on my doorstep with a smaller belt.

* * *

I wished I had saved Sam. I think I could have. If only he had talked to me.

Late November, I received the police report and the coroner's report. I read both beginning to end. I even took them with me to a session with Dr. Newland so she could explain every bit of medical terminology. These reports included verbal descriptions, witness statements, and a diagram showing the places where Sam's bones had broken and where he had hemorrhaged, but no photographs. For that, I was grateful.

According to the police report, surveillance video caught a glimpse of Sam in the stairwell on his way up about ten minutes before jumping. There was a small white terrycloth towel at the top of the parking structure where Sam had been, along with an open water bottle and an empty bottle of Vicodin. He appeared to have taken whatever was left before he jumped. I never did find an explanation for the towel.

Sam had suffered from back pain in varying degrees from the time he was thirteen. It was never diagnosed. It might have been genetic; his mother had had back troubles, too. It might have been an injury; he loved playing baseball, but he stopped his sophomore year of high school. It might have been stress-related; I didn't believe it a coincidence that his back pain started around the time of his parents' bankruptcy.

I had never known Sam without back pain. It caused a little hitch in his walk which I found endearing. I don't think he himself remembered a time when he hadn't suffered. There was a week, about three years into our marriage, when Sam was in such intense pain that he couldn't stand or sit. He crawled from room to room and lay flat on the floor. The pain might have been related to a weekend golfing, but it was undoubtedly exacerbated by the stress of changing careers. He had left a salaried position with a tax firm for a commissioned one with a brokerage house.

What I knew about that bottle of Vicodin that the police did not was that it would have been nearly full on the day Sam died. He must have been determined to end his pain. Sam had had two back surgeries, both for herniated discs, and the surgeon had prescribed the narcotic. But Sam didn't take it; he was deathly afraid of addiction. If he took any pain medication at all, he chose Advil. Indeed, the toxicology report confirmed that he had consumed significant levels of Vicodin, although whether it was enough to cause a fatal overdose remained inconclusive.

There is a gender gap related to suicide. Twice as many women attempt suicide, but twice as many men die from it. Statistically, women make attempts to end their lives in ways that leave room for doubt or a chance for intervention, such as an overdose, but when men decide to suicide, they get the job done. I will never know whether Sam was attempting a suicide in two ways—both the fatal fall and the overdose—or whether the Vicodin was a conscious attempt to reduce the pain of his fall.

Oddly, I drew comfort from the fact that he had taken so much Vicodin. When I perused the police report, I noted that there were twenty-eight minutes between his fall and when the emergency room doctor declared him dead. I hoped that the medication eased his pain in those lingering, excruciating minutes.

I wondered if he was at peace now, as they say, or whether his pain simply transitioned with him.

CHAPTER 16

THE FATHER DANCE

"Heyyy…" Zack intoned without introduction. He and I had appropriated the greeting that he and Sam used, Sam's bride and his best man consciously keeping his memory alive.

"Heyyy…" I responded, both smiling and sad. I was grateful Zack checked in with me consistently. I didn't feel obligated to tell him things were okay when they weren't.

Zack said encouragingly to me, "I know you feel lonely, honey, but you're never alone. Danny and Jason will be okay. We're going to make sure our boys have what they need. Our boys are going to be fine."

The personal pronoun stopped me in my tracks. *Our* boys? Zack was smart and reliable, but he had his own kids. I blurted, "Danny and Jason are not *our* kids, Zack. They're mine."

"Oh, I know, I just meant that it's on the whole family now to take care of them."

"No, it's not. It's on me. They're *mine*." It pained Zack for his nephews to have lost their father. I understood that piece. But I could raise them myself. I was in charge. This was not parenting by proxy. There was no democracy here, no commune, no kibbutz. "I appreciate that you care, and you're a wonderful uncle, but I am their only parent. I promise to ask for help if I need it. But Danny and Jason are mine."

Whenever I had referred to Danny and Jason as "ours," I meant Sam's and mine, but more frequently I found myself saying "my" and "mine." Only if Danny and Jason were in trouble did I refer to the boys exclusively as "Sam's."

* * *

My children's father now resided in a cemetery, a cold hard truth. I wanted Danny and Jason to see for themselves that Sam's grave was beautiful, not Halloween-movie creepy. But I wanted to go first without them.

Susan asked, "Want me to go with you?"

"I would. I haven't been back since his funeral."

"I'll pick you up tomorrow morning. Ten o'clock?" Susan's offer spoke to her generosity. She had felt guilty, but also relieved, when a family obligation had prohibited her from attending Sam's funeral. Cemeteries were nowhere she wanted to go.

The hillside was that unnatural green endemic to cemeteries in the desert, dotted with a few wilted-flower calling cards from visitors. I did not bring Sam flowers. I brought a rock. In the Jewish tradition, the rock represents enduring love, and mourners place a stone on the gravesite as a sign of respect.

We were alone at the cemetery, apart from the man sitting inside his white sedan a few car lengths away. Susan and I walked up to Sam's spot. There was no gravestone yet. The grass covering his grave was still torn at the seams and the ground not yet leveled by time and gravity. Toward the top of the grave sat a temporary placeholder, a laminated 3x5 index card with his name in small type: Samuel L. Maya.

It pissed me off.

When they talk about the stages of grief—denial, anger, bargaining, depression, acceptance—what they don't tell you is that these stages don't arrive in an organized manner, like a checklist. Denial and depression might blow in together like a storm, with dark rainclouds and wind whirling, or anger might drop out of the clear blue sky like a lightning strike. They are not tidy or predictable or compliant. Something about that index card unleashed my fury.

He couldn't have told me he was suffering?!

Now I was suffering. My *sons* were suffering. And there Sam rested, the reason for our suffering, appearing as innocuous as a card in the drawer of a librarian's card catalog. It was insulting. I didn't know if Sam was at peace or in hell, and in that moment I didn't care.

I looked at the rock in my palm. I didn't set it reverently near the nameplate. I took a step back and threw it at his head. I wasn't inclined to listen for otherworldly messages. If Sam had had something to say, he should have said it when he was alive. If he had wanted an opinion, he should have stayed. *He left me.* This reality cold-cocked me. Seeing him at the cemetery reinforced his absence everywhere else. I looked around for another rock. I hurled it. Plus a few more. Eventually, I sat down, listening to my own heartbeat, my own ragged breathing, feeling the emptiness and staring into the blue sky.

Susan stood to the side protectively, keeping a wary eye on the guy in the white car. He stumbled out drunkenly and flopped down next to one of the graves.

I appreciated the impulse. If there had been a drink powerful enough to dissolve the pain, I'd have been all about it. But there wasn't. And I didn't want to put myself, my children, or other people at risk. I didn't want to be that girl.

On the drive home, Susan remarked gently, "I haven't seen you that upset before."

It was a testament to our friendship that I trusted Susan to bear witness to my secret identity as the rock-throwing angry girl. A woman enraged is even less acceptable than the woman inebriated, and I had learned to bite my tongue. I couldn't hurt Sam by hurling rocks at him any more than he had already hurt himself.

"All I know," she continued with her eyes on the road, "is that when I get to heaven, Sam better be ready to run, because when I catch him, I'm going to kill him. And I'm not the only one, you know."

I smiled at the image of my loyal friend leading a legion of livid women chasing after Sam in eternity. Hell hath no fury.

It would have been nice if grief kept to the cemetery, but the stages seeped out into other places. Denial found me in the kitchen and jumped out from a recipe annotated in Sam's handwriting. Depression met me at Sam's favorite restaurant, in the wind, at the park. Bargaining surprised me in a song, a glance, a doppelgänger, a dream. Acceptance rarely, if ever, made an appearance. It would have been nice if I could have taken my grief to the cemetery and left it there, like a rock placed intentionally to honor Sam's memory. Even though I washed my hands of death on the way out, in observance of tradition, grief followed me home, an impish shadow refusing to stay where it belonged.

* * *

Sam wanted to be a very different father to his own children than his father had been to him. Alberto was proud that he had never once changed a diaper; Sam was proud that he was the first one to change Danny's diaper when we brought our newborn home.

"Just ignore him," Sam told me one afternoon after his parents had left. His father had said, "If she doesn't put that boy down, he'll never learn to walk." I was hurt that his father had criticized my parenting, and I was insulted because he made this comment in Spanish, thinking I wouldn't understand. (I was nowhere near fluent, but having taken a few college-level courses, I understood more than he gave me credit for.) Sam hugged me and said, "My father doesn't know the first thing about being a dad."

It is nearly impossible to hold a baby too much. As soon as they're ready to go, little ones will squirm their way out of maternal arms and into the world. And, for the record, Danny started walking at ten months.

Sam and I didn't argue very often, but when we did, he was immovable. Once, exasperated, I had burst out, "You're just like your father!" He looked stricken. Speechless. I had landed a devastating blow. I was shocked at the impact of my remark, so much so that I forgot what we were bickering about. He had tried to differentiate himself from his father, and with a handful of words, I had swept them back into the same rank.

* * *

When Sam was twelve, his father had run into financial trouble, succumbing to a combination of the vagaries of his Los Angeles–based manufacturing business and the volatility of a real estate gamble. At one point, Alberto loaded Sam and the family dog, a terrier mix they named Freddie Mercury, into the car. They drove out of town for maybe thirty miles, eventually arriving at a park. Sam thought he and Freddie would play, but his father forced the confused dog out of the car and sped away. Alberto could no longer afford to take care of the dog, and so, in an act reeking of desperation and shame, he abandoned it.

Sam watched in horror, devastated, as his little dog frantically followed the car. As they turned a corner he lost sight of his dog, and he and his father rode home in silence.

Soon thereafter, Alberto used Sam's bar mitzvah money to pay the bankruptcy lawyer. My father-in-law never quite recovered, emotionally or financially, after losing his home, his business, and his pride. He had lost everything once before, when he fled Cuba in 1960 after Fidel Castro had appropriated his upholstery business. Alberto had left his birthplace and his upper-middle-class lifestyle behind, seeking refuge for his wife and three-year-old daughter Miranda and a chance to start over. After the bankruptcy twenty years later, they moved into a one-bedroom apartment with Eleana's mother in the mid-Wilshire area of Los Angeles. Eleana secured a job in a small insurance office. Alberto never worked again.

From that time forward, Sam felt obligated to take care of his parents. When he was a student at UCLA, Sam signed his loan checks and scholarship grants over to his father so they could pay their rent. Over the years, we helped them buy used cars or pay for airline tickets to visit Sam's sister in Miami. It pained Sam to see his mother working into her seventies, but the social security checks weren't enough to cover their expenses. Sam and I started sending them a monthly stipend, so his mother could retire. At the time, I thought I was being a supportive wife and a good daughter-in-law, but after Sam's suicide, I saw things differently. I resented Alberto for putting financial pressure on Sam for almost thirty years. Teenagers aren't supposed to take care of their parents. It was backwards. I was also afraid—afraid that I could not afford to fund both my in-laws' retirement and my sons' education. I never discussed it with his parents. I just stopped sending them the monthly check. I didn't blame Sam's father for his son's death as much as I blamed Sam. Sam was the one who had said nothing. He was the one who had jumped.

Sam had lost respect for his father after the bankruptcy. Not so much for his financial failings—things might have worked out if the housing market hadn't taken a capricious turn—but for his lack of resilience. I wondered if, at some level, Sam feared that, despite his best efforts, he was becoming his father. That my return to work brought shameful reminders of his own mother's role in providing for the family. That he was afraid he would not be able to recover like his father, still hearing Freddie's footsteps, echoing in the distance.

CHAPTER 17

RECKONINGS

I think it was still November—so much was condensed into those embryonic weeks of grief—when Jane asked, "Would you be interested in joining our book group?"

I barely had the attention span to finish a haiku, but my friend invited me anyway.

"It's a nice group of smart, sassy women. We eat well, we drink good wine, and we laugh a lot. It could be a place where you'd feel normal and safe. You don't even have to read the book."

She knew I would like the people in the group and had faith that I would read again. She offered support without adding pressure. She made it easy to say yes.

The group tried to avoid books with suicide as an obvious theme, but suicide often featured as a dramatic plot point or a literary device: *The Great Gatsby, One Hundred Years of Solitude, The Secret Life of Bees.* I could go on. Jane cringed on my behalf.

I felt a similar impulse to protect my children from Disney movies; virtually every animated film featured at least one dead or missing parent, sometimes two. When I took the boys to see the remake of *Get Smart*, I expected it to be silly and harmless. Halfway through the movie, Maxwell Smart was hanging from a suicide prevention banner on a flying plane with the phone number 1-800-GET-HELP, and the audience burst into laughter. Danny and Jason did not. I couldn't wait for the movie to end. I would never have showed them *Dead Poets Society* or *Thelma & Louise*, and I felt betrayed by Hollywood, using suicide as comedy play.

The Reverend Doctor Matthew Potts describes grief as a reckoning with that which cannot be undone. Suicide's claim on Sam's life continued to interrupt us in songs, casual conversations, and newspapers. I already wished I could excuse the boys from Shakespeare and other required reading. There was no undoing of Sam's suicide.

I kept reckoning.

* * *

I couldn't say exactly when it happened—I was just glad to get to the therapist on the appointed day—but the first time Danny and Dr. Kimberly held their session in her office felt like a step forward. The journey from car, to front lawn, to office was remarkable. Danny told me they played games—Scrabble, backgammon, chess—all games Sam loved. In all the years Sam and I were together, I never won a game of Scrabble against him. Not once. After their first few years working together, Dr. Kimberly hardly ever won a game of Scrabble; Danny, like his daddy, was an excellent Scrabble player.

I didn't know what they talked about or if they did at all. Danny still refused to say the "D" words—*dead* and *dad*. I desperately wanted to eavesdrop on their conversation, but I also knew it was important to keep a boundary around his therapy sessions. I wanted him to feel safe to say whatever he needed to say. I told Danny that I wouldn't know what he told Dr. Kimberly, and I didn't. Sometimes after a session I'd ask, "How's Dr. Kimberly?" to which my taciturn boy responded, "She's good." That was it. If I had a specific concern, I would send Dr. Kimberly an email, but it was like dropping a rock down a deep hole. I didn't see it land. I might hear it clunk at the bottom, or I might not. I just had to trust.

I didn't trust trust.

I wanted certainty, control, and results. I didn't want to fail my son as I had failed his father. Danny's reticence echoed Sam's, and the silence terrified me.

Jason, on the other hand, was open with his grief. He was both perceptive and articulate. I would have hired a therapist for him, but he didn't need one. He did normal kid stuff *and* normal grief stuff: playing, laughing, crying, sacrificing Legos, and breaking rocks.

I also had a safety net for both boys in the form of Dr. Newland. If, in one of my sessions, she heard something that raised an alarm for her (sleep disruption, for example), she would suggest resources. Often she confirmed my instincts, which bolstered my confidence. Ideally, every member of a grieving family would have their own therapist, but the most efficient way to help an entire family is to support the surviving parent. It's the surviving parent who's behind the wheel when those spontaneous conversations arise. She might turn the music down a notch and drive the long way home in order to keep the conversation going. And it's the surviving parent who's tucking her grieving child into bed at night, when baths and books have been drawn and read, when the child says, "Daddy kept looking at me that morning. I think he was trying to say goodbye."

Jason didn't need to explain which morning he was talking about. I knew.

Whatever dishes I had left to clean or emails still unanswered were relegated to the bottom of my priority list. I snuggled next to my little one, and he told me what he remembered, the intensity of his father's gaze. "It felt like he was trying to remember everything about me."

Another bedtime, Jason asked, "Mommy, do you think if Daddy had loved me more, he wouldn't have killed himself?"

The one thing I knew beyond the shadow of a doubt was that his father loved him with everything he had.

"But wasn't I enough?"

How, exactly, could I explain to my son that sometimes love is not enough? That terrible things happened in this life. That we could not control other people, not even the ones we loved, and not the ones who loved us. We could only control ourselves. And sometimes not even that.

"Maybe he died because I wasn't good enough. Maybe if I had been a better kid then he would have stayed."

So many questions. So much guilt. I tried to convey to my kids how desperately their father loved them. I wished I had smacked Sam back to his senses.

Sometimes the conversation took a turn that surprised me. "Mommy," Jason began sweetly. "How do I know that Daddy is really dead?"

I assured him that trained professionals had confirmed this fact, but his frustration built quickly. He said accusingly, "You never let us see him! I wanted to see him, and you said no."

Guilty as charged.

"How did you know he was actually dead if you didn't see him yourself?" His voice rose in pitch. "Maybe the policeman was *lying* to you!"

There is research that supports the idea that it can be easier to accept a death if one sees the actual dead body. This can be especially true for children, who have little experience with death and dying. Children are confused by such euphemisms as "He's gone" or "He passed on" or "We lost him." Adults might be reluctant to say the words, "He died," but this clarity is helpful. Some grief experts recommend that children be allowed to see the body, depending on the age and maturity of the child and the condition of the corpse, because it helps them understand what happened. Often, however, children are kept away and not granted the opportunity.

After having read the police report and witness statements, I conjured a clear picture of Sam's body after the fall. It was not pretty, but it was not imprinted in my memory as it might have been if I had seen him myself. That traumatizing visual would have endured. Instead, when I remembered Sam, I called to mind his soft brown eyes and gentle smile, as he appeared in the family portrait taken just two weeks before his death.

Still, I appreciated that my child was flummoxed by the concept of death, never having seen a dead body. At one point in our conversation,

Jason dug a sharp fingernail into the back of my wrist. I still bear a small scar on that spot. He wanted me to feel his pain, attempting to transfer the pain from his body to mine. If only it were that simple. If it would have helped, I would have let him tattoo my whole arm with his tears.

Or maybe he was confirming my presence, testing for himself the very aliveness of my body with its pain and blood and capacity to heal.

* * *

"Mommy, do you think Daddy is in heaven?"

"Yes, I do."

"But how do you *know*?" Jason implored.

"I believe with all my heart that if there is a heaven, then your father is there."

He furrowed his little brow. "Jackson said that my dad is in hell because he killed himself."

This made me about eleven different kinds of mad. I had several choice words for Jackson and his parents, and I sure as hell did not need them feeding my son such hateful religious rhetoric. I had never subscribed to a theology in which an omnipotent God made us flawed and then punished us for our mistakes. I had never believed in a God who distributed disease among his creation. I had not grown up with a hellfire and brimstone kind of God, so I easily dismissed the idea of Sam in hell. Like my son, I had had a classmate from my schoolgirl days inform me that Sam's suicide landed him firmly in hell. I never spoke to her again.

I had been taught that life or the soul or consciousness or whatever continued in some form after death. I didn't think that Jesus arrived to tell us how to live our lives—or else. That kind of judgment came from church hierarchy as a means to manipulate people into (or out of) certain behaviors. I believed that when Jesus was talking about heaven and hell, he was more accurately describing our experiences on earth than anything after death, and that he was inviting his followers to live in a way designed to bring more peace, more love, more joy to all lives. Life was heavenly when participating in acts of affirmation or generosity, and hellish when gripped by jealousy or fear. If I believed in any God at all, it was a loving One who scooped us up after death, perhaps even more so for someone like Sam, whose suffering led to such a terrible, violent death.

Not that I condoned Sam's actions. He was wrong. He should have asked for help. If, after his death, he felt remorse for his mistake or anguish over the pain his children suffered as a result, then that would be hell enough.

"But Jackson said that everyone who kills himself goes to hell."

I felt the anger tighten my jaw. I would have liked to preach a little vengeance against self-righteous assholes who inflicted their insufferable arrogance against my grieving children. Such conversations reminded me why I refused to darken God's door, and why I would not be setting foot inside a church again.

"Jackson is wrong. Suicide is just like an undiagnosed cancer, or a sudden heart attack. It just looks so much uglier from the outside."

"What if I…" Jason started to ask.

"*Shut up!*" Danny shouted. "Don't *talk* about him!" As incessantly as Jason wanted to process ideas about death and remember his father, Danny did not.

"Gentlemen, we have to respect each other. Jason wants to talk about Daddy, and Danny doesn't. It's all okay. We just have to figure this out together."

Danny looked defiant. I glanced around the room to see what fragile objects might be within his arms' reach.

"How about if Jason and I go into my room and close the door so you can't hear us?"

"Sounds good!" Jason chirped. He hopped up and headed to my room.

Danny looked downcast. "But I want to sit in your green chair with you," he begged. "I don't want to be alone." It was impossible for me to be with both of my children simultaneously in the opposing ways that they needed me.

"How about this…Danny, you go into my room with your book and Parker, and Jason and I will talk out here. When we're finished, then we'll come join you."

It wasn't perfect, but it was the best I could do. If Sam had been there, he could have cared for one child, while I looked after the other. Then again, if Sam had been there, we wouldn't have been in this situation.

* * *

"Charlotte!" Engineer Jane confronted me one morning me after I had dropped the boys off at school. "I've been wanting to do something for you, but I'm a terrible cook, and I've noticed that you're always late getting the boys to school, and I thought Danny and Jason might like walking to school with my sons, even though they're in different grades, so I was thinking that if I was at your house at 7:45, then I could help you get to school on time." She interrupted herself. "I'm sorry. Is now an okay time to talk?"

Engineer Jane described herself as having "no social skills." She was abrupt, opinionated, and dogged. Our sons practiced karate at the same studio. When her son's tenured second-grade teacher became generally unfit for the classroom, Engineer Jane took it upon herself to document each day's negligences. She sat outside the classroom in order to substantiate reports of the teacher's odd behavior, and she single-handedly forced the district to retire the teacher in order to avoid a lawsuit, thereby saving several hundred youngsters from incompetence and a lost year of elementary school. She was a fierce advocate for causes dear to her heart.

For reasons I could not explain, I was one of those causes.

I smiled. "That sounds wonderful."

Engineer Jane showed up at 7:45 a.m. the next day with her sons in tow. "Good morning!" she called. "Where are your backpacks?"

Danny glanced at me curiously, and I shrugged. He collected his homework from the dining room table and slid it into his backpack.

"Lunches?" she asked.

I handed both boys a brown paper lunch bag.

Engineer Jane pointed at the untied shoes on Jason's feet and motioned for him to sit down while she knotted the unruly laces. Then she marched us up the street. Danny and Jason arrived to school on time for the first time in weeks.

I often think about Engineer Jane when people ask me how to help someone in crisis. Everyone has a gift to offer, no culinary or social skills required. Engineer Jane was on my doorstep at precisely 7:45 a.m. for months on end. I didn't know any other mom who could be any-where—with two kids in tow—and on time day after day. Danny and Jason didn't drag their feet when she was on duty. For that matter, nei-ther did I. But I didn't need a dozen drill sergeant moms on my door-step first thing in the morning. I just needed one. And Engineer Jane was there.

*　*　*

During one insomnia-induced internet research expedition, I stum-bled across the fact that—for men—the combination of chronic pain and clinical depression could be fatal. I stared at the glowing screen. Sam definitely had chronic pain, but he had never been diagnosed with depression.

I continued scrolling through the website. Men sometimes expressed their depression in ways that looked more like anger or aggression and less like ennui, in which case the underlying depression went undiag-nosed and untreated. Sam hadn't seemed angry; if anything, he seemed anxious. I kept clicking. Men were less likely than women to recog-nize or seek treatment for depression. This rang true for my husband. Somewhere in the night, I landed on this: Chronic illness can lead to clinical depression. *Could Sam's long-standing back pain have devolved into depression? Which, when combined with his pain, produced a circum-stance primed for suicide?*

We had dealt with Sam's back issues for so long that I primarily addressed the physical dimension to his pain. I hadn't contemplated the emotional components. Sam had had multiple herniated discs and one degenerated disc. He had resisted surgery for ages but relented when

Jason was just a few months old. He couldn't even lift our infant son into or out of a car seat. There was so much Sam couldn't do as a father, and he had hoped that a successful surgery would deepen his relationship with both Danny and Jason by expanding the physical experiences they could share—camping, playing catch or basketball—or just lifting them into the bucket swing at the park.

His first surgery was for one of the herniated discs. For three months, he wasn't allowed to lift anything heavier than a coffee cup. Like most men, Sam was not an easy patient. He refused to use the baby monitor, which I thought was a genius idea in 2001 (before everyone carried cell phones), and I felt bad if I couldn't hear him hollering for help from across the house. I schlepped everything—groceries, trash cans, car seats, an infant, and a very busy toddler. Three months later, however, he was still experiencing debilitating pain. Sam was discouraged, but he had a second surgery before Jason's first birthday.

The fact that Sam couldn't lift Jason for the first year of Jason's life embarrassed Sam deeply. Danny would clamber up next to Sam, and I would set Jason next to them—on the bed or the sofa—so they could snuggle and read. It was frustrating for him to watch me lift our sons when he could not. I tried to encourage him that fathering was more than literal heavy lifting. Even so, managing the children and the household chores without his help was exhausting me. At one point I told him, "For your third surgery, you'd better check into a hotel for three months, because I am *not* going to do this again." I was only half-joking.

After the first two surgeries, Sam managed with a regimen of daily stretches and the occasional ibuprofen, and he avoided activities that might put him at risk of further injury. He wasn't optimistic that a third surgery would yield an appreciable improvement.

Once, on a Cub Scout outing, Sam was sitting on a bench watching the boys take turns on a zipline. The dads took turns pulling each boy up to the top of the hill and then the child zipped down. The dads were working and sweating in the heat when one of them, with some edge in his tone, asked Sam to help. Sam stayed sitting. He shook his head apologetically and pointed toward his back, humiliated by the fact that he couldn't lift the kids. In retrospect, I imagine his shame was more intense than the pinched nerve.

In the summer before he died, Sam's back pain seemed to be flaring again. I noticed that he winced and flinched more than usual getting into and out of a chair, and especially his car. He stood frequently because sitting exacerbated the tension in his lower back. But he deflected conversation about his pain and ignored my suggestion to make an appointment with his physical therapist.

I had wondered then if he was thinking about the third surgery. I never dreamed that he would end his life instead.

CHAPTER 18

DECEMBER SOMEHOW

Grief warped my relationship with time. It was like having a newborn, when I counted its life first in hours, then days, then weeks. I was sleepless and bewildered. It was the longest two months of my life. Also, morning arrived with alarming regularity, and the electric bill couldn't possibly be due again, because I could have sworn I paid all the utilities earlier that morning, and all of them had Sam's name on the envelope, taunting me.

None of that changed the fact that I was desperate to make Christmas happen for my boys. I couldn't give them the only thing they wanted, so I shifted my focus to toys. If I prayed for anything those days, it was a Wii. The Janes circulated an email requesting leads on how to get hold of the scarce but coveted video game. Through tenacity and sheer luck, my mother found one. Who needed God when Grandma was on duty? Grandma, who hung our stockings off the fireplace awaiting Santa's special deliveries, and who, not knowing what to do with Sam's, packed his back into the box, as though we might forget that he was gone if his stocking was, too.

I retrieved it and hung it with the rest of ours.

One evening in mid-December the doorbell rang. We frequently had unexpected visitors in those early days of grief, sometimes bearing dinner, often with tears, a spontaneous and extended shiva. But when we opened the door, nobody was there.

On the doormat was a triangular box, a kit to make a gingerbread house, trimmed simply with a wide silver ribbon and a note that read "On the First Day of Christmas…"

A mystery.

The next night, the doorbell rang again. Also after sunset. Another package on the front porch. Two snowman mugs, a packet for hot chocolate tucked inside each one, tied with the same silver ribbon and the same simple white square of paper, reading "On the Second Day of Christmas…"

The third night, we were ready. I turned on the porch light and turned off the living room lights, so we could spy our secret Santa. The boys and I sat together on the sofa and waited. It grew darker. They grew bored, and then hungry. I went to the kitchen to put dinner together. When the doorbell rang, Danny and Jason ran to the front of the house. But all they found when they flung the door open were three large candy canes. Same silver ribbon. Same notepaper. Same message in the same black, felt-tipped pen: "On the Third Day of Christmas…"

The industrious elf delivered the fourth day's offering while we were out, probably at therapy. We arrived home to find four little tree ornaments, bundled in the silver ribbon. Same square of notepaper. Different color ink. *Was the handwriting different?* It was hard to tell, but it appeared to be in a child's hand.

Intriguing.

It seemed like the kind of effort Susan would coordinate. I mentioned the secret Santa to her, but she insisted that she hadn't orchestrated it. "Seriously," she said. "I *wish* it was me!"

Linda seemed as perplexed as Susan, and I doubted her sons could keep such a secret from mine. *Which Jane was the mastermind?*

The boys and I started to look forward to our mysterious deliverer. Jason and Danny wanted to catch the bearer of gifts, scheming a plan to snare the culprit. I started to warm to the idea of not knowing. Some evenings, I corralled the boys into the kitchen at the back of the house, so that the elf would have time to escape notice.

Somebody was creating a little light in our darkness with a simple and powerful message: "You are seen. You are loved." Over the course of the next week, we received nightly offerings. Always simple—six apples, seven clementines, eight packets of gum—each adorned with the signature silver ribbon, the white square note and the childlike handwriting.

It was a strange feeling, to be wrenched so hard by grief and darkness on the one hand and drawn so firmly toward light and hope on the other. To feel bereft and abandoned and at the same time held, grounded, and supported. 'Tis the season, as they say. The darkness is overwhelming and terrifying and completely unfair when the tender newborn enters the scene. It is hard to imagine that the infant hope will wield any impact. But there she is.

After eleven days of Christmas offerings, we weren't sure quite what to expect when we approached home on that twelfth night, but we were expecting something. I trusted there would be *something*, but after all the nights building up to that moment, would my boys be disappointed? They wondered aloud what might await us at home—chocolates? a dozen cookies?

When we pulled into the driveway, it looked like Santa himself had delivered the contents of an entire sleigh to our front porch. I could practically hear Rudolph's footsteps dancing on the roof. The elves must have worked overtime. There were twelve exquisitely wrapped packages—four gifts for Danny, four for Jason, and four for me. All different kinds of paper, every possible color of ribbon. Toys, games, goodies, and a Bruin baseball cap in my favorite shade of powder blue. One message: *Merry Christmas!*

Fourteen years later, I still don't know who gifted us with those twelve days of hope in the darkness. I don't even want to know anymore. The not-knowing has become my favorite part. Their lasting gift: I believe in Christmas magic.

***

Zack called. "What are you doing for New Year's Eve?"

"Hopefully, going to bed early."

New Year's Eve is a grown-up's holiday, a romantic night for couples, a new beginning together, sweet and full of promise. Linda and Ben had invited me to their party, but who would I kiss at midnight? Valentine's Day could be salvaged by my children's hand-drawn hearts and dark chocolate, but New Year's Eve had nothing for this newly single widow.

"The only redeeming thing about New Year's Eve is that when I wake up the next day, the year of Sam's suicide will be behind me."

"Sweetie, I get it. But I think it's important that you find someone special."

"I found someone special. And now he's dead."

"I'm serious. You're young, and you have your whole life ahead of you. You deserve all of life's pleasures."

"Honestly, I'll be just fine never having sex again."

"Don't say that."

"Plus, it would be awkward. At least one kid and the dog still sleep in my bed every night."

I didn't tell Zack that I drew comfort from the boys' warmth and Parker's soft snoring. I would miss them when they decided to sleep in their own beds.

I didn't set any resolutions or even have much hope for the New Year beyond time's obstinate movement forward. I was desperate not to get stuck in the past, like the widow from church who honored her husband by keeping the same furniture, the same dated wallpaper and décor, all a testament to the year of his death, as if she expected him to walk through the door any minute.

I just wanted it not to be 2007 anymore.

CHAPTER 19

NEW YEAR, NEW THERAPIST

Having been widowed was an effective way to gain closet space and lose weight, but I don't recommend it. I lost twenty-five pounds in the three months after Sam died. People around town told me I looked great. I didn't. I was lighter and bonier than I had been when I graduated from high school. Our grief-averse culture is so tongue-tied that nobody knew what to say to the widow, and our weight-obsessed culture is warped. My friends were alarmed. One Jane brought me a two-pound box of chocolate with a cautionary note: "Underwear falling off is NOT acceptable!"

Sam, too, had lost weight before he died. Not a lot, not significant enough to change the way his suits fit or dramatic enough for anyone to notice. If anything, the loss of a few pounds seemed to have made him happy; less weight on his frame meant less pressure on his back. It never entered my mind that his loss of ten pounds might have pointed to something more insidious, that anxiety was eating at him from the inside, that depression had claimed its toehold.

* * *

Danny and Jason bickered constantly. They used to play together happily (mostly), compromise (eventually), and take turns (usually), but after Sam's suicide, they couldn't even agree on what day it was. I didn't know whether it was grief or ADHD or an age-appropriate developmental stage. All I knew was that I needed help restoring harmony to my sad, struggling family of three. I had Dr. Newland, Danny had Dr. Kimberly, and now the three of us had Dr. Clark.

He looked like a family therapist from a movie: kind smile, intelligent brown eyes, a few weeks overdue for a haircut, tweed jacket. Dr. Clark usually started the session with some type of activity such as, "Draw a picture of the day your father died." Or an agenda: "Let's talk about who does which chores." In the first month, Danny quietly destroyed half a dozen stress balls, and I cried my way through a box of tissues. Jason provided the comic relief, pulling faces to make us laugh.

One afternoon, Jason and Danny and Dr. Clark were sitting on the carpet examining the family trees the boys had drawn. They were explaining the who's who, both emphasizing Parker's importance and the absence of Sam. With much gentleness, Dr. Clark told my boys, "Someday, you will reinvest in life."

Absolutely, I thought from my chair on the sidelines. *They need to do that. This is why we're here, so Danny and Jason can heal and learn to love again in their young lives.*

Dr. Clark caught my eye, and said quietly, "You too."

I smiled and shook my head. *No way.*

I had already invested once. I gave my whole heart; I was loved truly and well. It was too short, but it was mine. I didn't need another partner. I had two boys, a lovely home, good friends, my education, and an adorable dog. It was a full and beautiful life, and it was enough.

The fear that undid me was that my children might follow in their father's suicidal footsteps, that they might become addicts or get trapped in their own grief. Statistically, children who have lost a parent (for any reason, not just suicide) are at increased risk for a variety of dangerous behaviors, such as alcohol and drug use and, horrifyingly, suicide. That fear paralyzed me. It took my breath and darkened my vision. I resisted it like an oncoming migraine. I couldn't let it take hold, but the force of it was overwhelming. I had to believe that Danny and Jason would heal from this loss, that they would make positive choices, that my efforts to nurture their mental health would make a difference.

Dr. Clark's "You too" warned me of a double standard. I could not ask my sons to do something I was unwilling to do myself. I could not just tell them to continue to live full, joyful, purposeful lives. I would have to live one of my own.

* * *

Taking my boys to the park was usually a time when I could feel normal again for a couple hours—just Danny, Jason, me, a mesh bag of sand toys, and a picnic lunch in tow. It would have been just another day at the park that January afternoon, too, if not for the bride.

She and her photographer were at the edge of the lawn. The young bride looked beautiful, a shimmer of white silk against a gentle green backdrop. I felt wistful for a heartbeat, and then I remembered: *She doesn't know. She has no idea that whoever she loves is going to die, and when they do, she will be left alone with her heartbreak and a useless dress.*

It was so easy to say "I do" when "till death do us part" looked so far away.

I wiped the tears from under my sunglasses. If I had known then how painful it was to live with this loss, would I still have married Sam? *Yes.*

I looked back to the playground where my sons were creating an obstacle course, jumping from the slide and throwing a truck through the tire swing at the same time. Danny and Jason were my everything.

Would I have married Sam again? *Definitely, yes.*

* * *

I padded into the morning with my little black shadow at my side, his toenails clicking on the hardwood floors. I made my coffee and checked my email, filtering through school updates, work deadlines, and marketing campaigns, looking for Bess's message in my inbox. I knew she would be there.

"*We did an informal poll on whose husband was most likely to take his own life, and I want you to know that Sam came in last place.*"

I sent my reply almost immediately…*Dead last?*

My college roommate Bess was one of the few people with whom I could share my darkest thoughts. She was shorter than me but made up with attitude what she lacked in height. Though Bess was raised in Kansas, her Brooklyn home suited her edgy self. One of her eyes was brown and the other was a light golden brown; like the Australian shepherds who share this trait, she was a loyal friend.

Since Sam had died, Bess had been sending me daily emails. Every morning, I woke to her musings on caffeine, rescue puppies, or the antics of boys. "Mothering sons is a full-contact sport," she wrote once, making me snort coffee out my nose. Every evening, she sent a tirade on a work snafu, the latest update on the world's longest divorce proceedings, or snarky commentary on her New York Mets. When she asked whether I had given anyone "the 39-year-old widow speech," our code for "Eff you," I answered her honestly. I was navigating widowhood while she was navigating divorcéedom. She understood the single parent shtick. We shared sleepless nights and a reverent love for our children, which brought an intimacy unmitigated by the 2,500 miles between us. "Did I mention I love you?" she wrote again and again.

I began and ended every single day with her communiqués. Bess was as dependable as the sunrise: even during the holidays, even though she had a full-time job and two sons herself, even when she was traveling, even though her soon-to-be-but-not-soon-enough-ex-husband was unreasonably difficult.

Bess was also a gifted photographer. One evening's email consisted of a photograph: three green agapanthus stems not yet in bloom, one taller than the other two, the spring green buds on the verge of bursting open but still tucked inside, swollen with possibility. Raindrops stuck to the buds and stems, traces of a recently passing storm. She had titled the picture "after the rain."

I stared at the photograph on my screen, noting the resemblance between the fledgling African lilies and my little family of three. I was struck by a sense of wholeness looking at the trio. In that moment, I felt a sense of promise for my family. I hadn't thought much about the "after." There had simply been so much rain. Bess had faith in me, trusting that after the rainstorm that was Sam's death, the three of us—my little boys and me—would bloom again.

CHAPTER 20

FEBRUARY BIRTHDAYS

It was significantly less fun to celebrate the children's seventh and ninth birthdays without Sam. It was even less fun to celebrate Sam's birthday without him. I took the boys to Houston's, and we ordered a round of his favorite cheeseburger in his honor. Sam would have been forty-two. It had never sounded younger.

I've never been one to fret much over my age. There were worse things than getting older. Like not.

Thirty didn't throw me for a tailspin. Forty on the horizon didn't bother me. Going through the motions, living in a state of permanent nostalgia, resisting joy: those things scared me. I didn't want my sons to feel that when they lost their father, they lost their mother, too. I was less afraid of death than I was of disengagement.

Caroline invited me to celebrate her fortieth with a girls' weekend in Pennsylvania Amish country. Several things appealed to me about this trip: spending a weekend with women who loved me and who loved Sam, sleeping without being kicked, not cooking, not driving, visiting a place I'd never been, and celebrating my dear friend. The downside was the distance. Air travel hadn't frightened me before, but flying while widowed felt different. I was terrified about something happening to the kids—or to me—when I was impossibly far away from them.

"Well," Dr. Newland chose her words pointedly, "you could let inertia win this round, but that will probably make it harder next time."

I decided to go.

When the day arrived, I boarded the plane and stared at the book in my lap until takeoff. I was afraid that if I took a Xanax, I would be too knocked out to notice sudden turbulence or a sexual predator. I was afraid that if I didn't take one, I would hyperventilate or cry uncontrollably or throw up. Once we were safely in the air, I took a Xanax and stared out the window.

Caroline met me at the Philadelphia airport and embraced me in a hug so long she could feel my body trembling. Not until she sensed that I was steady did she release me.

She smiled broadly. "I'm so glad you're here."

The countryside was beautiful, if stark. The frozen ground was still hard and dormant in shades of brown and slate. With the land resting quietly, it was easy to succumb to a slower pace.

Caroline pulled up to a drive-through bank teller to get cash for the weekend, and a horse-drawn buggy was in front of us in line. I smiled at the incongruity of the scene. I hadn't realized that the Amish interacted with the modern financial world in this way, and I watched the driver in his black suit and broad-brimmed hat deftly place the canister in the pneumatic tube. It struck me that, as a widow, I felt similarly out of pace with the rest of the world. The difference between me and the Amish man was that I had stopped dressing in black. It may have appeared to the world as though I had reengaged with life, but my insides felt as barren as the chilled landscape.

Our bed and breakfast was tidy, simple, and warm. Esmé popped open champagne and handed glasses around. Before marriage and kids, Esmé wrote for a magazine in New York, and she peppered the conversation with fashion and practicality tips. "Every woman should own a pair of Dansko clogs."

We talked about the children—all of us had at least two—and our husbands, including my dead one. We talked about careers, education, working, staying home with kids full time, fashion trends, in-laws, travel, good books, good sex, bad sex, and no sex.

"You know what I'm jealous of?" Esmé said, looking at me pointedly.

I laughed. "Who in her right mind would be jealous of the widow?"

"I am," she said, full of sass and waving her champagne flute. "You're going to experience all that good stuff again—a first kiss, those butterfly flutterings of falling in love, the thrill of sex with a new partner."

"I just want one night of uninterrupted sleep."

She ignored me. "Maybe you'll meet him in Paris."

"Did you get that credit card with the miles?" Caroline smiled.

"What do you think Jacques is going to say when he finds out that at least one kid and the dog sleep in my bed with me every night?"

I had never been to Paris. Traveling was something Sam and I didn't do much. A few years prior, I had tossed around the idea of working abroad and going to Switzerland for a year. The boys were not yet in school, and I thought it would be an amazing experience. Sam wouldn't entertain the idea—wouldn't even consider going abroad for family vacation. Not only did his back hurt just thinking about traveling with kids and their accoutrements, but he was afraid of leaving the United States, likely due to his parents' experience in communist Cuba and one regrettable incident his sophomore year in college when his own Modelo-induced misdeeds landed him briefly in a Mexican jail. He and his buddies saved themselves with a combination of quick thinking, cash, serendipity, and Sam's fluent Spanish. I couldn't convince him that anywhere outside of America would be safe to travel. He refused to get a passport, so I let mine expire. If we weren't going to travel together, then what was the point?

After the girls' weekend, I began to think about traveling. During a sleepless night back home, I downloaded the forms to get myself a new passport. Then I found the forms to apply for children's passports. Normally, both parents' signatures were required, but I needed only my signature and Sam's death certificate. If I wanted to, I could take Danny and Jason to Europe or Canada or anywhere in the world.

Next I found the Dansko website and ordered a pair of clogs in a black and brown leopard print.

CHAPTER 21

WIDOW AND ORPHAN SCHOOL

One afternoon while doing his homework, Danny slid a yellow paper across the kitchen table. Not looking up, he said, "Can you sign this?"

It was a detention slip with the infraction described thus: "Carved name in desk."

I looked at him curiously. The child was usually Boy Scout–level obedient in school, and this evidence of his misbehavior left him on the verge of tears.

This was a delicate parenting moment, figuring out how to encourage my child to tell the truth when he knows that the truth will get him into trouble. How to remind him that he is deeply loved, even though he must face the consequences of his misdeeds. It can be hard to tell the truth knowing that disappointment or penalty will ensue. And I was disappointed. My own parents would have been furious if I had ever come home with a detention slip, so I already felt I'd made parenting progress. If this had happened before Sam's death, I would have been seriously miffed. In light of Sam's suicide, a detention was nowhere close to the end of the world. He was just a kid. A kid who was trying to learn to read and write and do math and be social and play baseball without the benefit of a father. And a kid who needed to learn to respect school property and to manage his anxiety in a different way.

"It's okay, sweetie. Just tell me what happened."

"I carved my desk at school."

"I see…." I paused. A lengthy pause can yield more insight than a litigator's line of questioning.

"I was really mad."

"Seems like you were."

"I'm just really mad."

He was miserable. He was so angry with his father, so hurt, so confused. I avoided saying one of the "D" words, in an effort not to upset him more. "I wonder if there was something different you could do with your mad instead of carving your name in your desk."

"I didn't carve *my* name in my desk."

I raised an eyebrow.

"I carved Spencer's name."

Interesting. Spencer was not a name I heard much. They were in the same Cub Scout den; otherwise, he and Danny didn't spend much time together.

"Why?"

"He was making fun of me at recess…" He hesitated. "Because my dad died."

The cruelty was a gut-punch.

"What did your teacher say when you told her?"

"I didn't. She just shouted 'Danny!' and I got nervous. And then she told me I had a detention."

It was all I could do to remain calm. "Did she come over to your desk? Or did she just talk to you from across the room?"

"She walked over, and she looked at it. And touched it. And then she went to her desk and gave me the yellow slip."

At one level it didn't matter what he was carving—it was all graffiti—but I couldn't let it go. I couldn't believe she wasn't curious about why Danny had carved another kid's name in his desk.

"Mommy, are you mad?"

I pulled him into a hug. "I'm not mad at you. I love you. You do know you're not supposed to carve names in desks, right? Not yours. Not Spencer's. You'll have to serve your detention. But I'm not mad."

Not mad at *him*, anyway. I was incensed that a teacher would hand my third grader a detention slip without having a conversation with him or giving him a chance to explain his side. I didn't necessarily disagree with the result. But what a wasted opportunity. Where was the attempt to repair the relationship between Danny and Spencer? What about the conversation with Spencer about not teasing orphans? How about helping Danny address the taunts of kids on the playground? With her rigid and myopic adherence to rules, she had entirely missed the teachable moment. I didn't care that he received a detention or even that he deserved it. But oh baby, was I ever mad.

In widow and orphan school, we learned how to hold our own grief with both tenderness and ferocity, because the world would not be so kind.

* * *

I could see the pain shimmering in Jason's eyes from ten feet away.

"Matthew started calling me 'dead father guy' at recess, and he won't stop!" The child in question lived across the street from us, and he waved at me energetically before darting inside. Matthew usually sprinted home and then waited for Jason, taunting, "I won! I won!" from his front porch finish line. That day, he had tracked with Jason on the walk home from school, hollering *dead father guy* at him from the opposite side of the street. *Dead father guy*? Accurate. Hurtful. But not remotely clever.

The kid had his own problems. He had moved to La Cañada the year before, speaking almost no English. When his kindergarten teacher asked for words that rhymed with truck, he bypassed "buck" and "duck" and went straight to something more illicit. Poor Matthew didn't get invited to playdates after that outburst. But my priority was my own kid, and now I was pissed. *It just really seems like—if there is an omnipotent and loving God—then She or He or WhoeverTheHellIsInChargeOfThisMess would give these kids a break. Haven't they been through enough?*

"Sometimes," I told my son as I shepherded him into the house, "the best way to take the sting out of hurtful words is to own them."

We cried, we talked. We crafted our own alliterative phrase: *dead dad dude.* We role played: I called Jason dead father guy, and he practiced saying, "That's right. I am the dead dad dude. *Mister* Dead Dad Dude, to you." He would be prepared next time.

* * *

On an unseasonably warm Saturday, we went to a friend's house for a swim (weird for February, even by Los Angeles standards). I plopped my pool bag on a lounge chair next to Linda. I had never looked better in a bikini—that is, if you consider "emaciated widow" a good look.

As Danny jumped from the edge, I noticed him pull one leg up sharply, and, instead of gliding across the water, he pushed up through the surface of the water quickly and dogpaddled back to the edge. By the time he had pulled himself out, I was at his side. He tucked one leg across the other so he could see the underside of his left foot, dripping water and blood. Danny seemed more surprised than hurt. Mostly, he was curious about what was so sharp near the edge of the pool. It looked like the remnants of a steel mount for a ladder that had been removed, the edges jutting up dangerously.

The Jane whose pool it was was a registered nurse and a doctor's wife. She exuded competence and calm. I moved aside so she could examine Danny's foot. I expected Nurse Jane to tell me she had the perfect salve and would bandage up my son herself.

It was another beautiful Southern California afternoon, the kids splashing playfully and the warmth inviting us to linger into the evening. There was already talk of firing up the barbeque. Nurse Jane looked at me and said, "You need to take him to the emergency room."

So much for my poolside reverie.

She wrapped the wound, and I helped Danny change into dry clothes. Linda offered to watch Jason, and I pulled a dress over my head and grabbed my keys. Ben accompanied us, because Danny needed two of us—a pair of human crutches—to help him hobble to the car. Sam should have been with us. It was hard to believe he was gone.

We arrived at the emergency room and waited. Eventually, a doctor came into the exam room, addressed a few questions to Ben, remembered something he forgot, and then excused himself briefly.

I looked at Ben. "Think if I had walked in here wearing only the bikini, he would have looked in my direction?"

Ben smiled sadly. "I'll wait outside."

Danny leaned against me, his injury somehow making him appear smaller.

The doctor returned momentarily. "Do you want me to wait for Dad?"

"That's not Dad." It irritated me that he treated me like a runner-up parent. It's also likely that I was a teensy bit hypersensitive because this was my first trip to that emergency room since Sam had been declared dead there four months ago.

The doctor raised an eyebrow condescendingly.

I explained, "Dad died in October."

Something in the examination room dynamic shifted, and he finally made eye contact with me. After a pause, he said, "I'm sorry."

It is hard enough to be a woman in a man's world. Harder still to be a widowed mom in a two-parent system. I was perfectly capable of having a coherent conversation with my child's physician and taking care of my son, and it annoyed me that I kept having to prove myself.

The doctor showed me where the tendon in Danny's foot had been nicked. "The good news is that it will heal well without surgery." He put in a few stitches, showed me how to wrap the foot, and gave us instructions. "No swimming for two weeks."

Danny asked, "Can I play baseball?"

"No baseball for at least three weeks."

Danny's face crumbled. For the first time all afternoon, his eyes welled with tears. "No baseball?" He was inconsolable. Baseball season would be half over by the time he was allowed to play again. Three weeks was forever in kid-time.

They say that time heals all wounds, but time was making this one worse. And there was nothing I could do.

* * *

One surprising aspect of being widowed was not only how quickly men started making overtures, but how many of them were married. Even more surprising was how long it took me to figure out that none of them actually wanted to go to coffee. Or to talk.

The guy from the grief group called. "Do you want to meet for coffee?"

He was so sad I didn't have the heart to hang up. I let him tell me his story while I folded laundry, creating stacks of Danny's and Jason's shirts on the kitchen island. His wife had died from cancer; he had two little boys. He was overwhelmed by office work and housework and grieving children. I understood. Widowed single parenting was like racing in a velodrome riding a tricycle. Not for the faint of heart.

He said, "I need to find a woman to be the mother for my kids."

That, I didn't understand. I didn't want a man to father my sons. I wanted to take care of my own kids and get a good night's sleep. The only hairy body I wanted in my bed was the dog's. I didn't have to negotiate or compromise on anything from choice of movie to bedtime to restaurant to vacation. I never had to iron his shirts. I was a pretty good mom, and I was starting to think I was a good enough dad, too.

I added grief guy's name to my contact list, so I could send him to voicemail if he called again.

* * *

Once Susan had reorganized my closet, she was dying to clear out more. She set her sights on some old DVDs, a mélange of superhero and original Speed Racer television shows, but I wouldn't let her touch them. Sam had grown up with those shows, and Danny and Jason loved them. The truth was I wasn't ready to let them go, either.

Susan remained respectful of my process, but I could see that it pained her that she could not, through the combination of interior design and force of will, protect us from the mess of our grief. She told me, "I've been working at Tim's house."

"Who?"

"Tim Stratz? The widower?"

I vaguely remembered that one of Susan's favorite clients had recently died. When Debbie was diagnosed with colon cancer, she and her husband had put their remodeling project on hold.

"He called me and said, 'I'm going to ask you a question, and I know it might be too hard for you, so please feel free to say no. But I was hoping that you might be willing to finish the project you started with Debbie.'" Susan paused. "Isn't that sweet? Of course, I said yes."

I smiled. Nobody rolled up her sleeves like my Susan.

"I'm picking up chairs for their dining room this afternoon. You can imagine what it's like over there without a mom."

"How old are the kids?"

"Fifteen and twelve," she said. "We're choosing paint, too. It's the same light green as your kitchen."

"Tickled Crow." I don't know why I remembered the quirky name for this specific shade of gray-green, but I loved the color. It was an easy green to live with.

"Tim is such a good guy. I told him about you, my amazing friend."

I didn't feel amazing. I felt like I was drowning.

"He said the nicest thing," she said, starting to tear up. "He said, 'Tell Charlotte I know what the nights are like.'"

She looked at me hopefully. I shook my head. Maybe it was unfair to lump her friend together with the guy from the grief group, but I wasn't interested. I already had girlfriends who knew that the nights were like suffocating in a watery cloud of octopus ink.

She continued, "It might be nice to talk to someone who's in the same leaky boat."

"Do *not* give him my number."

* * *

Another sunny day, plus a heated pool and a seventh birthday yielded an end-of-February pool party, but Danny was still on crutches and decidedly unhappy about it. Shortly after we arrived in our neighbor's backyard, he took a swing at me.

"Danny!" I caught his arm. I was stunned and embarrassed that my nine-year-old had tried to hit me.

I was not entirely sure what had set off my blue-eyed boy. It could have been that a bunch of kids were swimming and he wasn't allowed to, or that I embarrassed him when I caught him trying to push his brother into the pool. It might have been that I stopped him from getting another cookie. He ate all the comfort food I didn't have the stomach for. Whatever weight I had lost after Sam's death, Danny had gained.

"You stop it, Mommy! *You* stop!" He threw a cookie at me.

I had to get Danny out of there, but I couldn't leave Jason poolside without me. Linda offered to keep an eye on Jason so I could walk Danny home.

Home was across the street and down two houses, but it seemed much farther with Danny hobbling and hollering the whole way. Once inside, he completely unraveled.

Nothing consoled him. I was afraid to leave him alone. He tried to hurt himself. He hurled his crutches at the wall and walked without them. He cried out in pain and plopped to the floor, threatening to pull the stitches out of his own foot.

I didn't know what to do. At five feet, Danny was too big for me to control physically. I was afraid, and my heart thumped wildly.

I called Zack, putting him on speaker because I needed both hands to protect myself.

"How can I help?"

"I don't know! Take him away!"

"Charlotte, don't say that! He can hear you!"

"Zack—it's okay to let a child know when he's out of line! I don't care if they say *fuck*. I don't give a rat's ass if they break shit. But they cannot hit me!" I started shouting. "They cannot hurt each other and they absolutely, positively *cannot* hurt themselves!"

Danny lunged toward me again, and I caught his arm mid-flail. My skin was electric with fear; even the hairs on my head were standing on edge.

"I have to go." I hung up.

I didn't know what I thought Zack could do. I wanted someone to know how hard this whole grief scene was. My son's rage was more than I could handle alone.

Danny tumbled into the sofa, and I took a seat nearby. He looked at me through his tears, and said, "I wish *you* had died instead of Daddy!"

His words hurt, as he undoubtedly intended. Intellectually, and as a result of Dr. Newland's influence, I knew that what he meant was more like: *I'm in so much pain that I don't think I will survive and I don't know what to do with it and I need you to feel it with me!*

I could have killed Sam right then.

I needed a minute alone, just to take a few full breaths. I headed to my room.

He followed me screaming, still in a fury. "Don't go, Mommy! Don't *GO!*"

My phone rang. It was Zack. I let him go to voicemail.

I found my way back to the kitchen, the heart of our home. Danny pointed to a small black plaque hanging near the kitchen table. Displayed on the plaque was a decorative pink heart for Valentine's Day. Danny pointed to it and glared at me.

"Take it down!"

"What's wrong with it?"

"It's not broken."

Then I understood: the heart on the wall was whole, not broken like his.

"Do you want to draw the crack?" I asked.

He nodded, his face as wet with tears as if he had, in fact, been swimming with his friends. I took the heart off the plaque and handed it to him, along with a pencil.

"Not pencil. Pen."

I gave him a black pen. He drew a jagged crack down the center of the pink heart.

"That's better," he said.

He handed me the now obviously and permanently broken heart, and I fit it back onto the plaque, the essence of our lives on display. He was right, of course. Healing happens when we face our feelings, as Dr. Newland was showing me, and we were navigating gale-force emotional winds.

Danny crumpled into my arms, and I held him until we both stopped shaking. "You're surviving one of the worst things that can happen to a child," I told him. And then, looking squarely into his teary blue eyes, I added, "For rest of your life, you'll be able to look back at this time and say 'I survived my father's suicide. I can do anything.'"

***

I suppose I could have given myself similar advice. I could handle all the household responsibilities—mortgage, meals, manners—as well as going back to work part time, but the Cub Scout camping trips? I would totally have pawned that off on a husband if I'd had one.

It was early March, and we had sighted a brown bear across the lake from the campsite in the Angeles Forest that afternoon. Late that night, inside our cold and dark tent, Jason woke up and scooched his sleeping bag closer to me. He whispered urgently, "Mommy, I hear a bear."

I nestled him close, because the bear-like grunting had kept me awake most of the night myself. I had, however, already determined the source of the growls, and I knew they weren't a threat. Jason tucked his head under my chin, and I breathed in the top of his head. At seven, he smelled of dirt and sunshine.

"That's not a bear, sweetie. That's just Mr. Reyes."

Jason looked relieved.

"And Mr. Smith."

He smiled.

"And Mr. Lee." They weren't exactly the three tenors.

He giggled and snuggled back to sleep. His breathing relaxed into a soft, rhythmic pattern, and for the first time since my husband's death, I felt a little sorry for the women happily married to those apnea-afflicted men.

* * *

Danny was cleared to play baseball again. "Bye, Mom!" he called as soon as he saw Steve's car pull up. He slung his bag over his shoulder and ran out the door.

Steve and his wife Maris were not the kind of people I would have been close to in high school: he was captain of his school's baseball team; she was homecoming queen; I hid in the library. But life had its way of leveling the playing field. I had been widowed, Maris was fighting breast cancer, and our sons had landed on the same baseball team. In addition to being my financial advisor, Steve was now my son's baseball coach.

"Thanks for driving Danny to practice."

"No problem," he said, throwing Danny's bag in the trunk with the rest of the equipment. "You should come with us to the cages later."

I was confused. "Me?"

He shrugged. "Might not suck to hit a bucket of balls."

It hadn't occurred to me to take my anger out on several dozen unsuspecting baseballs. "Really?"

"Batting practice ends at 5:30. We'll have a bucket ready for you."

"Okay then." I changed out of my office attire and drove to the batting cages. I hadn't taken a swing at a baseball since I played on a co-ed intramural team in college.

Steve handed me a bat, and I took a few swings. He threw out a couple pitches, and I missed them, demonstrating why I was more suited for library life.

"Relax," he encouraged me. "Keep your eye on the ball."

I connected on a pitch.

"Atta girl!"

I hit a few more, and then he started the machine.

I had forgotten how good it felt to take a full swing, to smack the lights out of a baseball, to hear the satisfying crack of the bat. Suicide was a death complicated by the fact that the man I loved was the one who killed the man I loved. My anger responded to the physical release. With each swing, I imagined calling Sam names. *Asshole. Dickhead.*

I started sweating and settled into a rhythm: a ball popped out of the machine, and I swung back. For each pitch thrown, I hurled an insult back. I sent several expletives in God's direction. *Stupid plan. He had enough angels in heaven without having to take mine.*

And a few toward those little shits on the playground. *Leave. My. Kids. Alone.*

And more than one to the patronizing pea brain at the bank who insisted that I produce a legal form that did not apply in Sam's situation and would cost more in court fees to create than the account itself was worth. *That bitch. Dimwit. Fuck her. Fuck them all.*

In that moment, it was easy to forget Sam's gentleness, the night after nights he held me as I cried over lost pregnancies, the lullabies he sang sweetly out of tune because he had read that children who were sung to became musical, even when their father sang off-key. I would stand at the door of the boys' rooms listening to my husband sing "He's a Jolly Good Fellow" softly to our sons, amused by his spartan repertoire. Mad was easier than sad. It was simpler to forget the hours Sam spent coaching the T-ball team how to play his favorite game, a sport he gave up his sophomore year of high school because it hurt his back to swing the bat.

I swung for the fences instead.

Steve was right. It didn't suck. My hands tingled from the vibration of the bat. My shoulders were already sore, but I felt strong. I had envisioned the lifting of my grief sandbag as metaphorical, best addressed in the confines of my therapist's office, but the reality of rage was that it insisted on expressing itself elsewhere. And it wasn't easily tamed.

When we got home, Danny dropped his bag in the hallway and ran to search for his brother. "Jason! Guess what? Mommy doesn't hit like a girl!"

* * *

My anger intensified. I felt my hands prickle with rage when I saw dads walk into classrooms and living rooms. A pang of regret hit me in the stomach when I saw gray-haired couples shuffle along holding hands. Angry tears overflowed when I saw Sam smiling in a photograph looking joyful in perpetuity. *He had better not be at peace*, I thought. *His suffering better not be over. He does not belong in a better place. He belongs here with us.*

My skin practically sparked with a static energy. I worried that my temper might accidentally strike my parents or a Jane, unintended lightning rods. Angry does not make quality decisions, but it can spark an initiative for change.

What started as taking the dog for a walk one afternoon led to short sprints on the horse trail. Nobody could see me, how short on stamina I was, how quickly out of breath. I ran until I gasped and sobbed with each exhale. Nobody hushed me. I caught my breath and took off again. Alone on the trail, nobody told me the tired lie that everything was okay. I was not okay. Tears, sweat, and snot ran down my face and neck.

I heard footsteps overtaking me from behind, growing louder and faster. I stopped and turned to look, but nobody was there. My eyes stung with tears. *Fuck you, Sam. This time, I'm leaving you.*

I sprinted again, kicking up dust and rage. I was grief in motion.

Parker wagged enthusiastically alongside.

I returned home, lungs wheezing. After a shower and another crying jag, I noticed a sensation in my center that I hadn't felt in months: hunger. Like an old friend who had returned home from a long journey, my appetite showed up unexpectedly and somehow felt completely familiar. For the first time I could remember since Sam's death, I was looking forward to eating dinner.

CHAPTER 22

MARCH BIRTHDAY

Suicide's claim on lives is so ugly that people mostly speak of it in whispers. It was a relief to speak out loud with a fellow survivor.

Louis, who cut my hair, had been widowed to suicide. I was sitting in the salon chair when he told me the story. He said, "When I saw what my husband had done, I wanted to kill him!"

It was a natural impulse.

I had cut my hair short about a month before Sam's suicide. He preferred my hair long, but I cut it when I went back to work. I looked more professional with shorter hair, and frankly, I preferred it. When Sam got home from work that day and saw my freshly cut hair, he looked so disappointed. I felt defensive. It was my hair, and it would grow back. I thought, *Why should he care?*

Did my "attorney" haircut trigger his shame about my going to work again? Had my short hair exacerbated his depression?

Louis took a few lengths of my hair in his hand. "Okay, girl, we need to lighten up your hair."

I knew better than to argue. He was an artist, and he had told me more than once that my job was just to show up.

He sensed my reluctance. "I'm not going to go blonde on you, we just need to lighten things up."

"Let's start with my hair," I said, "and then we'll work on the rest of my life."

* * *

My high school sweetheart and I still talk twice a year: on his birthday in September and on my birthday in March. The last time we had talked, he had been groaning about turning thirty-nine.

"Are you kidding me?" I asked, surprised.

"Next year is the big FOUR-OH," he said. "It sounds so old."

"I don't think so. My thirties were better than my twenties, and my twenties were so much better than my teens. You couldn't pay me enough to be a teenager again. No offense."

"I guess." He didn't sound convinced.

"Oh definitely. I got married in my twenties and had my babies in my thirties. My life just keeps getting better. I *cannot wait* to be forty!"

Then my thirties ended with shock and tears, and I just wanted out of that decade. My husband betrayed me in a public and humiliating way, leaving me with two children and a big, fat mortgage. That, to me, was worse than turning forty.

Not to mention that Sam died at forty-one. Which suddenly made forty seem very young, and getting older like an exceptionally good idea. Aging was not a problem. It was the goal.

Something about forty felt like a fresh start. I was looking forward to my birthday with an anticipation I hadn't felt since I was a child.

I called Susan. "Would it be too weird to throw a fortieth party for myself?"

"Not at all! Can I help?"

"I'm thinking dinner with my A-Team. Maybe ten of us?"

"Madeleine's?"

Madeleine's was perfect—a French-American bistro in nearby Pasadena with a friendly staff, a full bar, and several private dining rooms.

I made the reservations and invited ten of my tried and true. I had a hunch that my friends had agreed to split the bill, and I didn't tell them that I planned to pay for the evening myself. I wanted to treat them, partly as a thank you and partly to demonstrate my burgeoning independence.

Sometime between appetizers and the main course, and after one or maybe two pomegranate martinis, I excused myself and found our handsome waiter. I patted his chest flirtatiously and said, "I'm the birthday girl and I should get what I want." I slipped my credit card into his shirt pocket. "The first thing I want is to pay for dinner."

He smiled and nodded.

"And the second thing I want is another pomegranate martini."

"The birthday girl shall have what the birthday girl wants," he assured me.

When the bill arrived, Steve reached out to take it. I put my hand over his and slid the leather folio back toward me. "Too late. This one's mine."

Linda protested, "Charlotte! We wanted to pay for dinner."

Susan objected, "But it's your birthday!"

I shrugged. "Shouldn't have let me to go the women's room alone."

I smiled at the waiter and added an extra tip before signing the receipt. I had pulled off a small coup. I was thrilled.

"I appreciate it. I do," I said, looking around the table. "But you have already done so much. You've taken me to countless coffees and fed my kids. I've cried on your collective shoulders for hours on end. You drove my kids to baseball and Cub Scouts. You organized my bills so I wouldn't forget to pay them. Steve put in a dog door so Parker would stop waking me up to go potty. Linda snuck into my house and logged onto my computer to nab a picture of the boys to make a locket for Christmas. I'll never be able to thank you enough. It's my birthday. Please. Let me pay for dinner."

What were they going to do, argue with the widow?

CHAPTER 23

SPRINGTIME

One Tuesday, Roger ended yoga class with this quote from Anaïs Nin: "And the day came when the risk it took to remain tight in the bud was more painful than the risk it took to blossom." The sentiment arrived like an invitation to a party I didn't realize I wanted to go to until I was holding the card stock in my hand.

***

"Charlotte!" I could hear the excitement in Jane's voice. "I'd like to take you and the boys skiing in Utah for Easter!" Designer Jane had helped me with my kitchen remodel. She thrived on updating living spaces into places of beauty, comfort, and purpose. I knew before seeing it that her ski home in Utah would be fabulous. And accented with a leopard print.

Danny and Jason had never skied before. I learned in the Swiss Alps, which might sound like advanced skiing, but really my parents, my sister, and I just happened to ski one time when we were visiting my grandparents.

Sam and I had skied together exactly once, long before we had children. At the end of the afternoon, the only run between the lifts and the parking lot was a black diamond. I started to take off my skis and trudge toward the gondola, but Sam insisted that we ski down. At some point I gave up and, with my skis over my shoulder, alternately hiked and slipped down the icy slope. By the time I had reached the bottom, I was about as serene as a cat who'd been dropped down a laundry chute. That our sense of humor survived that afternoon was a testament to grace and forgiveness. Still, we had never taken our boys skiing.

Danny turned out to be a natural on the slopes. He loved the freedom of flying down the mountain. I watched my son swish and tuck and wished his father could see him. Jason hollered with excitement as he zipped down the blue hills, but by early afternoon, he had discovered the bane of skiing: ski boots. Danny and I returned to the slopes, and Designer Jane took Jason home to play in the snow. They built an anatomically accurate snowman and snowwoman and then accessorized them.

As he drifted to sleep that night, Jason said, "Jane really loves us a lot, doesn't she?"

It was a beautiful moment, that feeling in our bones of being loved dearly, like a hot chocolate after coming in from the freezing cold. Sam's suicide brought with it an insecurity, the ever-present inkling at the back of my mind that all was not well, that I'd missed something terribly important, that calamity might strike swiftly and unpredictably. I sometimes wondered if I would ever feel truly safe again. But in that moment, we were warm and content. The tension was gone, shoulders relaxed, eyelids heavy. We were tired from playing outside in the snow, from feeling the strength and balance in our limbs, from moving in concert with gravity. There was something healing about the outdoors, especially in the mountains, the scent of pine, the exhilaration of experiencing something new together. It was an altogether different kind of exhaustion than the one from coping with the constant weight of grief. With her generosity and enthusiasm, Jane gave my little family a hint of adventure ahead.

* * *

In about early April, a single dad from the elementary school invited me to coffee. I told him outright, "I'm not interested in anything more than friendship," and he assured me that he wasn't, either. He had sole custody of his son and daughter, and he told me the crazy story of his now ex-wife.

"Meet me for coffee," he said, "Just friends." And I agreed.

It was nice to chat with someone who understood the single parent acrobatics.

We chatted on the phone another time or two, and then he suggested that we take all four kids to dinner.

Jim was a gentleman, opening the car and restaurant doors for me, pulling out my chair at the table. But when he pressed his hand against the small of my back, I tensed. I didn't want him to touch me. His sweet daughter looked at me longingly, and I wondered what her father had told her about me. I imagined she missed having a female compatriot in the midst of all the masculinity.

After dinner, a fellow patron commented, "You've got your hands full."

I wanted to explain, *This is not my family. We are not what we look like.*

* * *

Sam had taken his life at a crossroads, at the corner of Green Street and Hudson Avenue in Pasadena. It was an intersection that I otherwise would have passed on my way to Target and my local independent bookstore, both essential stops in the life of this mom. For months I avoided the intersection altogether. Then I begin to circle it like a shark. Once, I almost drove through but changed my route at the last minute. I knew that the only way to move forward would be to face into the pain, but I wasn't ready.

The first time I mustered up the courage to take Green Street all the way through, the light was green. I held my breath and zipped through.

I would never have driven through that intersection with the children in the car. Not that they would have recognized what it signified, but what if I had spontaneously burst into tears? What if I crashed? I could have asked someone to come with me, but I didn't want to. I wanted to take this step alone.

The next time I drove through, the light was green again, and I was oddly disappointed.

A few weeks after that, the light was red. I braked and peered up at the building. The light turned green, and I kept driving.

Sometime in the spring, I parked and got out of my car.

Sam jumped to his death from the top of a four-story structure in the financial district of Pasadena, across the street from his office building. On the street level, there is a single storefront, an elegant salon and day spa. The upper three levels are for public parking; it would have been easy to access the very top from the open stairwell. I imagined that Sam had come to this same conclusion while sitting at his desk and gazing out his office window.

I walked to the place on the sidewalk where it would have happened.

It struck me that Sam jumped at the intersection of two one-way streets. The thing about anxiety, depression, and shame is that they conspire to narrow the focus. Sam saw only one way forward. He had lost the capacity to think creatively and the flexibility to pivot. He was so focused on one path that he was blind to any other options. He descended quickly from one way (Surprise!) to no way (suicide).

Obviously, he didn't heed the big red sign on the corner bearing the message: *WRONG WAY*.

I didn't talk to anyone at the salon on the corner. I imagined the scene as described in the police report and felt the chaotic emptiness. There had been a blur of movement, followed by a loud crunching sound, and then yelling. A pediatrician who had been paying her bill ran out and began chest compressions. One witness called 911. Somebody took over the CPR. Sirens blared. I stood in the place where my husband's heart stopped.

I had a friend who knew the manager on duty at the salon the day Sam jumped. She had rushed out of the salon and to his side. According to her, Sam's eyes were open as he lay still and broken. Blood flowed from his left ear, forming a red pool on the sidewalk. I wondered what Sam might have thought in those final moments. Was he afraid? Was he in pain? Was he relieved? Did he feel regret? The manager told my friend, "When I looked at his eyes, I didn't see death. I saw youth."

So much life left in those eyes.

It must have looked odd to anyone who might have seen me standing alone on the sidewalk. There was no obvious reason for me simply to be there, not going anywhere. They would not have known the effort it took to stay still, or the progress it showed.

CHAPTER 24

A LITTLE ANGRY RUNS A LONG WAY

A random woman at the park once told me: "You've got to treat your sons like you treat the dog…. Take them for a run every day." This would turn out to be good advice for the mother of said sons, too.

I had always hated running. I never ran voluntarily, never felt inspired to run, never saw a runner who looked remotely happy during the process. I thought "good run" was an oxymoron. I had stumbled on running as a socially palatable form of grieving, a sweating out of tears. I ran alone. I didn't enjoy running, but I kept at it, because I felt better after a run—"run" being a generous term for my pace.

Every May, Paradise Canyon Elementary held a community "fun run," charting a course around the neighborhood. I hadn't run a timed mile since the presidential fitness test when I was in elementary school, but Sarah convinced me to sign up with her. "I'll stay with you. It'll be fun! Our goal will be to run the mile without stopping or walking." Sarah had a contagious laugh, and I couldn't resist her misguided enthusiasm.

When I first met Sarah, she described her family with a straightforward, "We have four kids." Months later, I would learn that her first husband left her when she was eight months pregnant. He had been having an affair with her best friend. She later remarried, and together she and her second husband had two "his," one "hers," and one "theirs," but she never differentiated the children in this way. She simply opened her tender heart and mothered them all, not allowing how they had arrived in her nest to define how she related to them.

The starting horn blew, and a jumble of parents and kids burst ahead. Sarah and I fell into a comfortable pace, keeping up a conversation to distract ourselves from the misery of running. The second half of the course featured a slight uphill grade, and Sarah began to tire. She had raced in the 5K earlier that morning. "You've got this!" she encouraged me. "Just go!"

I started to pick up speed. I set my sights on catching one runner ahead of me, and then the next. I heard my friend behind me, yelling, "Go, Charlotte, *Go!*" As I neared the finish line, I pushed harder. I had no idea what my time was, and I didn't care. I crossed the finish line gaining speed and confidence.

I was an unlikely athlete. Christian Science focuses on spiritual identity, almost to the exclusion of the body. It is a largely cerebral and almost wholly disembodied perspective. There was no discussion of nutrition, or cardiovascular health, or the mental and physical benefits of exercise-induced dopamine. The theology of Christian Science champions creation as described in the first chapter of Genesis: "So God created man in his own image, in the image and likeness of God created He him; male and female, created He them." Full stop. There was much to admire in this concept of creation, the idea that we people are made of the same divine essence as Spirit itself, the equal inclusion of both male and female, the complete absence of original sin. But it also created a dualism: "good spirit" versus "bad body." Mary Baker Eddy, the founder of Christian Science, wrote in her seminal text *Science and Health*, "Man is not material, he is spiritual." I heard this binary repeatedly, and I came to believe that my body wasn't the "real" me. Naturally, I then ignored any physical aches, pains, twinges, or even pleasure, because that was not my spiritual self.

I had never so fully inhabited my body as I did when I ran. I started to embrace the suffering of climbing uphill and the exhilaration of powering through a mile. I wondered if the real me could be both divine and material. I contemplated a God who cares not only for a person's spiritual development but also longs passionately for the physical well-being of Her sweet and dusty worldly creation.

* * *

I dreamt that I was hugely pregnant, about to give birth. I was alone in a bright white delivery room. No husband, no midwife, no doctor. No monitors, no epidural. I didn't call out for anyone. I knew instinctively that I was everything I needed.

Intuitively, I started to push. I was afraid, but I pushed through the pain and exhaustion. Tears ran down my face, and after one final push, my baby girl arrived. We were safe, and I was relieved. As I held her, I looked at her precious little face for the first time. She was not a newborn. I recognized her angular jaw, the light brown hair, the crinkles at the corners of her bright blue eyes. Her face was mine. The baby in my arms was me. I gasped and woke up.

I didn't need Carl Jung for this one: I was giving birth to my new life.

* * *

Mother's Day started off well enough. It was the first day since Sam's death that didn't begin with tears. My kids and my parents spoiled me. They gave me the newly released Kindle, and Danny and Jason used their own allowance money to give me a certificate to buy my first e-book.

I didn't cry until later that afternoon, when I thought about a man I didn't know and his two sons on their first Mother's Day without mom. I imagined how miserable Father's Day would be without Sam. I dissolved into tears and cried uncontrollably for half an hour.

I didn't have to know Susan's friend to know that Mother's Day would be unbearably sad. I didn't have to know his sons to empathize with suffering that would be especially sharp that day. I hoped that bearing a gentle witness would be a balm to their pain.

I tapped out an email to Susan. "Please let your friend know that I imagine Mother's Day completely sucks and there are people who care."

She responded almost immediately. "Okay if I forward your email to Tim?"

I must not have been thinking clearly, because I said yes.

* * *

The first time I completed the three-mile loop around the Rose Bowl without stopping felt like a medal-worthy accomplishment.

Sarah had rallied a few ladies to start a running group. Like a pack of She-Wolves, we ran together in the early dark, chasing down dreams and demons. The entrepreneur, the artist, the writer, the lawyer, the engineer. We were wives, divorcées, and a widow. We talked about career steps and missteps, mammograms, faith, and the fourth-grade California Mission project. All our frustrations, failures, and fears, along with our triumphs, pleasures, and dreams came out on the trail. It felt safe in those pre-sunrise hours. It was better than therapy. And cheaper. We laughed a lot, even while running.

This was the real miracle: I had *teenagers* at my house at *5:30 in the morning* to boy-sit so I could run.

My appetite increased. My anger subsided. I built up endurance. I found a community. My group of running girlfriends and I woke up at o'dark thirty to carpool to the Rose Bowl and power through a few miles while the kids were sleeping. We returned home in time to get kids ready for school and ourselves ready for work.

I was not out to break any records for distance or speed. I wasn't remotely interested in running an entire marathon, unless I could count that distance in installments over the course of a couple weeks. Shelly-Ann Fraser-Pryce didn't exactly have anything to fear from me. None of that mattered though, because what was happening was empowering. With every step, anger and fear shook loose, and somewhere along the trail, joy bubbled up. Joy in the very life I was living.

* * *

Just-friends-Jim invited me to go to Las Vegas.

For the record, I hate Las Vegas. It's too hot and too loud. I went for a conference once and decided I never needed to go there again.

"It'll be fun," he said. "Some of the other families from school are going, too."

As it turned out, not one of the families he mentioned was going to Las Vegas. Friendship was obviously not his agenda. I stopped answering his calls.

I wished I had removed my number from the school directory.

And I regretted having told Susan she could give my number to "just a nice guy" Tim.

* * *

Sometime after Mother's Day, I was standing on the back stairs of the karate studio—still in my suit and heels—when my cell phone rang. It was a local number I didn't recognize. I answered, thinking it might be work-related. It wasn't.

"It's Tim Stratz," said a pleasant voice. "Am I calling at an okay time?"

"No," I said. I watched my boys take their bows. "I'm about to pick up my kids. Can you call later?"

"No," he said, dispassionately. "I'll be in a basketball gym."

It was just as well.

After karate, there was homework, dog poop, and dinner. The meal train had stopped its weekly deliveries. There was something gratifying about going solo. Engineer Jane no longer walked us to school; she was simultaneously pleased and disappointed when I told her we would be okay on our own. After bath, teeth, jammies, stories, and lullabies, Danny was asleep in his bed and Jason in mine. The house was dark and cozy.

My phone rang after 10 p.m. "Hi, it's Tim. Is now an okay time?" I could hear a smile in his tenor voice.

"Sure. How was your son's game?" I plopped onto a worn brown sofa in the living room, and my companionable dog hopped up next to me. I petted his silky spaniel ears.

"Good." He paused, then proceeded without pretense. "So...can you focus?"

"No."

"Can you sleep?"

"No."

The nice guy was no bullshit.

Tim and Debbie were high school sweethearts who met when they were sixteen. He called her "my girl" with obvious affection. When she died a few days after her forty-first birthday, they had been together for twenty-five years. He didn't seem bitter, just sad and darkly funny. "I picked up the guitar again. It'll give me something to do after I get the boys off to college. I'll sit on the porch, sipping scotch and playing guitar, and wait for the rotten cats to die."

I told him how Sam had jumped out of the blue. "It would have made sense if he had just walked out the door. I mean, I'm tall and funny and smart, but if he had to leave, then fine. Go. But leave the children? I don't get it. What would it take for you to leave your sons?"

"I cannot imagine," he said, sincerely.

We talked about giving the eulogies at our respective spouses' funerals and laughed about the "head tilt," that universal gesture of pity that accompanies the rhetorical question, *How are you doing?*

On the question of cemetery plots, I told him I didn't even consider getting two. "Sam left me first. So I got him a single plot."

Tim said, "Debbie didn't even want one, so I got two."

I laughed.

He explained that a friend of his whose father died young suggested that it was nice to have a place to visit, and Tim wanted his sons to be able to do the same if they wanted to. When the cemetery offered a double plot, Tim took them both.

We talked about single parenting. "And the electric company keeps hassling me with those nasty red letters," he said with mock exasperation. "I have the money, I just don't have the time!"

His honesty was refreshing.

We talked for an hour. Susan was right—it was surprisingly comfortable to talk to somebody in the same leaky boat.

Tim asked if he could call again.

I didn't hesitate. "Yes."

CHAPTER 25

LIVING ON THE EDGE OF TEARS

Every Saturday marked another week without Sam, every 20th another month. Each one wounded my heart. The good thing about those calendared days—and upcoming holidays, birthdays, and anniversaries—was that I could brace myself for them. The unanticipated reminders sent me reeling. An anniversary card with Sam's handwritten "I love you, sweetie!" sabotaged me when I opened a drawer. It was hard to catch my breath. The stranger whose voice sounded like Sam's incapacitated me for the rest of the afternoon.

In June, with my sons' first Father's Day without Daddy on the horizon, I called a girlfriend whose Father's Day would also suck, and we concocted a plan. Genie (whose daughter would spend the weekend with her soon-to-be-ex) and I (along with Danny and Jason) would check into the Langham Hotel in Pasadena. It was an extravagant expense, but we hoped that the picturesque garden setting and a few bottles of wine would console us through the weekend.

Dr. Newland seemed doubtful. "You realize that it will be Father's Day there, too."

I did. There was no escape from our grief. It was the shadow that stuck to my heels, obvious on sunny days and invisible yet equally present on moonless nights. "We decided that Father's Day is going to suck wherever we are," I said, "so it might as well suck poolside and with room service."

She nodded enigmatically.

I met Genie on the very first day of law school orientation at UCLA. I met Sam on the second day. Those two days—and these two people—would remain the most vital of my entire J.D. endeavor. If I had known that then, I could have skipped the next three years altogether.

Genie was wickedly smart and uproariously funny. She was the only person I knew who could turn a wrong number into a husband, although in retrospect it might have been better if she had simply hung up. Genie kicked out the misdial a few weeks after Sam died, so we were sharing the single mom path.

Genie and I checked in early to our adjoining rooms, and the spoiling of ourselves began. We commandeered a couple of lounge chairs by the pool. Danny and Jason ordered cheeseburgers and ice cream shakes; Genie and I ordered frosted drinks with little umbrellas. She and I pulled books out of our bags but spent more time talking than reading. Every now and again, we hopped in the pool and splashed with the boys.

After a sun-soaked day, we got dressed and headed downstairs for dinner at the hotel's featured restaurant. Jason, who was barely tall enough to sit comfortably at the table without a booster seat, climbed into his chair and pronounced, "Father's Day is fucky."

This fact could not be camouflaged with white tablecloths and multiple forks.

Nine months earlier, I might not have known what to do if my young child had issued such commentary, but now, I smiled. "Yes it is, buddy. Yes, it is."

We clinked wine glasses against Coke bottles. "To F-Day!" We offered a toast and a roast for the dads in our lives—the live ones and the dead ones, for their goodness, their failings, the fathers we missed, the ones we wished would go away. We said everything out loud. Genie could talk about Sam without having to change the subject, without judging him or me or the boys, and I adored her for it. We talked and ate ourselves silly—appetizers, salads, desserts, the works.

Back in our room, I let the boys play video games on the TV while I took a hot bubble bath. Then they rented an overpriced movie, and we curled up in the king-sized bed to watch. I was asleep within minutes.

In the morning, room service delivered our breakfast. My sons were wide-eyed, noting the tiny maple syrup, minuscule Tabasco bottles, and the silver bud vase with a single yellow rose. We soaked up every indulgence and went back to the pool.

By late afternoon, we were happy and tired and ready to go home. We had survived the worst Father's Day and initiated our first F-Day, and we were looking forward to next June's decadence with more anticipation than dread. I was a little proud of myself on this score.

Not everybody appreciated when the widow started to laugh, even if only to break up the monotony of her tears. Some people liked her better when she was suffering.

It was especially discouraging when someone I thought was an ally seemed to disapprove of my healing process. They wanted me to heal, but not too fast. They wanted me to laugh, but not too loud. They wanted me to forget, but not too soon. They wanted me to remember, but without tears. I didn't think I should have to apologize for what my grief looked like. It was true that I planned our F-Day celebration without giving a single thought to honoring my dad or Sam's. My focus was exclusively on Danny, Jason, and me, and what a Samless Father's Day felt like to us. Neither my father nor my father-in-law objected to this plan, but there were others who felt entitled to share their opinions.

Maybe they were surprised to hear joy in my voice; maybe they thought me disrespectful. Maybe it was unnerving. Unseemly. Insulting. Maybe it was as simple and ugly as jealousy. Or maybe it was because they could ignore the day-to-day grief; they didn't have to check the "head of household" box on a tax return, and they didn't gaze into the eyes of their dead spouse's beloved children every morning. And every night. And all the moments in between. They had no idea how hard grief was or how strong we were becoming.

Dr. Newland was right, too, of course. F-Day away didn't entirely counterbalance the misery of Father's Day. My weekend also included this: both boys reported that they continued to endure death-related teasing at school; I ordered a memorial tablet for Sam's grave; I filed an extension for his final tax return; I called Social Security to figure out why they had reduced my income; and I accepted a Little League coaching award on behalf of my late husband.

Kirk was right; I was amazed at what I had done.

*　*　*

I didn't know this term "spiritual bypass" until recently, but it perfectly encapsulates how I thought grief should look before I learned better. As I understand it, the spiritual bypass skips directly from loss to recovery without processing the hurt in between. It's an attempt to move directly from feeling crappy to enlightened without going through the shitstorm. It is being told to be sunshine in moments when I was a storm—dark, swirling, chaotic. I couldn't be a gorgeous sunset when my teardrops were splashing in full force, falling unbidden, uncontrollable and cold. I was not in a place to draw inspirational pink and yellow streaks across a deepening blue sky. I was the darkest, cloudy black sky—no stars, no shape, hot, electric, loud. To be told otherwise made me feel worse.

My impulse was to turn away from the sunset seekers and in toward myself. This protective instinct served me, but there is a risk to riding out the storm alone. I knew I was not okay after Sam's death because I was paying attention. I knew I wasn't sleeping, that I was losing weight and struggling to catch a breath. Paying attention was, perhaps, the most important action I could have taken on my behalf. When I needed help, I sent my tethering anchor out. I learned where my safe harbors were when I needed to find refuge. The sturdy few who held my hand had heard my cries, and they didn't let me go.

The spiritual bypass misses entirely the opportunity presented by the storm: the invitation to chart a different course. It signifies the urge to go back to a normal that might not have been healthy, or even safe. It is not enough simply to wait out the storm. If there is to be any healing, learning to navigate the storm will be key. What a shame it would be not to be changed by the experience.

* * *

Eight months after Sam's suicide, I still didn't understand why. I started to realize I might never know.

I didn't believe that his financial problems or his back pain would have been enough to justify suicide. I didn't believe he would have left us. I started to believe that his intense emotional reaction was the result of some disconnect. Every part of our human physiology is wired for self-preservation. Even babies gasp for breath. People who cannot swim will flail around if they are dumped into the water. What biological switch of Sam's had flipped?

I found this definition of clinical depression on the Mayo Clinic website: "A mental health disorder characterized by persistently depressed mood or loss of interest in activities, causing significant impairment in daily life. Possible causes include a combination of biological, psychological, and social sources of distress. Increasingly, research suggests these factors may cause changes in brain function, *including altered activity of certain neural circuits in the brain*" [emphasis mine].

Depression itself changed Sam's brain.

I would yet grapple with other unanswerable questions, but in my heart, I began to trust that the man I knew had been overtaken by an illness that neither of us understood. According to the CDC, suicide was the second-leading cause of death for Americans ages ten to thirty-four (the first being accidents), and the tenth leading cause of death for Americans in general. There was a suicide every eleven minutes and, alarmingly, those rates were increasing. As I learned about mental illness and suicide, I realized that Sam must have been fighting a silent battle with depression.

Sam had to have been in a place where he couldn't see how much we loved him, or even how much he loved us. There was no way he would have left those boys if he had been in his right mind. If he had been himself, he would not have jumped. My reasoning always circled back to this place. The Sam I knew was a loving father, a passionate husband, and a kind man. It was not a question of intellect or attention or memory or capacity. It was a matter of mental health.

The Sam who jumped was a man who had been hijacked by mental illness.

When depression speaks, who knows what it says? It lies about things like worth and value and success. It makes dire predictions about the future. I don't think it always says things like "You're horrible," or "You've never done anything worthwhile your whole life," or "You have no reason to live." I imagine it's more insidious than that. It cloaks its deceptive messages in the language of the first person: *I am a failure. My family is better off without me. I don't deserve their love. I don't deserve to live. I can't do this. I don't want to.*

The Sam who jumped didn't even recognize himself anymore.

* * *

Suicide points out how interconnected we are: everybody knows somebody. There is no way for someone to complete a suicide without traumatizing a surprisingly wide circle. Beyond colleagues and casual acquaintances, anyone who happens to witness a suicide (or discover it after the fact) suffers as a result, as do first responders, police, physicians, good Samaritans. It's the kind of death I wouldn't wish on my worst enemy.

The paradox is that someone this deep in the throes of a depression sees only worthlessness. They believe that they are separate from the rest of us, that their death will have no impact (or that it will have a positive impact). This idea of disconnectedness is an illusion, of course. Every suicide creates a ripple, spreading dismay like a virus, as if the person's own distress then infects large swaths of humanity with helplessness. I believe that hearts touched by this particular loss would gladly have lent their hands to the struggle, if only they had seen it. That's why it is so important learn the language of sadness. I don't know anyone whose life has remained unaffected by suicide. Every life matters; every death hurts.

* * *

"Mommy," Jason asked one night, "what if I have the same sickness Daddy had?" His fear was palpable. Or maybe I was seeing my abject terror reflected back to me in his eyes.

"What is the one thing we wish Daddy had done differently?"

He paused thoughtfully. "Ask for help?"

"Exactly. Ask for help."

He nodded bravely.

"If you ever feel so sad, or just down and you don't know why, ask for help. Promise?"

"Okay, Mommy."

"There will always be help if you ask." I held my little one close, knowing that the asking can be the hardest part, hoping that he would trust me enough to ask if—God forbid—he ever faced such a time. "Ask as many times as you need to."

I didn't tell him that I had suffered from depression as a teenager. I worried that this knowledge would increase his own fear about his heritage and exacerbate his fear of abandonment. He was too young to carry such a heavy load.

I didn't understand at the time that I was clinically depressed. I just felt blue much of the time. I was sluggish and unmotivated, as though wearing a weighted cape I couldn't take off and, in fact, didn't realize I had on. I went through a lot of motions, but the days felt increasingly pointless, heavy and dark. So much so that my best friend told me I wasn't fun to be around anymore. And then she found new friends, leaving me despondent. I concluded that sharing my feelings was the problem and thereafter resolved to hide my pain. I didn't know what else to do.

I couldn't talk to my parents. They would have told me to pray about it. Or to write a gratitude list (even though I was already keenly aware of one hundred things that I was, in fact, grateful for). Under no circumstances would they have taken me to a therapist or a medical doctor. We didn't even have Tylenol in the house. I didn't know where to turn. The National Suicide Prevention Lifeline would not be established for another twenty years. And the Crisis Text number (Text HOME to 741741) would not be established until 2013, six years after Sam died.

I know now that the only way to get over it is to go through it. But this can be treacherous to do alone.

Most afternoons after high school let out, I would drive up Angeles Crest Highway, a curvy highway over the San Gabriel Mountains. My old Toyota Celica was a stick shift without power steering, so I focused on driving and feeling, changing gears, tears flowing, tasting the freedom and imagining the peace that might come if I just sped up, missed a curve and flew blissfully airborne a few yards before dropping into the canyon below. It would have been a painful death, but I was already in such pain, without an obvious light at the end of the tunnel, that I didn't linger on those details.

The thing that stopped me was picturing how shattered my father would have been. I didn't think he could have ever recovered. My suicide would have broken him. My mother and sister would have been devastated, too, but there was something about my hapless, rose-colored, rocket scientist father...

I pulled into a vista point, parked the car, and sobbed. I wept until I was wrung out, or until the sun began to set, or until a pickup truck pulled up next to me. When the driver, a muscled man in dusty jeans, got out and beckoned, I started my engine and eased back toward the highway before he could get any closer. I was afraid to roll down my window. I didn't want him to yank open my car door, or even ask with genuine concern whether I was okay.

My teenage depression lifted slowly, almost imperceptibly, until sometime during my college years I realized that I was returned to myself. Not until my work with Dr. Newland after Sam's death did I recognize the depression for what it was.

Mercifully, it has not returned, but I do not forget its grip.

My own experience with the darkness gave me insight into this terrible isolation, the excruciating pain, the desperation that Sam must have been facing. It made it so much easier to forgive Sam for his hopelessness than to forgive myself for my inattention.

CHAPTER 26

SUMMERTIMES IN MINOR
AND MAJOR CHORDS

In July, after several late-night telephone conversations, Tim asked if I would be interested in meeting for lunch. "Just to put a face to the voice."

We had had the friendship discussion. I had explained the Las Vegas debacle, to which Tim had responded with a salacious tale of woman who showed up on his doorstep late one night, well after dinnertime, wearing a negligée and pressing comfort food and boobs in his direction. "I was so surprised I just said thank you, grabbed the dish, and closed the door in the Casserole Lady's face."

We settled on a Thursday for lunch, but Jason woke with a fever that morning, so I moved lunch to Monday. At some point over the Fourth of July weekend, Tim sent a text message. *Hope the little guy is feeling better.* Texting was relatively new in 2008, and the cheery tri-tone alert lifted my spirits. I was touched that he'd thought of us.

When I mentioned to Susan that I was meeting Tim for lunch, she said again, "He's just a nice guy." Every time she said that, I pictured Tim as shorter, fatter, balder. By Monday, the nice guy was pretty much a troll.

I arrived at the bistro in Pasadena just before noon, not yet knowing that Tim was chronically early, and I breezed past the hostess stand to go wash my hands. I noticed a man sitting at the bar, balanced on a barstool, scrolling through messages on his Blackberry. He looked fit, like an athlete in business attire. *He is so handsome.* The thought surprised me. I hadn't noticed *any* man since Sam died. And then, *I wonder where Tim is?*

But the guy at the bar turned around and, in a now familiar voice, said, "Charlotte?"

Oh shit! Susan didn't tell me Tim was good-looking.

He started to move from the barstool, but I held up a hand. "I'll be right back," I said, and skirted into the women's room. I looked in the mirror. No mascara, as per usual, and I regretted that now. I smoothed my hair and went to meet Tim.

"Thanks for rescheduling," I said, as we shook hands.

"I figured you had changed your mind," he said, not unkindly.

"Life as a single parent." I shrugged.

He smiled. "The only friends I have left are the ones I can cancel on last minute."

The hostess nodded toward us, and Tim motioned for me to go ahead. She sat us at a quiet table in the corner, away from a group of businessmen.

Tim had green eyes and his dark hair was generously laced with white; he had the angular look of a model. He was a natural conversationalist, and he laughed easily. We reflected on grief and insomnia. We marveled at the healing effects of pets. And running. He had twice run the Los Angeles Marathon.

"I'd love to run Boston one day," he said, "but at my pace I'd have to be an eighty-four-year-old woman to qualify."

I laughed. "Did Debbie run, too?"

"No, she played basketball. She was a great point guard." There was such sorrow when he spoke of his wife. He shook his head, remembering. "I spent a lot of years in a gym watching Deb—and then Gregory—play."

I sensed the rhythm Tim and Debbie shared, growing together from the homecoming and prom years, through college, early careers, young children and family life, then catapulted directly into chemotherapy and hospice care. "She was short," he said, his affection shining through his glib commentary, "but I liked her okay." He teasingly described her "speech impediment."

"Wait," I asked, "the woman who couldn't say her Rs named her firstborn son Gregory?"

"Gwegowy Paul," he mimicked. "And Daniel Wyan."

That girl had confidence. I think I would have liked her.

We discussed suicide, naturally. Tim listened thoughtfully. He didn't appear uncomfortable and did not try to change the subject. "I don't know how you do it."

"I'm the luckiest unlucky girl," I said.

Tim looked at me skeptically, but also amused.

I explained, "Some people live their whole lives without experiencing unconditional love. Seventeen years was too short, but still. I had it."

He nodded thoughtfully, then asked about Sam's suicide.

"I believe Sam protected me, even at the end. He didn't do it at home. I never saw the body. The kids didn't find him, thank God. He left a note. He told me he loved me. He didn't blame me. Honestly, for as bad as it is, it's as good as it gets."

Tim described finding Debbie gone, just as the "crazy hospice lady" predicted, refusing to die while Tim was in the room, waiting instead until he was upstairs having a drink with his childhood friend Dyon. Only after Dyon had left and Tim returned to check on his wife did he find her lifeless body. "Dead as a doornail," he said. "Not her best look." I had the sense that this was the kind of teasing comment he would have volleyed to her during their years together.

"The worst was waking up the boys." He told them that their mother had died, and then he brought them to her bedside.

We always came back to the children, these wrenching moments, these difficult conversations, their wounded hearts. What we would do to spare them. If only.

I did notice, during that two-hour-plus lunch, that Tim was not wearing a wedding ring. I tugged uncomfortably at the gold band on my left hand, running my thumb over Sam's wedding band on my right.

As we were walking to our cars, Tim invited me to dinner on Friday. I said yes without even looking at my calendar.

* * *

"You didn't tell me the nice guy was nice-looking!"

Susan smiled mischievously. "He is kind of cute, isn't he?"

"Too bad he's Catholic."

"He's not that Catholic," she said.

I held up a simple sheath dress with a nautical pattern, and she nodded her approval. Susan was helping me decide what to wear on my first post-marital date.

Sometime between Monday's lunch and Friday's dinner, I had loosened Sam's ring from one hand and slipped my engagement ring off the other. I gently placed both rings together in my jewelry box and closed the lid.

Tim picked me up at my home. I met him outside on the sidewalk. I didn't want my sons to know I was meeting a man. *A date!* I had told my boys that I was at book group. Tim had told his boys he was out with the guys. We were sneaking around like teenagers, only this time we were lying to our children instead of our parents.

On the drive downtown, I glanced over at Tim's profile and thought, *He is the most handsome man I have ever gone to dinner with. I hope he likes me.*

Tim chose Pacific Dining Car, a steak house downtown, where Los Angeles musicians, actors, and athletes wishing to remain anonymous dined, a restaurant where the widow and the widower could also go incognito for the evening. Tim's hand hovered protectively behind me as we walked toward the front door, and I found this gesture endearing.

He was engaging and kind to everyone he encountered: the valet, the hostess, the bartender. The way he talked about Debbie was real. He adored his wife, but he didn't canonize her. "I loved my girl, but she was a bitch—she'd hit you in the back of the head with a pass if you weren't ready."

He had an irreverence to his faith. He said, "Jesus is too busy in the Middle East to worry about my problems." He made me laugh, or maybe it was the wine.

If Tim harbored any anger, he directed it toward cancer itself.

I didn't know what to expect from dinner with the most eligible widower in town, but there was something about his tanned skin and the grace in his movements. I was drawn into his green eyes, and I felt a fluttering in my stomach. Sitting across the table from Tim, I felt like a kid pretending to be grown-up. There I was, dining with a handsome man, laughing and crying and sharing a bottle of Pinot Noir. I could hardly believe it. I ran my fingers along the stem of the wine glass, too skittish to eat much of the filet on the plate in front of me.

Tim held my hand as we walked from the restaurant to the car. We drove home, still chatting. He was the consummate gentleman. He stopped the car in front of my home and turned off the engine. He seemed to hesitate, then turned toward me. Nervously, like an awkward teenager, he said, "Can I kiss you?"

I realized I wanted him to. "Yes."

He leaned in and brought his hand to my chin, pulling me gently to him. His hand was warm. I brought my fingers to his jaw, strong and freshly shaved, a hint of scotch on his breath. We closed our eyes, our noses pressed together softly, so close that our eyelashes brushed against each other, and then our lips touched. It was our first kiss, a sweet kiss, simple and unadulterated, lingering only for a moment. A kiss for one night, with potential for more.

A kiss that gives me butterflies still.

Insomnia had stolen many nights since I had been widowed. But that night I couldn't sleep, not because I was anxious or grief-stricken, but because I was excited for what life might yet have in store.

* * *

The next day, Tim went to the Sierras for a mountain biking weekend with his guys. I kept checking my phone, hoping for a text message.

Later that night, finally, the telltale three-tone text ring: *You are a terrible distraction.*

I was not the only one who had been preoccupied by the previous night's kiss. Tim would later share that after an afternoon of riding mountain trails, as they were nearing the last mile, he went literally head over handlebars. Instead of focusing on the trail, he was thinking about a kiss.

The nice guy likes me! It was my happy little secret. I didn't even tell Susan.

* * *

Tim and I had graduated from adjacent high schools, but we had never met then, likely because he attended the Catholic boys' high school. St. Francis High School had a reputation for being home to athletic knuckleheads, and I stayed far away from them. My family kept a safe distance from Catholics in general. Christian Science is one of those minority denominations that stirred up controversy and misunderstanding, so I had spent my lifetime defending it. Not to mention that religion almost became a dealbreaker when Sam and I were engaged.

Tim would tell you that I asked whether I would have to convert to Catholicism on our first date. This is pure hyperbole. It was our second date. Maybe the third.

What was undoubtedly true when I met Tim was that I was an unenthusiastic Christian, at best. I could not reconcile a loving, omnipotent God with Sam's suicide. Atheism made more sense. If I had any conversations with the divine, they were antagonistic. I never said prayers with my children anymore, not even at bedtime. Prayer Warrior Jane brought my concerns to her temple from time to time, and that was as close as I needed God to get to me. I felt gratitude and I kept my spiritual practice with my bowl, but I gave up all things church.

I was intrigued by the fact that Debbie's cancer didn't send Tim's faith into a death spiral. Even more impressive to me was that, according to Tim, Debbie herself wasn't angry. She was sad because her sons were eleven and fourteen and she would miss so much of their growing up. But she wasn't bitter or angry.

Tim joked: "I have an uncle who goes to church twice a week—once to drop off my aunt and again to pick her up." This was not just a convenient punchline; it was true. Yet Tim found solace in his faith. He didn't expect not to have difficult times and seemed to accept that suffering was part and parcel of the whole experience. He drew strength from community, and he continued to attend mass after Debbie's death. He said sitting in church was hard when he and the boys felt self-conscious; everyone felt sorry for them. And yet he also felt that his presence supported others in church who were going through their own difficult times.

Tim's faith pointed outward; his practice of Christianity was fundamentally for the benefit of others. More than service (although service was essential), he believed that the purpose of spiritual formation was to become a better person *for the sake of others*, especially those among us who were marginalized and suffering. It wasn't about personal morality, or spiritual healing, or living life in such a way as to procure entrance into a humanly conceived heaven. It was about using our talents and honoring our experiences by getting to work, ushering more heaven into the here and now, for other people. This shift in perspective would eventually redeem my relationship with Christianity.

Meanwhile, my Bible and *Science and Health* sank to the bottom of the stack next to my bed, underneath the resources on parenting, estate planning, suicide and children's grief, and several novels. Books had often provided comfort, confidence, or escape, and normally I would have devoured several books in a month. As much as I loved reading, when I cracked open a book and my fingers lingered over the cool pages, I often found myself staring into space. When I returned to the page in front of me, the words seemed unfamiliar, as though I had not just scanned through them. I started again at the top of the page, trying to focus. Sometimes, I closed the book and returned it to the pile. That my collection of unread books was growing indicated that I hadn't given up on reading yet, and there was hope in that.

* * *

Tim sent an early text: "*A new day... Watching the sunrise over the mountains...*"

Me: "*Beautiful!*"

Him: "*You make it so.*"

The morning sun scattered pink and orange light over the foothills. I rather liked knowing that Tim was thinking of me as the new day began.

* * *

I adored my married friends, but I was closest with the single-or-soon-to-be-forty-something-moms who lived a similarly harrowing existence. When Genie's three-year-old daughter asked, "Mommy, what's a bitch?" and followed with a furrowed brow and the question, "Why does Daddy call you that?" things got real. Genie was up to her eyeballs in restraining orders, divorce pleadings, and child custody disputes. It was such a hot mess that the widow track looked enviable by comparison. At least my husband wasn't a deadbeat, he was just dead. There was no bickering, no legal maneuvering, no negotiations. The retirement accounts, the life insurance, the family home, were all mine. If I wanted my kids to go on a field trip, I signed the permission slip, and they went. If I decided they needed therapy, I made the appointment, and it was done.

I was just a weensy bit jealous that she had every other weekend to herself. For thirty-six uninterrupted hours, she got to do whatever she wanted—to choose the movie, to take a bath alone (or not), to drink a bottle of Sauvignon Blanc and eat an entire baguette with brie for dinner, to sleep past sunrise. There was something to be envied about the divorced path, especially for the kids. Both Danny and Jason wished that Daddy had just left, not died. "Why couldn't you and Daddy have gotten a divorce? At least then we would have gotten to see him." They had a point.

It all sucked. Just in different ways.

I met Genie for dinner on her birthday, but I kept getting distracted by the text messages on my phone.

Tim: *What are you wearing?*

Me: *Green lace thong. Matches your eyes.*

Tim: *Oh my...*

Me: *Something to think about...*

Tim: *Drop dead legs...*

I had forgotten how much I enjoyed flirting—the innuendo, the suggestion, the silliness, all from a safe distance across town.

I confided in Genie that I had met someone, and I showed her our exchange. Her eyes lit up. She disappeared into her bathroom and returned with a box of condoms. "You are going to need these more than I do!" she said, tucking them into my purse. It had been a long time since I thought about birth control. I had married young and then spent the better part of my marriage trying to get pregnant. I didn't really know what to expect from dating. I didn't know what Tim expected.

But I thought it could be fun.

* * *

Pasadena announced its first-ever marathon, and Sarah and the She-Wolves signed up for the half-marathon. Then we started training.

Tuesday and Thursday mornings, Sarah picked me up for a pre-dawn three-mile loop around the Rose Bowl or for sprints at the high school track. Saturday mornings we ran long. These distances sounded crazy to me. Four miles? Five? In a row?

But we did it. Together, we ran. Our motto: No Mom Left Behind.

In July, I registered my half-marathon as a fundraiser for The American Foundation for Suicide Prevention; Jason named the team aspirationally: "Sam's Suicide Stoppers." I imagined that Sam would be both mortified that I spoke openly about his suicide and optimistic that my talking about it in a larger forum might stop another person from taking the same leap.

I sent an email to a large group, explaining that I would be running this half-marathon, which for those who had known me for any length of time was almost as shocking as Sam jumping off a building. I included the link for the fundraising site. I hesitated before including Tim in the email, but then I added him and hit send before I lost my nerve. He was one of the first to hop on the website and contribute to the cause with an encouraging note, "Many are with you."

Genie sent me a text: *Tim! OMG!*

* * *

The first book I remember devouring again was a memoir Genie recommended, *Here If You Need Me* by Kate Braestrup. Kate had been widowed with four kids, and she *decided* to attend seminary because that was what her husband had planned to do after retiring as a police officer. He had been killed in a car accident, so the suddenness and violence of his death resonated with me. Also, her kids were young, like mine. It dealt with the messy, ugly, painful stuff of life along with the lovely, the hilarious, and the kind. *Here If You Need Me* addressed themes of spirituality but didn't offer simplistic answers. One moment I especially enjoyed was when Kate bristled at a Baptist classmate who suggested that *God's plan* was for her to become a minister: "Surely, God was not so urgently in need of Unitarian Universalist ministers that he needed to kill a father of four in order to make one?" This was exactly the kind of snippy remark I would like to have made. I loved her voice and her perspective. And I melted when later (Spoiler alert! She falls in love again), she explained: "I can't make those two realities—what I've lost and what I've found—fit together in some tidy pattern of divine causality. I just have to hold them on the one hand and on the other, just like that."

For someone who had grown up with tidy patterns of divine causality, where goodness negated badness (and vice versa), it was a relief to hear that the mess didn't negate the existence of the sublime. It felt like a guilty verdict had been lifted. Sam didn't die because I didn't love him enough or because I failed to pray fervently enough to the right god or because I lacked the key words to say to Sam at a pivotal juncture. His death was not the result of a cosmic plan or an epic fall from grace.

His death was. Love was.

Both were true.

And neither one negated the other.

* * *

Tim and I met for dinner again at the end of July, fabricating plausible excuses to be out for the evening. I don't remember being so instantly attracted to a man as I was to him. My high school sweetheart was my best friend for three years before we kissed; Sam and I were law school classmates for months before he asked me out. I was drawn to Tim immediately. It was unnerving.

When he dropped me off at home, I hesitated before asking him a question. It was awkward. I was nervous, but I felt like I had to ask. It was the responsible thing.

He eyes widened curiously.

"Is your wife the only woman you've ever slept with?"

He smiled warmly, paused before answering. When he did, he seemed embarrassed, almost apologetic. "Yes."

It was so sweet, a love that most people never find in a lifetime. They were high school sweethearts, together for twenty-five years. They broke up once, but it sounded like that lasted about seventeen minutes, just long enough for Tim to get to his car, cool off, and walk back to her front door.

"What about birth control?"

He hesitated. "I had a vasectomy after Daniel was born." He winced when he said it, but in that moment, vasectomy was about the sexiest word I had ever heard.

I pulled him into a kiss. "It's going to happen."

He looked like a deer caught in headlights.

"Don't worry," I said, patting his chest. "Not tonight, but it will." I wasn't intentionally pacing our budding relationship, which would have been sensible in light of our mutually vulnerable hearts, as much as I was just trying to juggle kids, mountains, and beach. Between his summer travels and mine, it would be several weeks before we would see each other again.

"I'm kind of a fur ball," he said. "Are you going to be okay with that?"

"I don't know," I said. I hadn't thought about it. Sam wasn't particularly hairy.

"I'm like a chia pet."

He cracked me up.

CHAPTER 27

FAMILY VACATIONS

In a gin-inspired moment after Sam's death, José and Zack and I had decided that our families should get together beyond bar mitzvahs and funerals. We envisioned a "cousins' week" to honor Sam and to spend time with each other. "And if you don't want to go, then *fuck* you!"

We raised our cocktails and toasted "*Fuck* you!"

My little ones parroted, "If you don't come to Daddy's week, then *fuck* you!"

Sam would have been horrified. Oh, well. Fuck him.

José rented a house in Lake Tahoe and flew in from Miami with his wife and two sons. Danny and Jason and I caravanned for the ten-hour drive from Los Angeles with Zack and his wife Lilith and their twins. We rotated kids and drivers for the sake of sibling harmony and adult sanity.

When I was with the cousins, I realized that I had come a long way in my grief. I had started to incorporate Sam's death into my decision-making and even into who I was. I couldn't pretend his death didn't happen. There was no back to life as usual; there couldn't be. But Sam's absence was jarring for the cousins. Seeing Danny, Jason, and me without Sam forced them to navigate this loss; we reminded them of what they could otherwise forget for weeks at a time. They had some grief ground to catch up on. For us, it was awkward to be the living reminder of the loss, but it was comforting to be around the people who knew and loved Sam best. They didn't trip over saying his name or hesitate to tell stories about him. We laughed, remembering his penchant for superheroes and comic books, and we marveled at the fact that he never met a trivia question on the Dodger jumbotron that he couldn't answer, even though his team was the Angels.

I didn't mention that I had met someone. It seemed premature; after all, Tim and I had only shared one lunch, two dinners and a dozen phone conversations.

The dark cloud over this trip—the one we couldn't bear to speak of—was that Zack's sister canceled at the last minute. She was losing her battle against cancer.

I knew my first wedding anniversary without Sam—August 1st— would fall in the middle of the cousins' trip, but it had been the only week that worked with everybody's schedules. Zack reassured me that the day would be bested with a combination of fishing and horseback riding, but as the day drew closer, I found myself dreading it. The day reminded me more than any other that I was no longer married. It would have been my—or was it still our?—sixteenth wedding anniversary. But with Sam dead…what was our anniversary, exactly?

Realistically, the best I could expect was to breathe my way through the day. I was secretly hoping for a text message from Tim, but the cell reception was so poor at the house that I didn't receive texts for hours or until we drove into town. Sometimes at night, the alarm clock buzzed with electric static for a second or two, followed by the distinctive tri-tone alert signaling a playful note: *Maybe I could distract you from your book?* But Tim was on vacation with his kids at the beach, and I doubted that he remembered my first not-an-anniversary.

What I really wanted was for the cousins to watch my kids so I could go for a run. I needed a six-miler during the week to stay on pace with the She-Wolves' training schedule. We were almost halfway to our half-marathon. I went downstairs, running shoes in hand.

The adults were in the kitchen drinking *café con leche* and mulling over ideas for breakfast. When she saw me, Lilith said something pointedly bitchy, and Zack whipped his head around to stare at her.

I can't remember exactly what she said. I just remember being stunned. It might have been as benign as packing SPF 50 and snacks for her two but not the other cousins. It might have been a muttered, "How come she gets to leave her kids with us?" My heart clenched. I heard my pulse throbbing in my ears. I laced up my shoes and ran out the door in tears. I cannot remember where my boys were or what the plan was for the morning. I only remember thinking, *Today? Seriously? Of all the days to pick a fight, she chooses my wedding anniversary?*

I thought someone said they'd watch my kids. I thought I had told somebody, "I'll be back." Nobody remembered hearing me.

I ran down the street into the August heat, armed only with a water bottle and my iPod. The road curved right and I turned left onto a dusty trail. I headed uphill. I didn't know where I was or where I was going, and I didn't care. I turned on Jason Mraz and listened through "We Sing. We Dance. We Steal Things." Twice. I paused only to rewind "A Beautiful Mess." That song gets me every time. I ran the tempo of a fast waltz with anger. I sweated tears and kept climbing. I went right back to the place of disbelief and anguish. I was in Lake Tahoe with Sam's cousins, and he was dead and gone. *This was my life?*

I was angry at Lilith. How *convenient* that she could forget that Sam was dead. How *nice* that she had a partner to cover for her. I didn't have the luxury of ignoring Sam's death, because he was my reality every fucking day.

It would have been my sixteenth wedding anniversary. I was grateful for the first fifteen years. But I had wanted more. I still wanted more.

I panted and gasped. And I kept running, my lungs straining in the thin mountain air. Pine needles crunched with my every step.

At some point I turned back and found my way home—red-faced from the heat, but composed—no longer angry, but tired and thirsty. My nephew was the first to spot me, and I heard him yell, "She's here!" After an hour, my family had become concerned, and they spent another half an hour looking for me. They were relieved to have me home safe. If they were annoyed with me, they didn't express it.

That afternoon we were shopping in town when my phone rang. I stepped away to take the call. Tim had remembered my wedding anniversary. I shared the highlight of my day—eight hard miles at altitude, a new personal best. It was something of a rollercoaster to navigate both the grief and the emerging new love interest with piss-poor cell reception. I had only known Tim a short time, but he was on the same roller coaster, and there was some comfort in that.

He called back immediately after we hung up.

"Did you say I love you?"

I was certain I didn't, but he had thought he heard me say those words.

"Okay," he said. "I just didn't want you to think I ignored it if that's what you said."

He was a tender heart, this Tim.

"When I'm ready to say those words," I said, "I promise I will say them to you in person."

We finished our phone call, carefully choosing our goodbyes. My heart was lighter for hearing his voice, and I wondered...*does he love me?*

Later that night, in a quiet moment over a glass of wine, Zack explained his wife's vitriol. In the Bible (Deuteronomy 24:5–10), there is a specific instruction that a man should marry his brother's wife upon his brother's death. To be clear, the purpose of this Levitical arrangement was to provide for the widow's security in a patriarchal society. Somehow in Zack's grief-addled brain, he had interpreted this archaic text as a directive for him to take responsibility for me and my boys. When I had refused to move to the West Side, he began a campaign to convince Lilith to uproot their family and move closer to me, so he could fulfill his biblical obligation to Sam.

No wonder she hated me.

* * *

When their world has been upended, children need continuity, stability, and predictability. I was grateful that my children didn't have to change schools or friends or even their pediatrician. Some of the other post-marital decisions were more difficult. Did we do what we used to do with Sam without him? Did we try something new? One of the first questions Danny and Jason had asked after their father's death was "Can we still go to Bruin Woods?" That decision was a unanimous yes. We had attended the UCLA family camp in Lake Arrowhead, together with many of the same families, every summer since Jason was three and Danny was five. After the first summer, the boys cried all the way down the hill, and we started counting the fifty-one weeks till we could go back to Bruin Woods again. When I regretted having attended law school, I reminded myself that those three years were my ticket to family camp (not to mention my actual family) and worth the collateral brain damage.

It was our fifth summer at Bruin Woods, and the boys dashed off across the lawn to find their friends. A Jane stood in front of us in the line for check-in. She gave me a warm hug and then asked, "Is your husband parking the car?"

She didn't know.

Those were pre-Facebook days, and even though we got a week's worth of quality time together on hikes and lounging poolside, we didn't keep up during the rest of the year. I had not sent holiday cards that year. What would I have said? "Our *ho ho ho* went *boo hoo hoo*?"

I took a deep breath and delivered the bad news gently. "Sam died in October." I was getting better at this. I managed not to cry. "He took his own life." It was hard reliving the shock of Sam's death through my friend's eyes, but it was also cathartic to tell the story and to hear how fond she was of Sam.

The kids were sorted into age groups (from toddler "pooh bears" to teenage "grizzly bears" and every bear in between), led by UCLA student counselors, who were a seemingly endless source of energy and smiles. The boys enjoyed their normal summer routine, a week crammed full of swimming, boating, hiking, zip-lining, archery, pottery, disco bingo, and scavenger hunts.

We missed Sam, of course. We had to change to a smaller cabin for our three-person family. The new cabin was situated at the edge of the property in a quiet spot shaded by tall pines. I liked the seclusion of it. On the parent/child overnight camping trip, Jason was proud that I (the only mom in the group) found the best spot to pitch a tent, flat and upwind from the smoke.

I spent much of the week poolside, cocooned by girlfriends who listened to me and encouraged me. They took pictures of my kids because I had forgotten my camera. They shared recipes and book recommendations.

It was a real vacation for me: I read, I slept, I didn't drive, I didn't shop for groceries, I didn't plan a menu (or anything else, for that matter), I didn't make a single bed.

Neither did I mention to anyone that I had met someone. They were still reeling from the news of Sam's death. I left my cell phone in my cabin during the day, but I was thrilled to find flirty text messages from Tim in the evening: *I'd like to rival your Tuesdays.*

* * *

At the end of our week at Bruin Woods, the boys were reluctant to leave, as usual, but I was anxious to get home. I had a date with Tim, and we weren't going out. We would be dining in.

I had arranged for Danny and Jason to have a sleepover at Uncle Zack's with their cousins. Zack and Sam had slept over at each other's houses every weekend growing up, and they both hoped that their children would develop a similar closeness. I gave Zack the barest details of my plans—"I just need a night without kids"—and he was only too happy to accommodate.

Tim had likewise enlisted his sister to take Gregory and Daniel overnight. "Don't even come back for a toothbrush," he told her.

Tim picked me up and brought me to his hillside home, situated at the top of a canyon. The entry was on the top floor, with the bedrooms on the level below. The paint and hardwood floors looked mostly new, slightly scuffed at the edges. The décor was sparse; this was the remodeling project Tim and Debbie put on hold when she was diagnosed with colon cancer. But when I walked in, I didn't focus on the house because the French doors opened to a spectacular view of the San Gabriel Mountains.

He gave me a tour of the top floor, where the living room and kitchen and dining room were. I had prepared a picnic-style dinner—brie, a baguette, and homemade gazpacho—but I wasn't in the mood for that yet. I set the basket on the kitchen counter. "Are you hungry?" I asked.

"Yes," he said, turning me toward him and kissing me. His skin was tanned from a week at the beach, and he exuded that relaxed aura of sunshine and sand.

I said, "I want to see where you send me your notes from."

"Goodness…" He took my hand and led me downstairs.

The evening spread before us like the landscape, suspended in time, uninterrupted by demanding clients or little voices calling from down the hall. Our first night together. His bedroom was like a grown-up treehouse; the north and east facing walls featured floor-to-ceiling windows, revealing a wrap-around porch surrounded by leafy elms and a dense pittosporum.

Among the things I didn't expect from widowhood—the lost friends, the overwhelming generosity of near strangers—was the desire for intimacy with this man I had only recently met. I was struck by his goodness and his good looks, his integrity, and his love for his family. I trusted him. The gravity of the risk I was taking with my body—and with my heart—did not occur to me until later.

Wordlessly, we slipped into his bed. His chest against mine, I could feel his heartbeat on my skin. I responded instantly to his touch. Tim was an attentive lover, and it felt natural to lose myself in him.

Later, we ate our picnic dinner on the secluded patio outside his bedroom, scented with vines of night-blooming jasmine that twined around the trellis. He was wearing shorts, and I was wearing his shirt. By then we had built up an appetite.

As the sun set, casting a warm orange glow against the mountains, I retreated back into his arms, still longing for him, and we made love again. There was so much we didn't know about each other, but in that hidden moment, as we tenderly traced each other's scars, it felt like we had all the time in the world.

When I picked up the boys from their sleepover with their cousins the next morning, Zack handed me a *café con leche*. "How was your evening?"

"It was nice."

"Did you sleep well?"

I smiled. "Hardly at all."

Zack grinned conspiratorially. To his credit, he didn't say "I told you so," but I was wrong when I said I could live happily never having sex again.

CHAPTER 28

BACK TO SCHOOL

When I received the postcards with the boys' teacher assignments in late August, my first thought was, *Sam didn't live to see his sons start second and fourth grades.*

I would never get used to this.

The boys' backpacks had been sitting idly by the living room window since June. I kept meaning to clean them out, and I could no longer postpone this task. I unzipped one. Inside was a spiral notebook and a science project. It appeared that the boy had dumped a cup of rice into a brown paper bag. The grains were fat, like an Arborio rice but longer. And a grayish pearl color.

And, I realized with a wave of nausea, they were wriggling.

It was not a rogue science experiment; it was a neglected lunch bag filled with maggots.

The widow had fallen to a new low. It had taken me so long to clean out my son's backpack that there was a thriving larva colony in his Jansport.

I grabbed both backpacks and ran outside. I took the entire cornucopia—pens, pencils, rulers, creepy crawlies, priceless works of art—and tossed it all into the garbage.

"Okay, girlie, you have *got* to get a grip!" I reprimanded myself out loud. Just to make sure I heard the message.

When I told my therapist on Tuesday, she shrugged it off. "Bugs are no big deal," she said. "If anything, it's a good sign when you can let mess happen."

"I know, I know," I said, waving her off. "A clean house is a sign of a messy mind," echoing a statement she often repeated. "But I might be willing to make the sacrifice."

Then I paused and dropped my head into both hands. "I kind of thought I'd have it back together by now."

"It's only been eleven months."

"All the king's horses and all the king's men…"

Dr. Newland looked thoughtful. "I've been wondering if you'd like to upgrade to double sessions."

"Am I that bad?"

She smiled and shook her head. "Not at all. It just takes you one whole session to cover the children, and I feel like you need more time for you."

"Okay," I said, feeling discouraged. "I hardly ever take Xanax anymore, so that's something."

"That's good."

I reached into my purse and held up the container. "I carry it around with me like a security blanket, and that's usually all I need."

* * *

On the September day that we were to unveil the memorial tablet, Danny refused to leave school. After some cajoling, he agreed to come to the ceremony. When we got there, he refused to get out of the car. Reluctantly, he gloomily followed his brother up the grassy slope.

We were an intimate gathering, unlike the funeral from nearly a year ago, just me and my kids, Zack and Lilith, Sam's parents and my A-Team. It was blazing hot, and Rabbi Jonathan was late. He was predictably stuck on the 405 Freeway. I was annoyed with the rabbi, not so much because of his tardiness—Sam's family had conditioned me to "Jewish standard time"—but because he hadn't once reached out to me in the previous eleven months. Maybe he had called Sam's parents, I didn't know. All I knew was that I had asked him to check on me, and he hadn't. Not exactly great marketing for He-Whose-Name-I-No-Longer-Revered.

We waited impatiently in the heat. A sapling grew on the sloping hillside, but it was young, too small to offer shade. Eventually, the rabbi arrived, sweating. He murmured an apology, recited a few prayers, and conducted the ritual unveiling.

The gravestone was beautiful, in a depressing bronze sort of way:

Sam Maya
Loved husband, father, son and friend
1966–2007
"Let it not be a death, but completeness."

I had selected the phrase from a poem by Rabindranath Tagore because I liked the idea that death was not all that defined the man. The poem began, "Peace, my heart…" I felt sadness about Sam's suicide, anger at God, fear for my sons, but not much peace. Perhaps I would grow into peace.

Danny took a step forward to examine the gravestone, and his next step landed forcefully on it.

My father-in-law flinched.

The child who refused to say the "D" words trampled his Dead Dad with enraged feet.

I let him.

Alberto looked at me, horrified. "You have to stop him!"

"I'm not going to."

I remained calm. Danny couldn't hurt the marker or Sam with his size six stomps.

Alberto grew agitated, shaking his head, muttering in Spanish, glaring at me, but I didn't yield. Danny's stomping was the perfect expression of little boy grief.

I had known this day would be difficult, that it would bring Danny's intensity to the surface. I was proud of myself for standing up to Sam's father and protecting my son's feelings. I was getting better at honoring the boys' feelings, as I was learning to hold my own.

There is a sense in which anger keeps us as firmly connected as love does. In some ways it was easier to be mad at Sam than it was to love him after he left us. But anger embedded me firmly in the past. Anger fueled the fantasy that Sam would know how much we had suffered at his hand, but I would never get that gratification. I could not both cling to anger and live in the present. I had to choose. To make my peace with Sam, I would have to let my anger go.

* * *

My romance with Tim felt illicit. I hadn't told my kids or my parents. I didn't mention it at summer camp or book group. Susan knew about one lunch and a dinner. Genie knew we'd been flirting shamelessly. As far as Zack knew, I'd had a one-night stand, of which he was completely supportive—complicit, even—but the more time I spent with Tim, the more it felt like start of something. I wondered if, in that case, Zack would feel less supportive of me and more protective of Sam.

It felt presumptuous to say I was seeing someone, when I didn't know where things were headed. Tim might yet decide I wasn't for him. Or that he wasn't ready. Or that his kids weren't. Tim shared office space with Debbie's parents and both of her sisters. I didn't know them, but I was sure they would have opinions.

I hadn't talked to Tim about defining our relationship. I didn't want to think so hard. I wasn't convinced I wanted the complication of a significant other. Life as a single mom was complicated enough. But I liked Tim. He made me laugh. He was smart. He was handsome. His formerly dark hair displayed a presidential progression: primarily pepper with a dash of salt when Debbie was diagnosed, and more salt than pepper a year later when she was gone. And those green eyes of his…

But it was hard to find time together. We always had at least one of our young boys with us, shuttling them between school and sports and scouts, and without even a hostile ex to take the kids every other weekend. Not to mention, I had a dog to walk, he had a cat box to clean, and we both had jobs.

At dinner one night I suggested, "Let's go away for a weekend."

"What's on your mind, sailor?"

"Yes, that," I laughed. "But I'd also like to get to know you without the editorializing from the public and without the pressure of running home to relieve the babysitter."

He smiled. "Have you ever been to Cambria?"

We coordinated calendars and made plans. I told my parents I was going on a girls' weekend with Genie. Tim told his he was going fishing with the guys.

We talked endlessly on the drive up the California coast, holding hands and snacking on firm red grapes. Tim had rented a two-bedroom house for the weekend, which seemed extravagant. "So you can have your privacy," he explained, and then laughed, "and in case things don't go well."

Things went well.

Each morning, he woke me with a kiss and brought us coffee, mine with almond milk and his black. Sweet and decadent.

We took long walks up the coastline. We decided to make it a priority to get away like this, just the two of us, once each quarter. At brunch on Sunday, Tim happened to see the mechanic who worked on his car; turns out, two hundred miles wasn't quite enough distance to keep our relationship confidential.

* * *

"Hey." Zack's voice was clipped and tense, a harbinger of bad news. It was not the playful *Heyyy* that he used with Sam. "She's gone."

We had seen it coming—the growing masses, the desperate treatments—but it was still a shock. His younger sister, who was stunning but struggled with self-confidence and anorexia, who was whip-smart but played dumb, who only dated Adonis-looking men but had finally found one worthy of her. She had spent so much of her life fighting against her own body, and when she had finally learned to love her whole self, cancer turned her body against her. She died at thirty-six, leaving her husband and their three-year-old.

First his cousin and then his sister. Poor Zack.

"You know what's really unfair?" he said, despondently. "She was fighting for her life, and Sam threw his away. He just threw it away."

My heart started to pound. I hesitated before responding. "Sam was fighting just as hard," I retorted. "The difference is that he was fighting alone. He didn't have doctors or therapists or medication. Nobody was bringing him casseroles. Or setting up prayer chains. Or offering to drive carpool. He didn't lose his hair. He lost his mind."

The line went silent.

I thought back to Sam's suicide note: *They need you without the burden of me*. What Sam thought he was doing when he jumped was lifting a burden off his children. That was the choice he thought he was making, but he was wrong. This was why I bristled when a priest said, "He gave his life for us." Or when anyone said they'd give up their own life, as if it were a badge of honor or the highest demonstration of love. "I'd jump in front of a bus for my kid" never landed on me the same again after I'd met a child whose mother had done just that while the child watched in horror.

But there would be no benefit to arguing this point with Zack.

After a pause, I softened. "It's too much." She was my little cousin, too, a mere teenager when I first met her. "I miss her already."

As soon as I heard the sad news, it was Tim I wanted to talk to.

Tim spoke with a candor about death and dying. He described orchestrating the care and treatment for Debbie during her illness, but also managing the distraught extended family. "My father-in-law said Debbie just needed to get up and move around." As though the physicians had missed this step. As though, through sheer love and force of will, she could beat the cancer back.

When Tim described how much weight Debbie had lost, how little control she had over her own body, I imagined her a fragile little bird, wearing a diaper.

We talked about the unexpected death versus the anticipated one. One wasn't necessarily better or worse. Hearts were equally broken.

We talked about the goodbye. "It's not like the movies," Tim said. "You see it coming, but you don't get that Hollywood goodbye. The last note I received from my wife was: *Call me, you bum!*" He smiled. "She wasn't exactly Saint Debbie."

There was no single farewell accompanied by a poignant musical soundtrack. There was her last word, "Beautiful," as she sat in a wheelchair looking at the view of the mountains from her back patio. There was a moment, after she stopped speaking or opening her eyes, when she stubbornly refused to move her hand for the hospice nurse to adjust her IV. Only in response to Tim's voice scolding her—"Don't be a pill."—did she allow the nurse to do her palliative work. There was a child's footsteps scurrying down the stairs, too overwhelmed by the thought of what lay on the other side of his mother's bedroom door to stop and say anything. In those lived moments, though painful in what they portended, there remained a dwindling hope for more time. Only after Tim kissed her forehead, cool and stiff, could he understand what had formed a series of goodbyes.

"We live lifetimes saying goodbye without even realizing," he said.

* * *

I met Tim for lunch one day at Green Street Tavern, a new and relatively unknown place in Pasadena. I didn't know quite what to make of us. *Are we an "us"?* But when Tim reached across the table, I didn't hesitate to place my hand in his, the warmth of his hand both a comfort and a pleasure.

It was unnerving how easily I trusted Tim, how naturally I confided in him. Was it simply that we both understood grief?

Tim called me shortly after we had left the restaurant. By the time he had returned to his office, there was already a voicemail from one of his high school classmates. "Hey, Timmy! I just got a call from my aunt, and she said that she saw Tim Stratz in Old Town Pasadena with a tall blonde. Give me a call, buddy."

Living in a small town was great for prayers and casseroles, but it was a liability when the widow and the widower were trying not to be the subject of gossip.

Tim, Debbie, Sam, and I had all lived and worked locally. Three of the four of us had attended local high schools. Tim and I could not go to any restaurant in the area without seeing *somebody* one of us knew. We might even have tolerated the lack of anonymity, if not for the kids. The last thing either one of us wanted was for one of our four boys to hear through the rumor mill that mom/dad had a new boyfriend/girlfriend. It reminded me of what the police officer had said, "You do not want them finding out from someone else."

We would have to do what the celebrities in Los Angeles did when they didn't want to be caught by the paparazzi: go downtown. Nobody went to dinner in downtown Los Angeles in 2008.

Also, we were going to have to tell our children.

* * *

I sat at the edge of Danny's bed, preparing to read a chapter of *Harry Potter and the Goblet of Fire*. Parker sailed up onto the bed. For a small breed he had no trouble leaping up to nap on beds that weren't his. Jason gently stroked his silky black ears; those ears were better than therapy.

"So," I said, hoping I sounded casual, "I met a man I like." I wasn't sure how the boys might respond to this idea.

Danny's eyes narrowed. "Is he your boyfriend?"

The word "boyfriend" seemed too juvenile for a man in his forties, but for simplicity's sake, I said, "He is."

"When am I going to meet him?"

"We thought we'd all have dinner together this weekend."

"Where?"

"Café Bizou."

"Can I have the steak *au poivre*?"

"Sure."

"Okay." He looked at the book in my hands. "Can you read *Harry Potter* now?"

That was easier than I had anticipated.

Jason piped up, "I want sanddabs!"

I smiled. My little one appreciated the California delicacy, a sweet and flaky flatfish. Also, the potato crusted salmon had already crossed my mind.

* * *

I stood nervously on the sidewalk in front of the restaurant with my sons. Danny was shy about meeting Tim and his kids, while Jason was intrigued by this development.

I spotted Tim as he walked toward us, a son on each side. The three were smiling and chatting amiably. The older boy was almost as tall as his father and lanky. Gregory was the basketball player; he moved like an athlete, with graceful loping strides. Daniel was shorter and stockier, bouncing on the balls of his feet, quickening his pace to keep up with his father and brother.

Not until introductions had been made with handshakes all around did Tim greet me with a quick peck on the cheek. I felt four sets of eyes watching us intently. Tim calmed me with his warm smile and his hand lightly guiding me at my waist.

It was one thing to imagine our collective seven-, nine-, twelve-, and-fifteen-year-old sons...but another thing entirely to sit with our brood around one table. Four was a lot of boys. I felt especially intimidated by the teenager.

Gregory was polite to me but warmer with the boys. He had his mother's round brown eyes, and he easily struck up a conversation with Jason about sports. At one point, he asked Jason what his favorite entrée was, and then Gregory ordered the sanddabs, too. Daniel seemed less inclined to engage with either me or my boys, instead directing his comments to Tim and Gregory, which was awkward since he was seated between Danny and Jason. Daniel was a lefty, and occasionally, his elbow bumped into Danny's; that might have been the only interaction they had. I watched Daniel enjoying his steak *au poivre*, appallingly open-mouthed. I thought about how Tim had described young Daniel dissolving into tears as he walked toward the altar during his mother's funeral, and I couldn't help but feel empathy toward this boy, notwithstanding his regrettable table manners.

On our drive home afterward, I asked my boys what they thought.

Danny shrugged. "I liked the steak *au poivre*," he said.

Jason said, "Two Dannys is too confusing." His insight would prove prescient. As a practical matter, I began referring to the one I gave birth to as "Danny" and the one Debbie gave birth to as "Daniel," but this distinction was often too subtle to eliminate confusion.

Later that night, Tim called to share his boys' assessments. "Daniel told me, 'She's mostly hot, Dad. Too skinny.'" Funny, but sad. Skinny was not a positive trait in his mind; as his mother's sickness progressed, she had grown thinner.

Gregory had said, "Dad, it just looks wrong." His comment struck me as both diplomatic and true. His mother was a petite brunette, and to see his father with a tall blue-eyed woman didn't quite compute. It wasn't personal; I just wasn't his mom.

* * *

When the widow and the widower started dating, people had opinions. And they weren't shy about sharing them:

"It's too soon."

"It's about time!"

"Good, the boys need a father."

"You'll be good for them. Children need a mother."

"How did you meet this guy? Be careful."

"Seems like a recipe for disaster."

"Wait until after Sam has been gone for a year."

"Wait until the boys go to college."

"What a waste if you're not having sex with that man."

"What does she want from you? I don't like it. You're turnkey."

"Just because you kiss her, Timmy, doesn't mean you have to marry her."

* * *

When José was in Los Angeles for business, I met him for a loop around the Rose Bowl. It took me two miles to build up the courage to say, "I think I've met someone special."

He didn't hesitate in his response. "Good for you!" He smiled broadly.

"I'm worried the family might not like it," I said.

"What?" he exclaimed mockingly. "God loves you more when you're miserable?"

I laughed. "Do you think Zack will feel that I've somehow betrayed Sam?"

José stopped running to hug me. "Sweetie," he said, "we have all been praying for this day."

CHAPTER 29

OCTOBER AGAIN (2008)

Rainer Maria Rilke wrote, "Let everything happen to you: beauty and terror. Just keep going. No feeling is final." Everything had happened, and we kept going.

Jason once drew a picture of the day his father died. On the left side of the landscape page was a gorgeous fall day: blue sky, green grass, bright yellow sun, flowers, a little brown snake, and a frog. He then drew a line down the center and scribbled black haphazardly. He pressed the crayon stormily until only a small nub remained and the right side of page was covered in darkness. That was exactly what the day felt like. After that day, there were details and entire sequences I could not recall, but when I closed my eyes and returned to that fall day, I felt again the hollowness and a visceral longing for everything we had lost.

It was hard to believe Sam had been gone almost an entire year. The word "anniversary" didn't convey the right amount of heartbreak when observing the anniversary of Sam's suicide, so we made up our own: "deathaversary."

"Deathaversary" emphasized the gravity of the day. The passing of a year without Sam was not exactly a special occasion, and yet, when I acknowledged how far Danny, Jason, and I had come in the process, when I thought about how proud Sam would be, when I noticed that we could still laugh and love and run and find joy—that was worth celebrating.

There were many ways we could have observed Sam's first deathaversary, including doing nothing at all. I was not in the do-nothing, say-nothing camp. American culture tends to err on the side of reticence in the face of grief. I preferred a clumsy attempt to give voice to the unmentionable over a resounding silence. It meant that someone cared enough to notice my pain and to risk trying to help.

As I thought about Sam and his love of baseball, I decided to host a game in his honor. I wanted Danny and Jason to know that there were people they could depend on, including the many who loved and missed their father. Almost two hundred people showed up to the elementary school baseball field for a sunny afternoon of eating Cracker Jack, laughing, remembering, and playing baseball.

As I tucked tired, content boys into their beds that night, I was filled with gratitude for the many hands that had carried us through the previous twelve months.

* * *

My childhood friend Julie, the one who had been Jason's teacher, invited me to attend church with her around Sam's first deathaversary. She knew that spirituality had played a vital role in my life, but she also knew that I hadn't exactly been on speaking terms with God. If I spoke of Him at all, it had not been kindly.

I cannot now recall the exact words Julie used, but there was something so open about her invitation. She acknowledged that church might be the last place on earth I would want to be, but suggested that— with or without church attendance—our families could go to brunch together. I trusted that whether I accepted or declined, our friendship would remain intact.

As soon as she extended the invitation, I realized that church was exactly where I wanted to go. It was as though I had been treading water for so long I had forgotten that I could swim to shore, but now I could see Julie waving from the warm sand, where she had set out a beach towel for me next to her own.

That Sunday morning, I dressed the boys in collared shirts, and we ventured into God's house. The Presbyterian church featured a buttressed ceiling with a simple cross behind the altar. Gleaming copper organ pipes adorned the chancel, and as I sat in the pew with my sons and my friend, the organist began to fill the sanctuary with music I knew by heart. Nothing touched me more deeply than music, and this service featured selections on both piano and pipe organ, along with a full choir and a beautiful *a cappella* solo. It was hard to resist.

The readings included the story of Jacob, a man who was returning home to reconcile with his brother. Jacob had betrayed his brother, and he was afraid of retribution. He felt very much alone. The night before meeting his brother, Jacob wrestled with a man (in some Bible translations, an angel) who threw Jacob's hip out of joint, but Jacob held on to the man-angel long enough for the man-angel to give him a blessing. The next morning, his brother welcomed him with open arms, but Jacob walked with a limp for the rest of his life. Some experiences leave us changed forever.

Pastor Henry was a commanding presence. He spoke with the hint of a Texas drawl and began to share his own story. His firstborn had died from cancer when the child was ten. It had been more than a decade since his son's death, and still the pastor's voice cracked. *This man*, I thought, *understands my pain*. His was not that god-has-a-plan-whatever-doesn't-kill-you-makes-you-stronger-bullshit kind of faith. He had endured the light-swallowing-middle-of-the-night darkness and emerged with a different kind of faith.

He described standing on his back porch, night after night, raging at the heavens with raised fists. He compared Jacob's wrestling with the man-angel to his own struggle with God after his child's death. He explained that by wrestling with the man-angel, Jacob was holding onto his connection with God, and the upshot of this encounter was to be blessed. The pastor's anger did not sever his connection with God; on the contrary, the wrestling was a sacred component of the relationship.

I had spent much of my lifetime in church, but this was the first sanctuary to hold both my reverence and my rage. I realized that this God Pastor Henry spoke of could handle my anger without abandoning me. He was like Sam holding my hand during an argument.

And, I realized, I was still in relationship with the divine. All those times I was calling God names, all God heard was me calling Him. All those times I had been pushing God away, She was still drawing me close.

CHAPTER 30

SOCCER SEASON AND RELATED HAZARDS

A friend who lost her teenage son to suicide warned me that the second year was worse than the first. "Everybody thinks you're over it, that you've survived the hardest year of your life, and now you're okay. But the truth is it still hurts, sometimes more than ever."

* * *

Jason and I were in the bleachers at the Jackie Robinson field in Pasadena watching Danny practicing with his soccer team early on a Wednesday evening in late October. My sister and brother-in-law didn't have any children of their own, but Uncle John, himself a soccer player, had stepped up to coach Danny's team.

A Jane and I sat in the stands chatting about the challenges of working part-time—"It's the worst of both worlds. I feel like I'm shortchanging my boss *and* my family."—and joking about the perils of wearing pumps to soccer practice, while the younger brothers climbed up and down the rough cement steps. Suddenly, her son screamed. We looked up to the top of the stands, and we saw him stand, blood dripping from a gash in his forehead. I stood up to help Jane. Again, I heard the distressed cry, "Mommy!" but Jane was already tending to her son. More urgently, "*MOMMY!*" and I turned to see Jason staggering toward me. He, too, had blood streaming down his face and neck. His shirt was spattered red. For one horrifying moment, I thought a sniper was taking out kids in the stands. The reality was a banal and unfortunate coincidence of aging sports facilities, jagged concrete steps, and young boys with more energy than balance.

Uncle John agreed to take Danny home after practice, and I rushed off with Jason. He had an open gash in his cheek. Blood was everywhere. As I buckled Jason into the car, his eyes went wide, and his lips quivered. "Mommy…am I going to die?"

"Oh sweetheart, no. I've got you."

I phoned Tim from the car. It felt natural to call him.

"Just so you know," he told me, "you have the right to request a plastic surgeon if Jason needs stitches." I hadn't known.

He offered to meet me at the emergency room, but I declined. I was a mom. I was a lawyer. I wished Jason had his daddy for his sake, but I could do this myself.

"Okay, keep me posted."

The receptionist at the ER smiled as she handed me the paperwork, noticing the bright red stains, and I realized I had chosen the wrong day to wear a pale beige suit.

I started checking boxes. I completed Jason's information, and then mine. On the father line, I wrote: Deceased 10/20/2007. That part never got easier.

While the nurse examined Jason's wound, I requested a plastic surgeon.

"I just stitched up the other boy myself," she said.

"I'm sure you did a nice job, but I would still like the plastic surgeon."

"It's not like he's a girl," she said, shrugging.

I couldn't believe this nurse was arguing with me. Jason's cut was in his cheek, within an inch of his left eye; there were muscles and nerves *and his eye*. People like her were the reason I had a permanent crease in the skin between my eyebrows. "How long for the plastic surgeon to get here?"

Reluctantly, she made a call. Then she turned to me and said petulantly, "Twenty minutes."

"I'll wait."

The plastic surgeon spent the better part of the next hour reassuring my son, carefully cleansing the laceration, which had gone through to his cheekbone, and suturing the layers back together. Fifteen stitches later, Jason was gauzed up and ready to go.

"One day the girls are going to be kissing all over that scar," I teased him.

"Ewww…that's gross!"

By the time we got home, Danny was asleep, and Uncle John was snoozing on the sofa. He gave Jason a bear hug before heading home himself.

Jason, though exhausted, was revved up from his evening. His baby cheek was swollen and purple, and child-sized butterfly bandages covered the surgeon's handiwork. "Mommy, you didn't cry or anything at the doctor's. You don't even care about me!"

He had no way of knowing how much I ached when he suffered. "My sweet boy," I said, taking his little hand in mine, "I love you more than anything in all the world. I cannot take care of you if I'm falling apart myself. I save my tears for later."

"Ohhh…" he said pensively. "There are bunches of ways to love, like hugs and baking cookies and sewing Softie." One of the Janes had sewn his yellow blanket back together after he had shredded it.

"Exactly."

"I love you, Mommy." He fell asleep within moments. I sat on the side of his bed a few minutes longer, stroking his warm forehead and watching his chest rising and falling. He was sleeping in his own bed now, a sign of his growing confidence. I kissed his brow and breathed in. He was growing up, but he was still my baby.

I cleaned up the kitchen, took out the trash, and finally peeled the contact lenses off of my tired eyes. I crawled into bed, where Parker was already snoring softly, and made a call to the man who had said he would wait up for me.

Tim answered on the first ring. "Long day?"

"Seriously. You saved us, though." I told him everything, and that's when I felt safe enough to cry.

* * *

The Pasadena Marathon was canceled due to dangerously poor air quality. Fire was raging in the Angeles National Forest, and the air was thick with smoke and disappointment. All those miles run, only to have the finish line evaporate. I wouldn't sign up for another half. Any training run longer than seven miles had rendered me useless for the rest of a Saturday, which wasn't conducive to single parenting. It would be too much for me to train for another half-marathon.

Once the air cleared, I would start running again, but only for short distances.

* * *

We She-Wolves and our families gathered poolside at Sarah's house two weekends later to honor the training we had done, despite the canceled event, and to celebrate our friendship. It was also the first time I was introducing Tim to some of my friends. Sarah's tanned husband, with his windblown surfer hair and Ben, pale and slathered in SPF 50, cornered Tim at the edge of the deep end of the pool. Tim would joke about "the interrogation" later.

"Your friends are protective of you," he said. Then added, "That's a good thing."

Another evening, as a friend of Tim's welcomed us into her home for a party, heads turned pointedly in our direction. I felt like the blue-ribbon heifer at the county fair. I overheard a woman ask, "Is it true that Tim has a girlfriend?" before another guest shushed her and nodded in my direction. His friends were protective, too.

* * *

Once, when I was making dinner, I accidentally called Tim, Sam. I was mortified, but Tim was forgiving. He kissed me and said, "I think it's just a sign that you're becoming comfortable with me."

Another time, when we were on the phone, he referred to me as Debbie. I let it go. I wasn't offended. People were hard habits to break.

* * *

Every morning began with a note from dear Tim. The first time he referred to me as "My Love," I thought, *I am not the luckiest unlucky girl, after all. I'm just plain lucky.*

CHAPTER 31

WINTER BLUES

"You might need to work on setting some boundaries with the extended family."

This is the problem with therapy. A good therapist makes you work. As if the holidays weren't exhausting enough already.

* * *

Our holidays, though beloved, were tinged with sadness without Sam. We were blessed with a cornucopia of grandparents and aunties and cousins who held onto us and didn't let us go. But it was complicated: we celebrated Christmas with my family, Hanukkah with Sam's family, and Thanksgiving with everybody.

I wanted Danny and Jason to have a relationship with Sam's family, which meant spending time together. The *abuelas* and *tías* needed to plant lipstick prints on those smooshy cheeks and feed them arroz con pollo. And by the time I coordinated times, places, and holidays and then drove all over the greater Los Angeles area, I was spent. But then I had to deal with the emotional fallout. I held my boys as they cried. Jason, the carbon copy of Sam, said, "Why do they all say I'm Daddy?

I'm *me*!" Danny was worn out by the feelings. "It makes me so sad to see *abuela* and *abuelo* so sad."

Not to mention that I missed Tim. I wished we could spend a holiday together, but between celebrations with his family, mine, Sam's, and Debbie's, Tim and I were left celebrating apart.

I didn't want to draw boundaries. I wanted to expand them.

* * *

In January, 2009, Tim and I took Daniel, Danny, and Jason to a camp for grieving children. Gregory was a sophomore at St. Francis High School and in the middle of basketball season, so he stayed home with Tim's father. I was starting to get an education in the gravity of high school athletics and the rigidity of high school coaches. I also had the impression that if it hadn't been basketball season, Gregory might have found another reason not to go.

We all piled into Tim's car and drove to the camp in the Malibu mountains. Jason chatted amiably with Tim and me along the winding drive, while Danny quietly observed the terrain, maybe listening, possibly daydreaming. Daniel sullenly tapped out text messages on his flip phone. He hadn't warmed to the idea of driving together, and he resented me for taking the shotgun seat.

I felt ever so slightly guilty about leaving our collective children at bereavement camp while Tim and I escaped for a couple nights at a beachfront hotel. But only for a hot minute.

* * *

The camp was a healing experience in many ways. Our boys spent time with other children who had lost either a parent or a sibling. They listened to others' stories; if they chose to, they could share their own as well. It was a safe place to talk about all of it. Or none of it. They found that they were not alone. They saw other children carrying a variety of grief-filled sandbags, and they did some heavy lifting of their own. Also, they had fun. They played games. They stayed up past bedtime. They discovered loads of nutritionally void snacks they never ate at home. They got to feel normal in a community of kids safely grieving terrible losses.

After that weekend, Jason came home with questions about his father's death: Where did Daddy jump from? Was there blood there? Is it still there? How do you know? Have you been there? Can I go there?

I had known this day would come.

The next morning, I took my son to Daddy's "jumping spot." Jason stood on the sidewalk and looked up to the top of the structure. Then he looked down to the ground. It was a long way to fall. He walked up to the corner of the building and kicked it with his size 1 Vans skater sneakers.

We had come on a mission, armed with a few pieces of fat sidewalk chalk, but first we needed permission. I opened the door to the salon, greeted by soft music and the scent of citrus and lavender. Jason and I approached the reception desk, where two women were standing, welcoming us with pleasant smiles.

I took a deep breath. "Hi. Could I speak to a manager?"

Their smiles cooled, and the taller one said, "I'm the manager."

I introduced myself and my son. "I'm so sorry to bother you." I hesitated. "My husband jumped from the parking structure about a year ago."

She inhaled sharply and glanced from me to Jason. She seemed to recognize him. Her eyes softened and warmed as she held back emotion. I didn't know whether she expected to see the widow of the man who ended his life that Saturday morning. She appeared never to have imagined seeing this little boy, dark hair and brown eyes—a three-and-a-half foot version of his father. His cheeks and fingers were round and soft, two permanent teeth coming in slightly crooked, adorably awkward in his mostly baby-toothed smile.

"I don't know if you were here…" I began.

"I was working that day," she said.

"I am so, so sorry." I paused and inhaled slowly. "We have an odd request. My son would like to know where exactly his father fell."

She nodded. She came out from behind the desk, and the three of us stepped outside. She pointed out where Sam landed on the sidewalk in front of the spa. "Right about here."

"If it's okay with you, we brought some sidewalk chalk. Jason would like to write his father a note."

"Yes. Of course."

I thanked her, and she hesitated, as if deciding whether to say something. Then she turned back towards the salon and disappeared inside.

Jason squatted down to write with his orange chalk. He seemed so small in the cemented space at the base of the gray structure, a crouched figure wearing a dark blue Angels t-shirt. He started writing.

D...A...D...

"Dad is a ..."

Suddenly I panicked. I didn't know what my little darling was about to write here on the sidewalk for God and everyone to see.

"*Sweetie pie*! You know you can't use any of Uncle José's Colorful Words, right?"

"I know, Mommy."

He finished writing his note: *DAD is awsome*. Spelling had ceased to take priority in our life as a grieving family.

He stood, satisfied. I smiled. He smiled.

We stood on the sidewalk together, looking at his love note. Then he put his sticky little hand in mine, and we walked back to the car.

"Can we go to the cemetery now?"

I marveled at my brave little boy and his ability to hold the full range of his feelings. "You got it, buddy."

When we got there, Jason ran up the grassy hill, and together we found his father's grave. He had a stone in his pocket, on which he had written in red Sharpie the note "I love Daddy." He set the message on Sam's grave marker, then knelt closer and whispered, "I miss you, Daddy. I really miss you."

* * *

I knew I was returning to myself when I started reading again. Although I preferred the tactile experience of physical books—the smell of the paper, the crackle of a new spine opening, the smoothness of the page or folding of a corner, even the giving away of the book to someone who would enjoy it—there was one aspect of the Kindle that I especially appreciated. I could sit in bed, already cozy in jammies, browsing through the new releases or bestsellers, and then download and start reading, without dragging the boys with me to the bookstore or finding a sitter to watch them.

Tim called it my Ken-doll. As in, "I'd like to distract you from that Ken-doll."

And the truth was, with Tim in my life, I wasn't reading nearly as much as I otherwise might have.

* * *

February sucked. Sam would have turned forty-three. Both boys' birthdays were the week after Sam's; they turned eight and ten without their dad. By Valentine's Day, I was ready for a week's worth of Tuesdays.

Scheduling therapists started to feel like a part-time job in itself. I had Dr. Newland for me, Dr. Kimberly for Danny, and Dr. Clark for the family. Jason had been struggling in school, so I added Dr. Vincent for him. And Leonard was the therapist who came to our home twice a week to work with Danny and his rage. We had *his, his, his, her,* and *our* therapists. I was spending so much money on therapists that I despaired of being able to save for college.

One afternoon I was driving the boys for their sessions with Dr. Vincent and Dr. Kimberly, and even though they both had a nice rapport with their respective therapists, they didn't share my predilection for self-care. On their scale of things they'd rather be doing, therapy was preferable to homework but not as good as playdates. They sat in the backseat contentiously.

Then the bickering started.

I was sickened by the knowledge that their relationship had dramatically deteriorated after their father's death. They seemed to take their grief out on each other.

Their volume rose, and in my rearview mirror I saw Danny reach over the empty middle seat aiming a fist toward his brother. Jason was small relative to other eight-year-old boys, and Danny was big for ten; the difference between them was close to eight inches and twenty-five pounds.

I checked the clock. I didn't have time to negotiate a truce and still get to their appointments on time, so I shouted, "Stop it!"

This is rarely an effective parenting technique, but I was too overwhelmed to muster a better approach. Also, I was clipping along at forty miles per hour, hoping to catch the next green light.

Danny lunged again, and Jason screamed, drawing his knees up defensively and leaning to the side to get as far away from his brother as possible.

I reached back to wave my right arm in between the squalling boys, keeping my left hand on the wheel. I glanced into the rearview mirror. Danny had begrudgingly withdrawn his attack and sat fuming with his arms crossed.

We arrived safely, and the boys retreated to their separate therapy sessions. I sat in the waiting room for the hour, grateful for the quiet. Both boys seemed fine after their sessions. No sooner had we returned home, though, than the phone rang.

"Can you come back to the office?" It was Dr. Vincent.

"Right now?"

"Yes," he said. "I need to see you right away."

I called a Jane to watch the boys and drove back to the therapist's office, panicking. *Something terrible has happened to Jason…something so bad that his therapist has to tell me in person. Is another kid tormenting him? Has a coach abused him? Hasn't this child been through enough?*

When I walked in, both Dr. Vincent and Dr. Clark were waiting for me. They looked stressed. Dr. Vincent could barely look me in the eye. My stomach dropped.

Dr. Clark invited me to sit down.

I looked from one therapist to the other, bracing myself. Finally, Dr. Vincent spoke. "Jason told me today that you hit Danny in the car."

I felt like I'd been slapped. "What?"

"As a mandated reporter, I am obligated to report suspected child abuse."

My whole body started shaking. The words *"suspected child abuse"* echoed in my ears.

And then he told me that they had already reported me to the Department of Child Protective Services. *Were they serious?*

"I-I-I did not hit Danny. I would never," I stammered. "I was driving, and they started bickering and Danny tried to hit him. I had one hand on the wheel, and I reached behind me to get between them *so that Danny wouldn't hurt Jason.*"

I was beside myself. It was all I could do to maintain a modicum of control. Were they going to take my boys away from me? Danny and Jason were my everything. I was working my tail off to help these boys heal, running them all over town to therapy, to ADHD evaluations, and their fucking therapists—the ones *I hired to help* my sons and me—reported me to DCPS without even asking *me* what happened?

I was livid. And terrified.

Someone from DCPS called the next day. I answered his questions, and that was the end of it, as far as they were concerned. But I felt completely betrayed.

Within days, a painful rash appeared on my shoulders.

The next day, I was sitting in my doctor's examination room wearing a flimsy paper gown, so she could look at my shoulders. She immediately stopped small-talking and made that frowny doctor face. She flipped through my chart and jotted something down. Without looking up, she asked, "Are you under a lot of stress?"

Where would I even begin? "I guess."

She looked up from the chart to me and suddenly remembered. She had been Sam's doctor, too. Gently, she said, "You have shingles."

"Isn't shingles for old people? I'm only forty."

"Old people or inordinately stressed-out ones." She handed me a prescription and encouraged me to find ways to relax. "I don't care if you have a glass of wine every single night."

Between the DCPS incident and the shingles, I was a virtual powder keg of grievances by the time Tuesday came around. I still felt like firing both Dr. Vincent and Dr. Clark. Dr. Newland encouraged me to up my self-care game instead. "What are you doing for yourself?"

"My Charlotte Shabbat has gone sideways with Jason's 'late-bird' school schedule," I admitted. Danny started school at 8:15 a.m., but Jason didn't start until an hour later. "Sometimes my parents come over for dinner Monday night and spend the night to cover Tuesday morning logistics. Otherwise, I miss yoga."

She nodded.

"But get this," I said. "Cute Tim offered to come over after he gets his kids to school on Tuesdays mornings. He'll watch Jason, and I'll be able to go to yoga again."

Dr. Newland looked pleased.

For all that I shared with my therapist, I didn't tell her that sometimes Tim came to the house at lunchtime when all four boys were securely at school. Occasionally, we had lunch. More often, we didn't. After our noontime tryst, we would head back into our respective afternoons happily hungry. I had forgotten how much fun it was to fall in love. It seemed too precious—and too fragile—to say out loud.

CHAPTER 32

SUSHI TUESDAYS

The yoga pose Warrior I exudes strength, balance, and bravery. Meanwhile, the inner warrior struggles to hold her stance, inhaling, exhaling, trembling, and repeating the mantra to herself *I can do this, I can do this.*

* * *

Dr. Newland surprised me with a request at the end of one of our marathon Tuesday sessions. She and a hospital chaplain were coordinating a presentation on children's grief. "I'm wondering whether you would be interested in speaking at the conference with us?"

"Seriously? I'm just a mom."

She shook her head dismissively. "Every week, you tell me what grief honestly looks like. You're a natural storyteller. I think you will bring them hope."

I was nervous about speaking to a group of therapists. I had never taken a single psychology class.

"Do not underestimate the lived experience."

"In the same way that mothering sons has sort of given me an honorary degree in orthopedic surgery?"

She laughed. Then she looked at me pointedly. "You've faced Sam's suicide honestly, and you have held your sons in their grief. You have honored your husband, and you are building a new life."

I raised an eyebrow. "Is Tim what Dr. Clark meant by 'reinvesting'?"

She smiled. "Also," she continued, hesitating, "the conference is on a Tuesday, so I'd have to reschedule you either way."

I laughed, "Okay then. I guess I'll be Exhibit A."

When the day came, I told my story of lost and broken things, of reconstructed Legos and expanding hearts. I explained that my healing began in earnest when I implemented my Tuesday rule: "*Unless you are in fact on fire AND I gave birth to you, it can wait until Wednesday.*" And that, in addition to yoga and therapy, the best Tuesdays featured a pedicure and a sushi lunch. Obviously, I had violated my Tuesday rule that day, but if sharing my journey would help another struggling parent or child, then it was worth it. The audience was engaged and appreciative, and it was invigorating to hear myself speak my story in public.

After my presentation, the chaplain said, "You have no idea the healing power of story." Then she added, "When you write your book, the title should be *Sushi Tuesdays.*"

CHAPTER 33

ONLY FOUR REASONS

Tim and Jason created their own Tuesday routine. One morning, Jason said excitedly, "The Timmer is going to play me chess today!" Sometimes they played their guitars. Sometimes they looked at photographs and talked about Sam. After about an hour, the Timmer walked Jason to school.

Once Tim reported that Jason had asked, "When we get married, will Danny and I go to St. Francis High School?" Tim thought it was adorable that Jason had said "we," as though marriage would mean the union of all six of us.

In a way, Jason was right. I came as a package deal: Jason, Danny, and me. So did Tim, Gregory, and Daniel. Tim and I prioritized all four kids. Whenever we made plans together—to meet for dinner, or to get away for a weekend—he always said, "There are only four reasons why I might not make it."

I had not uttered the "M" word in front of Jason, but in his eight-year-old estimation, marriage was simply the normal arrangement between moms and dads. It melted me that Jason felt included in our love, but it also frightened me, this explicit acknowledgment that my relationship with Tim directly impacted my children. What if things

243

didn't work out? If I broke my own heart, that was on me. But if I broke my little boy's heart, would I ever forgive myself?

I had given Tim a key to my home so he could lock up when he took my boy to school, but the house was the least of my concerns.

When I met Tim, I was a forty-year-old single mom with two young kids to raise, mortgage payments to make, and dogshit to pick up. I wasn't looking for someone, and I had no time for games. In a way, it was liberating. If I liked him, I'd spend time with him. If I didn't, I wouldn't. As it turned out, I did like Tim. A lot. I felt safe with him. He spoke the language of grief and loss, and he made me laugh. Next thing I knew, I had given myself completely to him, and there was no turning back. One way or the other, love would break my heart.

Our relationship was still new, but we were battle tested. We had lived "till death did us part," and we were keenly aware of how special it was to love and to be loved. I didn't take Tim for granted. How would we choose to define our relationship?

I had loved Sam and would always love him. His love grew me into who I had become, and I would always be grateful to him. He was the father of my children, and that shared experience would forever be part of who I was and would be. Similarly, Tim once described watching Debbie give birth to Gregory and said wistfully, "She was my hero." Even as Tim relayed his birth experience, I pictured Sam from that moment in my life, giving birth to my firstborn, watching my husband turn to mush when he held our newborn Danny in his arms.

And yet, I couldn't imagine being with anyone other than Tim. He was the love of my life. I hadn't expected to find love again, and now it took my breath away.

Sam's cousin once said to me, "I know you and Sam had a good marriage, but don't you kind of think that you and Tim are meant to be together?"

I appreciated her confirmation that this love was not just the product of my imagination or simply the aftereffect of a shared grief. Marriage seemed like a natural next step, but with our children's hearts on the line, the stakes were high.

* * *

During the week, Tim and I spent evenings separately. He ate with his boys at his house, and I ate at home with mine. I thought it would be nice to try having a family-style dinner, and we chose a Friday evening so as not to disrupt the school schedules.

I was entering uncharted territory. I put together a beautiful menu: the crowd-pleasing Chicken Marbella, basmati rice, and a child-friendly Caesar salad. I wanted Gregory and Daniel to feel welcomed and comfortable, and I spent much of the afternoon preparing.

Tim and Daniel came over together, but Gregory drove separately because he was bringing a friend. As we waited for Gregory, the younger boys grew hungry. And increasingly grouchy. Almost half an hour later, Gregory and his friend arrived.

"Yeah. Sorry. We stopped to eat first." Gregory held up an empty Chipotle bag. "Where's your trash can?"

They stopped to eat dinner on the way to dinner? I didn't need Dr. Newland to interpret this message. Gregory wanted nothing from me, not even food. Which was a significant scorn coming from a teenage male athlete. His friend, at least, was gracious, but Gregory picked at his plate and didn't engage anyone other than his friend. Within minutes, the two had excused themselves and headed back out for their evening.

I was offended. Even as a teenager, I never would have swung through a drive-thru on my way to a dinner that somebody had prepared for me. *After*, maybe, but not before. It would have been easier to take if Gregory had just canceled, or if he had told us that he was going to eat with his friend, so the little brothers didn't starve waiting for him. To make matters worse, Tim was protective of Gregory. "You know how teenagers are."

But I didn't.

* * *

When she was gravely ill, Debbie had told Tim that he should find love again.

He assured her that he would not.

To which she replied, "Don't be an idiot."

According to Tim, Debbie did not believe in soulmates; she believed that people had a greater capacity for love than simply finding "the one" perfect match, and lucky are those two who stumble into each other. Debbie encouraged Tim to open his heart again, and I couldn't help but admire her love for him in that gesture. I don't know whether Tim would have allowed himself to love again if Debbie hadn't given her permission. I'm not sure he believed it possible. But she had known.

She had even created a "Do-Not-Date List"—only half-jokingly— comprised of four women Debbie deemed unsuitable for Tim's future dating purposes. One, for example, was a high school classmate who was uncompromisingly bitter about her husband's premature death. Another divorced friend began flirting with Tim in the next room while Debbie was still alive.

Debbie did ask Tim to find someone who already had children of her own. She believed that only a mother would understand how much Gregory and Daniel meant to her and would treat them accordingly. This made sense to me. I knew my parents loved me, but I had no idea how much until I held my own child. Motherhood blurs the lines between us; I feel my child's pain in my body, and his joy makes me smile.

I knew that when he looked at Gregory asleep on the sofa in his sweaty basketball uniform, Tim didn't see a 150-pound knucklehead who couldn't be bothered to turn off the television; he saw his baby boy. He still turned to mush. And because I was a mother, I was, with practice, able to see past the eye-rolling teenage exterior and to muster compassion for this child who was not mine.

* * *

In February, 2009, I wanted to take all four boys skiing for Presidents' Day weekend, but Gregory couldn't go because there were basketball tournaments in play. Only those dedicated few who forsook all other activities for the sake of sport would be rewarded with a chance to play varsity. High school coaches had no sense of humor (nor sense of family, it appeared). Gregory stayed, and the rest of us headed to the mountains.

I was still optimistic that if Gregory gave me a chance, he would discover that I wasn't the worst affliction in his life. I left him a loaf of homemade banana bread (with chocolate chips) and a note wishing him luck at his games. Little did I know that Gregory didn't like banana bread. I should have left him Chips Ahoy.

Up in Mammoth, a ski resort in the western Sierras about 325 miles from Los Angeles, the rest of us had time and space to build up appetites and a dozen casual meals together. All five of us took to the slopes, Daniel on a snowboard and the rest of us on skis. Daniel took a hard fall on his snowboard but recovered quickly. The three boys were exhausted and hungry after a day of sunshine and snow.

It is not atypical for children who have lost one parent to have no interest in sharing their surviving one. Daniel, Danny, and Jason jockeyed for our attention. Tim and I just wanted each other. We curled up on the sofa after the boys were settled, he with a glass of Scotch and me with a glass of Pinot Noir, enjoying being under the same roof for a few days, even though we slept in royally separate beds, like the Queen and Prince Philip.

Every morning, Tim brought coffee to my bedroom. It was delicious to be awakened with a kiss and caffeine before setting foot on the cold floor.

On our second day, Daniel turned in his snowboard, and asked me to teach him to ski. Danny and Jason flew down blue slopes with Tim while I helped Daniel navigate a wide bunny slope. At first his movements were tentative, but he soon found his balance. He looked frequently to make sure I was watching him, and he seemed to thrive on compliments and encouragement. I enjoyed getting to know Daniel. He was like an exuberant puppy with a renegade tail, haplessly knocking into things and spilling everywhere but so sweet I had to smile. After lunch, we joined Tim and the other kids and skied together, the boys eyeing each other, competing for kudos and seats on the ski lift.

Overnight, Daniel became rude and surly, snapping at Danny and Jason, refusing to look at me. Beyond normal thirteen-year-old peevishness, he seemed to be racked with guilt, as though he had cheated on his mother by having a nice time with me, so he made it up to her with venom. After a morning grousing about his skis and being frustrated by the younger boys' proficiency on the slopes, Daniel decided to go back to the apartment and plant himself in front of a violent video game.

I understood that he was struggling to keep pace with a life that had changed significantly in a short time. Daniel had been shielded from the details of his mother's cancer, and his eleven-year-old self had not understood how gravely ill she was. Less than a year after his mother's death, his father introduced a new girlfriend. It was a lot.

Young Daniel was also acting out the adage: *If I don't love you, you can't hurt me.* The last woman he had fallen head over heels for broke his heart. It wasn't her fault that she died, but she had left him nonetheless. If he didn't want to experience that pain again, the obvious antidote was not to love in the first place. I didn't think his pushing away was conscious. I did believe, however, that as the adult in the room, it was my job to see what was happening for him. His behavior wasn't a personal attack. He was grieving. I cared about him, just as Debbie had known I would, and I tried to help him through the process by bearing witness to his pain.

I would be lying if I said he didn't hurt my feelings. He did.

Dr. Newland helped me develop my capacity to be both attentive to his distress and mindful of my own. His words, even if intended to hurt me, were not about me. His actions were unfiltered grief. My role was to respond with kindness.

* * *

Tim's athleticism attracted me. Sam had struggled to get in and out of the car; Tim rode his bike or ran just about every day and still had energy left for me. Most weekends, Tim rode thirty, forty, fifty miles with his friend Dyon, or longer when they were training. The two had been riding together since they were ten, and they had served as each other's best men. Dyon was the first person Tim called after Debbie died, before he even woke up his children.

When Tim was on the bike, he didn't send his usual texts, and I wouldn't hear from him for long stretches, especially when their route took them on remote roads with poor cell reception. I worried: collision, heart attack, skidding off the edge around a steep downhill curve. I pictured a vivid and morbid litany of horrors. The realities of Sam's car accident and his suicide—and my own nearly fatal tubal pregnancy—did nothing to soothe my overactive imagination.

In early March, 2009, Tim and Dyon drove up to Solvang, a little town north of Santa Barbara, where they would ride a century (one hundred miles!). On the day of the ride, he sent his sweet good morning note early, and off he went. It was after 4 p.m. when I heard from him. He sounded tired and happy. "Only one flat!" he said.

I was relieved.

"Dyon and I decided to drive back home tonight. Can I come see you after dinner with my boys?"

"Please!" I was thrilled.

I did the dinner-bathtime-bedtime dance with my boys. Meanwhile, Tim's flirty text messages started accumulating:

You're distracting me again.

Trouble coming your way!

"Something in the way she moves…"

It was after 10 p.m. when Tim finally arrived at my house, freshly shaven and showered. "My god," he said, looking at me, "I've never known anyone with such blue eyes." The man gave me butterflies. He pulled me into his arms and kissed me.

We didn't even pretend to watch a movie or sit and chat, we just went straight to bed. I felt sexy and safe with him. It was always hard to let him go and then spend the rest of the night alone, knowing he was just across town, also alone. I wished I could curl up in him all night and wake up by his side. I rested my head on his chest, felt his heart beating and breathed in the scent of him.

Tim held me close and whispered in my ear, "I love you, Debbie."

I held my breath.

He drifted to sleep, snoring softly. I was suddenly wide awake.

There is such profound isolation in being called the wrong name. *Was he thinking of her when he made love to me?*

I was sick to my stomach. I kept thinking, *Don't cry*. But I couldn't help it. Silent tears trickled down my face. I didn't want to be the Debbie substitute, Deb 2.0. I wanted him to love me as Charlotte, not as the next best thing.

Tim startled awake and bolted upright. He kissed me again, seemed to notice my tears in the dark, hesitated, and then collected his clothes from the floor. "I have to get home." We never spent the night at each other's houses; we had our four reasons. He dressed quickly and left. I heard him set the alarm and lock the door.

I buried my head in a pillow and sobbed.

A few minutes later, his text message: *Goodnight, my love.*

I didn't answer. I could still hear his voice saying, "I love you, Debbie."

I was nauseated. I couldn't sleep, could barely breathe.

Sometime past midnight, I showered and washed away our love-making, but when I crawled back into bed, his scent still lingered on the sheets.

I stared at the ceiling, tears rolling down my cheek and behind my ears, soaking the pillow. I thought, *I want more than a lover, I want love. Have I been such a fool? I should never have let a man into my life.*

And then I thought, *I cannot let the boys see me like this. I have to get a grip. I have to sleep so I can function in the morning.*

There's Xanax in the medicine cabinet.

I hadn't taken a Vitamin X in months, but I needed to sleep, even if only for a few hours. I took one and surrendered to the night.

I woke up groggy and checked my phone. I had slept through the morning greeting from Tim. It made me feel hollow. I tapped an unembellished *Morning* and hit send.

I managed through the morning feeling wrung out. I was a single mom, and I had work to do: Cub Scout project, grocery store, dog.

The tri-tone alert sounded several times over the next few hours.

Tim: *Loving you, my Charlotte.*

Tim: *Thinking about a kiss…*

Tim: *I miss your voice!*

Tim: *Where'd you disappear to?!*

Eventually I responded: *Scout hike!* It was a lie.

Then I turned my phone off. I was too hurt to talk, and I didn't know what I would say. If I lacerated his heart with my tongue, I would ruin what we had. If, indeed, we had what I had thought we had.

After settling Danny and Jason into bed, I turned my phone back on. I'd missed two calls from him and several more text messages.

Him: *Aren't those boys asleep yet?! Call me!*

My heart lurched. I didn't call.

I brushed my teeth, crawled into bed with a book. Tim called again, and I answered. "Hi." It was all I had the voice for.

"Oh. My. *God!*" he said playfully. "Where have you been all day? I've missed you like crazy!"

My eyes filled. I didn't want to lose him.

"What's wrong, sweetheart?" he asked.

I could hardly speak.

"Tell me," he said.

My hurt tumbled out. Tim listened. "I don't want to be your Plan B," I said.

When he spoke, his voice sounded gravelly. "All I can say is that I must have been so tired from riding the century." He paused. "Will you let me come see you after I settle my boys?"

An hour later, Tim arrived at my doorstep. I was a mess. He swept me into a hug, and I melted into his shoulder, feeling the warmth and strength of his arms around me.

He pulled back and cupped my face in his hands. "Look in my eyes," he told me. "I love you. I don't remember calling you Debbie. I am so sorry. I wasn't thinking about her. I don't want her back. I'm not trying to replace her. I am yours. All yours. I am in love with you, Charlotte. Only you. Not because I want someone or anyone. I want you."

CHAPTER 34

SUMMERSCAPES IN BLUES AND GRAYS

G enie, who had grown up vaguely Jewish, surprised me with this: "I've decided to get baptized. And my daughter, too." She was now finding comfort in her local Episcopal church. She continued, "I was hoping that you would be Claire's godmother."

"But I've never been baptized," I objected.

"I already asked the priest, and he said it's fine."

I was reluctant. Even though I had been attending church regularly, I was troubled by the fact that I wasn't allowed to receive communion. I had begun to speak with God again, but I'd fallen off the Christian Science path. I wasn't fully Presbyterian, and I didn't want to join the cultish-feeling Catholic church. I didn't know where I belonged.

"Are you sure you want *me* to be the godmother?" I asked.

"Yes," she insisted, "you are the most spiritual person I know."

Her adamance surprised me. And yet her confidence brought an immediate sense of belonging, even if it wasn't to an official denomination, even if it was just my friend, her four-year-old, Jesus, and me. I said yes.

As I thought about Claire's upcoming baptism, I suddenly realized what to do with the diamond heart necklace that Sam had never returned.

When I walked into the jewelry store, I caught the eye of the man behind the display case and asked, "Are you the owner?"

"Yes," he said.

"Hi, Sam. I'm Charlotte." It felt bittersweet to hold those two names together in one breath. These inevitable moments where death intersected life now peppered my daily walk, and I found in them a combination of wistfulness and self-assurance.

I held out the necklace, and the jeweler recognized his own design. Sam looked at me sadly and reached over the glass case to shake my hand. "Your husband was such a nice man. I was surprised when I heard what happened."

I smiled sympathetically. "You and me both."

An hour later, I walked out with two necklaces: a little silver cross for my soon-to-be-goddaughter, already gift-wrapped and ready for her baptism, and a diamond cross set in white gold for me. The idea of my exchanging the anniversary necklace for one symbolizing my deepening relationship with the divine would have appealed to Sam. But I confess that I also found a warped joy in the heretical thought that my late Jewish husband had just gifted me a sparkly cross.

* * *

In the summer, Tim rented a house at the beach in San Diego for that one obligatory "dark week" for high school sports, the only time he and his sons could travel without crushing Gregory's varsity dreams. Danny, Jason, and I joined them just for a weekend, as the six of us had not quite achieved joint summer vacation status.

What would have been my seventeenth wedding anniversary fell that weekend, and I had anticipated that Tim and the distractions of four boys would carry me through. But the day took the wind out of my sails. Grief had its own agenda.

The grief migraine is a thing unto itself. No aspirin relieves it. The only cure is to listen to what must be heard and to feel what must be felt. Nothing else abates the pressure. I drew the blinds, closed my eyes, and surrendered. I felt the weight of another unreached milestone.

My whole body felt heavy, pulsing with an ache for something lost. I breathed slowly, and in the background, I could hear the muted cheerful voices of all the boys with Tim.

Once the house quieted, I imagined the group of them jumping in the waves, playing smash ball on the sand, skin browning in the sun. I thought, *Sam loved the beach, too.* It was hard to imagine that he was gone. The disbelief washed over me. This happened less frequently now, but like a rogue wave, it occasionally caught my breath.

The previous week, a neighbor told me that she had seen Sam race down the street the day he died. He must have been seized by the moment shortly after I left with the boys. She said, "It was so weird for Sam to drive recklessly."

Sam must have been hell-bent on accomplishing his own suicide. Once he had seen his opportunity, he acted quickly, before changing his mind. Before giving me the chance to change it for him.

"Sam was always so conscientious," she continued. "He saved my kids from that van. Remember?"

I nodded. Her kids had been riding their bikes to school when a van full of school children had made an illegal U-turn in their path. Safety Sam ran into the street to get the driver's attention. He was so upset he called the number on the van to report the driver, and then he called the school district.

"I'm sorry I didn't tell you before," my neighbor said.

"I'm glad to know now," I told her. I was grateful when people handed me these artifacts, so I could fit the pieces into the archaeology of Sam's suicide. It comforted me when others remembered his gentle side.

"Are you feeling better, Mommy?" Jason crept in and clambered up onto the bed.

I was feeling better, in fact—the repercussion of lifting the grief sandbag and allowing grains to fall.

"Come down! The Timmer has an idea for dinner."

I noted the scent of charcoal. "What is it?" I asked, realizing I was hungry.

"You'll see!" he said, bounding off again, leaving a slightly sandy residue in his wake and charming me with even these gritty aspects of mothering boys.

* * *

I took my little family of three up to Bruin Woods in Lake Arrowhead the following week. The highlight of the week was the talent show. One family wrote a play every year. Some kids played musical instruments or danced. Everyone on stage was received as a celebrity, surrounded by approval.

Danny and Jason had worked on a drum-guitar medley for three months, and they wanted Tim to see them perform. Tim had a business meeting that afternoon, and the drive from his office was eighty miles. It would take an hour and a half without traffic. Then, after navigating the winding mountain roads, he would have to find the wooded amphitheater in the dark. The show coordinator had put Danny and Jason near the end of the show, and I hoped it would give Tim enough time. I sat on a wooden bench with my boys at my side in the cooling, pine-scented air.

"Is the Timmer here yet?" Jason asked, tapping my arm excitedly.

"He's on his way," I said, hoping that the three-year-old on stage with wild blonde curls who laughed uproariously at his own joke had several more in his repertoire, but he ran back to his parents, smiling gleefully. I glanced at my phone. At this pace, Tim would miss the boys' performance.

An angelic teenager sang something from *Phantom of the Opera*. A grandfather sang a sad Irish tune, ever so slightly off-key. An autistic boy played the piano to wild applause.

The emcee introduced them: "Next up, Danny and Jason Maya."

On stage, Danny adjusted the stool in front of the drum set; the ten-year-old was just visible over the adult-sized drums. Jason plugged his guitar into the amplifier and nodded to his brother. I looked over my shoulder again, and Tim appeared. My heart quickened. It was hard to believe that a man who wasn't Danny and Jason's father would have gone to these lengths. He stuck out among the dusty sweatshirts in his crisp white shirt. His hard shoes clicked incongruously on the asphalt path. Heads turned. When he saw me, Tim smiled and made his way to me. He sat next to me, and I nestled closer to him, marveling at how happy I felt as I laced my fingers into his.

Danny and Jason began to play "Smoke on the Water." The crowd erupted.

Both boys were grinning like Christmas when they returned to our seats. Danny gave Tim a high-five, and Jason squeezed himself between Tim and me.

CHAPTER 35

OCTOBER AGAIN (2009)

Fifty people showed up for Sam's second deathaversary baseball game, and it felt somehow lonely. It seemed like people assumed we were fixed. We weren't. We could never go back to our lives before. It had simply taken us two years to get this far.

I was grateful for those who showed up. But the many who didn't made me sad. I felt like some had already forgotten Sam. Others avoided saying Sam's name, and I had the impression that they were afraid to remind me that he was dead. As if I could forget. They could forget, but I saw Sam's fingerprints all over my life. I wondered if he had died from something else—car wreck, cancer, assassination—whether people would have been more compassionate, or whether they could only hold on to grief for so long.

I felt protective of Sam. He deserved more than to be reduced to the last act of his life, this bleak shadow of himself. Or to be summarily dismissed as "chickenshit" or "crazy." People tried to explain his suicide as financially motivated. Somebody who had never met him told me once that he was bipolar. If his death could be traced to his frailty, then it was his own damn fault. They seemed intent on applying a logic that went like this: "If Sam was bipolar and I'm not, then I'm not at risk of suicide." Or they wanted to convince themselves that their financial or relationship security inoculated themselves against the chance of mental illness. What seemed to terrify them about Sam's death was that there was not one single factor that definitively resulted in his suicide. Instead, a complicated combination of factors and circumstances made the rest of us feel defenseless against the possibility in our own lives. If it could happen to Sam, suicide might happen to anyone.

Even though I understood this intellectually, two years after Sam's death, I was still secretly hoping that I would understand *why*.

The slippery thing about depression is that everyone experiences it during their lives without necessarily reaching a dynamic that requires clinical diagnosis. I ran up against the limits of vocabulary to describe definitive characteristics. It was like trying to piece together a puzzle, with no edge pieces and some pieces missing, and no picture on the box. At what point does somebody just need to cheer up? At what point does everyone need to take a break? At what point is anyone close to breaking?

What bridged the gap between the Sam I knew and the Sam who took his own life? I knew he had back pain. I knew he was struggling at work. I knew he was stressed about money and was disappointed about my needing to work. These stresses were normal. Where did the gray areas of everyday stress switch from pearly to pewter to bleak?

I remember a professor once saying that practicing law requires the ability to hold two mutually exclusive ideas in mind simultaneously. Coming to terms with Sam's death felt the same.

One of my lasting visuals of Sam comes from when he and I had been dating just a few months. We were in our first year of law school, and I happened to see him walking out of a moot court competition. He didn't see me. He and his partner had just left the simulated courtroom, deep in conversation. They turned down the hallway, walking away from me. He looked handsome in his suit, a tall and lean outline in navy blue, and he had that funny gait, just shy of a limp. Even so, he exuded confidence, intelligence, and an unrestrained joy. As he walked out of the building, I thought, *That man is going to make a wonderful husband and father.*

And he did.

Sam loved us with his life, and he hurt us with his death. He was kind and devoted *and* he hurled himself off a building. Both sides of him were true. They didn't make sense together, but there they were.

CHAPTER 36

FRACTURED FRIENDSHIPS
AND UNLIKELY ALLIES

I dreamt that Sam and I were flying together. I dozed off for what felt like just a few minutes, and when I woke up, he had vanished. I reached out to touch his seat, and it was cold. He was nowhere on the plane. Even his carry-on bag had disappeared without explanation. I traveled the rest of the way by myself.

I woke up with a knot in my stomach, feeling freshly abandoned.

* * *

Occasionally, I took Danny and Jason to mass with Tim, Gregory, and Daniel at the Catholic church. I didn't love it. I found the service exclusive. The congregants responded spontaneously, but I couldn't figure out how they knew what to say or when to stand or kneel. I recognized the Lord's Prayer, but then they raced through it so quickly I couldn't keep pace, as if the point of the prayer was simply to finish it. Nobody sang.

I liked being together with Tim and our collective brood of boys. We might even have looked like an intact family, with four children in stair-steps. Gregory guided the younger boys along, and Daniel tapped on his phone, as though texting with Jesus. Danny daydreamed. Jason squirmed. Tim held my hand, and we spent an hour together in relative peace.

When it was time for communion, all six of us processed forward; the three of them received the eucharist, but the three of us crossed our arms over our chests. This body-of-Christ moment that should have felt unifying, didn't.

One Sunday, Catholic Jane sat with her husband and their seven children a few pews in front of us. After mass, she grasped my hand and whispered urgently, "I have been praying for you!" She smiled genuinely and pressed a flyer into my hand. "I thought you might like to come to this workshop with me," she said. "It's called Marriage is Forever." Then she kissed my cheek and raced after her youngest, who was dodging the clutches of an older sister.

Marriage is forever? The simplistic message bugged me. *No, it isn't*, I thought. *Marriage only lasts until the dickhead jumps off a building. Then the marriage is over.*

Was Tim forever married to Debbie?

I was in love with Tim, but we were tending to four young humans whose hearts had been upended by trauma. Would marriage be in their best interests?

Maybe it looked nice all dressed up in church for an hour, but this widowed family life was fraught with contradictions. When I got home to my separate unmarried home—the one to which I held sole and exclusive title and for which I alone paid the bills—I tossed the church flyer into the garbage.

* * *

My two reasons were settled into bed for the night, and I was looking forward to seeing Tim. *When are you coming over?* I texted him.

No response.

An hour went by.

Finally, the phone rang. "I'm sorry. I can't get away tonight. I'm feeling like a delinquent father." He sounded somber. "I want to see you, but my boys need me home."

"Are they okay?"

"Gregory finally confided in me, through tears, that he was afraid of losing me." Then Tim told me that Gregory said, "I can see that you're happy with her, Dad, but you're all I have left. And I don't want less of you because you're spending time with them."

I felt like a jerk.

Tim continued, "He said, 'She's a nice lady and everything, but please just do whatever you're going to do after I go away to college.' I'm sorry. I need to spend more time with him."

My hands started to tingle, a premonition of bad news.

Then he told me about Daniel. I knew that Daniel felt bereft over his mother's death and betrayed by his father, who assured him that his mother would be okay when she was dying. He felt abandoned when Tim spent time with Danny and Jason, even if Daniel himself didn't want to spend time with Tim. He complained relentlessly to anyone who would indulge his belief that his life was a hopeless series of unimaginable tragedies and that Charlotte was, in all likelihood, an emissary of Satan. He often commiserated with a stormy girl whose parents were divorcing.

There was more.

Parenting children with smartphones was uncharted territory in 2009, and Daniel hoarded his privacy like contraband. "Daniel has been texting someone he met in a chatroom online," Tim said. "And now that someone has Daniel's personal information. Where he goes to school. Everything." Tim had spent the afternoon talking to the principal of the school, the local police, and Daniel.

My hands went numb. The child had put himself in danger that he didn't understand.

I wanted to support Tim—and Daniel. And I also worried about the influence of his older boys on my younger ones. *Would blending our families even be a good idea? Was it too much stress on the kids? Were the risks too high?*

265

* * *

Tim stayed home every night that week. When we ventured out to dinner Saturday night, he was quiet and withdrawn.

"Hello? Where are you?" I waved my wine glass at him.

He smiled wanly, then reached across the table to hold my hand. "We need to talk."

Nothing good can come from this, I thought.

"I went to the doctor today."

Oh shit.

"I noticed blood in my…"

This isn't happening. Tim pressed my hand with both of his.

"I don't want to put you and Danny and Jason through this. I know what it was like to watch Debbie go through her treatments, to watch her die."

I can't believe this.

"I love you too much to put you in that position."

I shook my head no.

Tears started to well in his eyes. "I don't think we should keep seeing each other," he said.

"What?"

"You don't know how miserable colon cancer is." Tim already recognized the signs.

"It's too late for me not to be heartbroken," I said. "I'll be devastated if you die and miserable if you break up with me. Please don't. Don't leave me."

"You'll find someone else."

"Is that supposed to make me feel better? I don't want someone else. I didn't even want you. Remember?"

He smiled a real smile.

"Let me be with you, Tim. I love you."

I reached across the table, and he held my hand. We would hold on to each other despite an uncertain future. There was nothing like a cancer scare to remind us to love with urgency. As though Tim and I, of all people, needed the reminder.

After dinner, we went to my house. At one point, he asked for a toothbrush. I pointed toward what used to be Sam's side of the vanity, where I kept the new toothbrushes. As Tim was opening the drawer, I remembered the condoms in the back of the drawer. I laughed, thinking about Genie's silliness the night of her birthday.

Tim looked to me for explanation.

"You'll see. Genie gave me a little something. It's in the back of that drawer."

Tim held the box of condoms. He looked unconvinced. "Is it Steve?" he asked, seriously.

"Steve?" I was confused. "She gave me those…for *you*."

"Do you have a thing for Steve?"

"My kid's baseball coach?"

"It's obvious he has a thing for you."

"He's a friend!"

"Friends don't install dog doors, or drive the kids to baseball, or manage their financial accounts."

"That's *exactly* what friends do."

"Are you sure you don't have something going on with him?"

"I don't know why you won't believe me. I'm not attracted to Steve, I'm attracted to *you*."

He left without even a kiss. The evening's turn took my breath away. I didn't want to lose him, but if we didn't trust each other, we had a bigger problem than colon cancer. I tossed out the condoms and willed myself to sleep.

When his doctor called with test results, Tim turned out to be fine. As part of my "health by stealth" campaign to introduce more fruits and vegetables to everyone's diet, I had been juicing beets. What Tim thought was blood in his stool was likely the dark red cancer-fighting superfood. The fact that he had leapt from one abnormal bowel movement to his imminent death—catastrophizing, Dr. Newland called it—highlighted how strong the undercurrent of his grief was, and I had to wonder whether he was ready to move forward in a new relationship.

Tim's comment about Steve was also concerning. I had glimpsed Tim's jealous streak before. "Debbie called me her 'gween-eyed mon-stuh'," he told me, which I had thought was cute and silly. Once when he was leaving my house, he said, "Remember, don't talk to strangers—or anyone you know." I had dismissed it as flattery. When he commented, "I wouldn't wish Sam dead, but it does make my life easier," I had laughed it off as gallows humor. After the prophylactic argument, I realized there was something more there.

I thought Tim's accusation was patently unfair until a few days later, when Steve's wife confronted me. It wasn't just Tim who saw something inappropriate about Steve's attention toward me. "My husband is attracted to you," Maris told me. "You have to stop talking to him. Please."

I felt sick. I would be sad to lose both her friendship and his. I hadn't experienced Steve's friendship as anything else. Maybe I had been naïve. And yet it felt arrogant to approach every man I came into contact with—through my kids' school or sports, at the law firm or in grief groups—as though he wanted to hit on me.

I distanced myself from Steve and Maris, and I moved my account to a different brokerage with a female advisor. I especially missed Maris's gentle emails at odd hours. I was willing to make the sacrifice—for Tim's sake, for Maris's, and for mine—and Tim seemed relieved. But I worried that his jealousy would undermine our relationship.

* * *

It was easier to imagine marriage when I was in my twenties, when I had no mortgage and no children, just one man-hating tabby cat. The idea of marriage in my forties was complicated by four kids, my mortgage, his small business, one lapdog, and two gorgeous but destructive rescue cats. Beyond flexibility and a sense of humor, this situation would require more therapists.

I had been urging Tim to find a therapist for himself and also for Gregory and Daniel, but our culture rewards men for stoic self-reliance and stigmatizes matters related to mental health. When Tim saw that his insecurity was threatening our relationship, he agreed.

Tim had been skeptical. "I don't intend to be in therapy forever," he said. So he liked when his therapist established an end goal from the beginning of their work together. Tim often seemed exhausted on the days he had a session; facing into the pain—whether anxiety or unresolved grief—is surprisingly physical in its exertion. He appreciated hearing his therapist's perspective and learning coping strategies, as well as having a confidential space to process his thoughts. He acknowledged that working with a therapist helped reduce his stress. He was sleeping better. But he was still reluctant to engage therapists for the kids. His father-in-law, Ted, had discouraged Tim from "letting" the boys see therapists because "that goes on their permanent record." His comment illustrated how deep-seated the stigma can be.

I was mortified. What record did he mean? Medical records? School records? Criminal records? The point of therapy was to stave off poor grades, declining health, or otherwise undesirable behavior. Grieving is a *normal* response to the death of a loved one, and even garden-variety grief can benefit from professional help.

Gregory was mostly ignoring his grief, which wasn't particularly alarming, but after Tim discovered that Daniel had been engaging in self-harm and sneaking alcohol, Tim found therapists for both boys.

After a few weeks, Gregory's therapist reported that he was, for the first time, actively grieving his mother's death. Gregory seemed calmer and softer, as though he had been holding his breath for so long that he had forgotten what it was like to fill his lungs with fresh air. Tim told me, "Gregory and I talked about his mom and the future she would have wanted for all of us. At the end of our conversation, he said, 'Charlotte's good for you, Dad.'"

A good therapist is a godsend.

Daniel's therapist was initially helpful in response to a scary cutting episode. "That knife looked mighty friendly," Daniel later told me.

He had felt so numbed by life that feeling physical pain was somehow comforting. The therapist, who had lost his own mother to cancer at a young age, provided a safe space for Daniel to process Debbie's death and encouraged Daniel to express his feelings in healthier ways. After a few months, however, he still seemed stuck on a hamster wheel of grievances. It was hard to tell whether the therapist was helping guide Daniel through his grief or whether their conversations had devolved into mutual bitch sessions. When scheduling appointments became challenging, as happens with busy teenagers, Tim stopped trying to wrangle the calendar.

Daniel's relatives, on the other hand, were losing patience with his complaints about me.

Debbie's mother was direct. "Oh, stop it. Be nice to her and to your father."

Debbie's sister was similarly sturdy: "She loves your father. Get over yourself."

Debbie's niece, who had had a harrowing experience of her own with a stepparent, told him, "She's kind to you. Be grateful."

Debbie's cousin said simply, "Don't be a jerk."

Daniel didn't especially like these responses. Coming from Debbie's own family, though, the messages were powerful.

* * *

On the night his daughter died, Ted told Tim that he was too young not to find love again. After Ted had met me, he again pulled Tim aside. "Timothy, let me tell you something." He had been bossing Tim around since Tim was a teenager. "That's a special lady. Don't you let her get away."

Debbie's own father had been accepting of me since day one. Arguably, before day one. Ted was inclusive, always ready to pull up another chair to the table. He was one of the most grateful people I had ever met. He valued community in all its iterations—family, church, locale—and had served as mayor of South Pasadena. It was hardly surprising that the Rotary Club honored him with a Lifetime Service Award.

Tim and I attended the awards dinner. When I looked at the program, I noted that Ted's biography read: "wife Joan, three daughters, and eight grandchildren." Something seemed off. Ted's daughters had two children each; that meant six grandchildren, not eight. I turned to Tim and pointed out the typo in the program.

"That's not a typo," Tim said. "Ted wanted to make sure that you and Danny and Jason knew that you were included."

I was speechless. Tim and I weren't even engaged, but Ted welcomed me and my boys into his family with an open heart. He later introduced me to one of his colleagues as "Timothy's very, very (pause) very, very special friend."

Neither Ted nor Joan ever confused their grief over their daughter's death with their happiness that their son-in-law had found love again, and I found their approval deeply gratifying. That Ted's vision of family already included Tim, me, and our four boys made a future together seem not only possible, but almost inevitable.

CHAPTER 37

WARNING: DECEMBER WILL BE
HARDER THAN IT LOOKS

By the end of 2009, the holiday orchestration was starting to require both a conductor and a referee. We had *all eight* of our collective parents—mine, Tim's, Sam's, and Debbie's. It was an incredible gift. And a logistical nightmare.

Each family came with its own holiday traditions. Our collective four children wanted to keep their celebrations intact, and they did not want to share. If they were curious about the others' traditions, they were careful not to say so.

It was lovely that the families included us, but I would quickly overextend myself trying to meet the requests of this largesse of family. The ever-sensible Dr. Newland reminded me to draw the boundaries one holiday at a time. "Figure out what to do this year, worry about next year then."

"Sounds easy in theory," I said. "But there could be casualties."

She shrugged noncommittally.

I was especially sensitive to the feelings of Sam's and Debbie's parents, but as for the rest of the family, all I would commit to was to show up on time-ish with a salad and tongs.

I had always wanted a boisterous family, but with everyone involved, the situation had advanced into unadulterated insanity. There were moments when I missed my growing up years, those quiet celebrations with only my sister and our parents.

Nothing with four kids was simple, not even the car ride to grandma's. Did six of us pile into one car, with bickering over who was squished and who called shotgun? Did we take his and her cars instead? What about parking? Did we let Gregory drive himself and make the younger boys come with us? The upside to multiple cars was that somebody could pull the ripcord if he or she (me!) needed to get away. We tried different combinations; none was ideal.

It was impossible to please everybody. We tried anyway. We had three Thanksgiving-related events over the course of the holiday weekend, the smallest of which was a dinner I hosted for twenty-seven. By Sunday, I despaired of ever figuring out how which cousin was related to whom. I hoped only that they would be kind to my children.

And yet I loved seeing Tim with the family. Tim was the uncle who danced with giggling children all over the backyard, and when they asked for a cookie, he said, "Okay, but just one" while holding up three fingers. The little niece's eyes widened with understanding and looked for approval from her mother, who was smiling and shaking her head because she, too, had once been the baby Uncle Tim spoiled with his silliness.

"I don't even like kids!" he protested, and my heart skipped with a love I hadn't known was possible.

* * *

Christmas Eve presented a stalemate: Debbie's aunt hosted an annual party that night, but my family had always celebrated our everything on Christmas Eve, as the Europeans do.

I wanted to be with Tim, but I couldn't be in both places at once.

I hosted my family's Christmas Eve with my parents and sister and brother-in-law, for our traditional Swiss fondue and my father's rendering of "A Child's Christmas in Wales." Tim, Gregory, and Daniel went to the aunt's house for handmade tamales, a Christmas custom in Southern California. They left early to join us for caroling and my sister's killer brownies.

It was a compromise that frustrated everyone.

We celebrated Christmas Day separately, united only in our mutual avoidance of church. I spent the day in a swirl of Razor scooters, ribbons, and Swiss chocolate, trying to distract myself from the fact that Tim was otherwise occupied with both his family and Debbie's. At the very end of the day, after the boys were settled for the evening, we would share our moment. By then, our collective children would have overindulged themselves on filial attention and Santa's surprises.

I, too, was hoping for a special gift. Tim was a romantic. Unlike Sam, who proposed to me on a wave of emotion but without thought of an engagement ring, Tim had carefully planned his proposal to Debbie. He didn't want to exchange our Christmas gifts in the midst of the wrap-ripping-ribbon-wrangling chaos. He wanted to set aside a quiet moment together.

Genie mused, "Do you think he's going to propose?"

I hoped so. He had told me he wanted to someday. We were in love and had no philosophical aversions to marriage; marriage was familiar and comfortable territory. Tim and I were products of successful marriages, both our previous ones and our parents', and this history surely gave me an unreasonable confidence in a shared future.

If neither of us had had young children, or if all of our children had been adults, we almost certainly would have been engaged already, but children changed the calculus. The watershed question became whether our sons would be stabilized by our marriage or further unmoored by the addition of a stepparent and two more brothers.

Putting two families of three under one roof would not transform us into one happy family of six, and I wasn't inclined to take this disruptive step without the gravity of marriage supporting us. Living together felt precarious. If our children thought they had the power to form a wedge between us, they might exploit it.

Tim arrived holding a gift behind his back. "Merry Christmas, my love."

We sat together on the sofa, and he handed me a carefully wrapped box about the size of a one-pound box of See's Candies. *Not a ring box.*

I pulled off the white satin ribbon, still hoping for an engagement ring. I opened the padded blue lid to find a classic and elegant strand of pearls resting on velvet.

Not what I had hoped for.

The iconic necklace was lovely, and I was impressed that he had noticed I didn't own pearls. I tried to mask my disappointment.

A thought arose—*the children hold a higher priority in my relationship than I do*—and my stomach sank. *Will it always be this way?* I knew Tim was devoted to me, but the question of marriage was singularly convoluted.

* * *

The one room I hadn't quite finished after my remodel was the living room. We lost steam at the end of construction, as one does, and shortly thereafter we implemented the austerity measures. After Sam's death, I wasn't in the mood to choose color palettes beyond black. Now, I was thinking about it.

My living room featured big windows, beautiful light and hardwood floors, ideal for train tracks and Legos. As Danny and Jason were growing up, they needed less space for Thomas the Tank Engine and more for a drum kit, guitar, and fellow band members.

I wanted a space to socialize with my friends, too, something warm and welcoming. I called Susan to discuss ideas, and in about four minutes my interior-decorating friend showed up with furniture catalogues, fabric samples, and a tape measure.

Still, I hesitated. If I were to marry Tim, I didn't want to spend money on furniture for a house I would soon leave. It would be hard to leave my custom kitchen…and my long tub…and the meticulously planned closets. But Tim's house was bigger, and we would need the space for our family.

I asked Tim for his thoughts on decorating my living room.

"You should! You love your home. Enjoy it."

This wasn't the answer I had been hoping for. Tim's enthusiasm made me feel lonely. I didn't want to invest in a divided future, but he was afraid to disrupt the children. I didn't like that idea of living apart until the kids were grown. I believed Tim and I could make a shared life work for all of us, but for now, we would stay on separate tracks.

I looked through the drawings and samples again. My favorite piece was a padded ottoman in a light green and brown leopard print that none of the men in my life would have chosen. I called Susan and placed the order.

* * *

There was a quality of loneliness to this netherworld of not-quite-wife and yet-still-widow. Not exactly single, and not entirely partnered.

Sometimes, I felt something—a shadow or the echo of footprints following a few paces behind me. Once in a yoga class, I felt the support of someone holding my Warrior I arms from above; I was relaxed, my arms lifting upward effortlessly, as though Sam was reaching to me from heaven. I threw wishes in his direction, when Danny or Jason wanted something—a win for the team, or a starring role, or a special award—hoping that Sam might exert some heavenly influence for their benefit. I wished he could see them at performances or graduation, or ordinary vanilla days, and especially on days when they were hurting. The hardest kind of day was when I watched Danny being rolled into an oral surgery for an impacted baby tooth. I sat helplessly alone in the chilly waiting room, hoping beyond reason that Sam was watching the procedure and would intervene in order to keep my son safe.

* * *

It was a Friday night and already dark. The pinewood derby race was the next day. Danny was running out of time.

He had built the first-place car with his father mere months before Sam died. The following year, the car he built with my father placed third. This year's car hadn't even qualified at the trial run. Danny narrowed his eyes, holding the offending car in one hand.

I braced myself for an evening of consoling a frustrated and potentially volatile child. Danny stomped out to the garage. I followed him.

He stood at the old workbench in the garage, focused on a freshly cut rectangular block of pine. When he heard my footsteps, he announced, "I'm going to build a new car." Then he started over again.

I held this when he asked, "Hold this." I handed him the tools, sandpaper here, a screwdriver there. He worked single-mindedly, barely looking up until it was complete.

"What are you going to name your new car?" I asked.

He didn't hesitate. "Recovery."

Indeed.

To witness Danny feeling his disappointment keenly, then finding his resolve and allowing hope to propel him forward, the magnificence of it took my breath away. It didn't even matter that Recovery didn't bring home a ribbon on derby day. What mattered was that Danny had stayed in the race.

CHAPTER 38

WRITING A BLENDED FAMILY PLAYBOOK

Four miles, I concluded, was the perfect running distance. The first mile sucked every time. The next one was hard, but doable. Especially with an encouraging voice at my side, like a She-Wolf. Or Sara Bareilles. Mile three was magic, a synchrony of breath and motion. I surrendered to that moment where power met stillness. The last mile was a variation on a theme. Whether a steady climb or a slower pace, I found my way back home.

***

When one of Tim's friends shared the news that she was engaged, I was excited. She had a contagious joie de vivre. She was the kind of person who rented a giant bounce house and catered a full sushi bar for her Superbowl party. And I was sad for me. It reminded me of those opposing emotions I felt when I saw round, glowy pregnant women during my miscarriage years.

She and her fiancé planned to keep their separate houses and commute back and forth, depending on work schedules and custody arrangements, until their youngest child graduated from high school. They had committed to five years of creeping along Los Angeles freeways.

I was lucky that Tim's house and mine were close, but Jason's high school graduation was nine years away. It felt like too long a time to live parallel lives.

* * *

At the Presbyterian church, I would sit alone in the pew while those who had been "baptized in the name of Christ" proceeded to the altar for communion. At the Catholic church, "only those baptized Catholic" and something else I could not quite catch were eligible to receive the eucharist. I would cross my hands across my chest so the priest knew to withhold the bread and wine. The Jesus I had read about in the Bible included everyone at his table, especially the rejected, the marginalized, the vulnerable—and the widowed, for Christ's sake—but these Christians had a lot of rules. I wanted to join in the reverence and the mystery, but I didn't qualify under their rubric.

After church one Sunday, Pastor Henry invited me to coffee, and I agreed.

I arrived early to get a table at the locals' favorite coffee bar. I often saw someone I knew there, sometimes resulting in an impromptu PTA meeting or a spontaneous playdate. I was looking forward to chatting with the Presbyterian minister, but it took him a while to cross the concourse; he seemed to know everybody.

The table in the quiet alcove was well-suited to pouring out my heart, and he was as thoughtful a listener as one would hope for in a minister, his eyes filling with emotion as I spoke. I traced for him my denominational lineage and the series of events that landed me in his church.

"I want to participate in the communion," I told him, "but I've never been baptized in that splishy-splashy way."

Pastor Henry smiled.

"And it seems to me that Jesus invited everyone to his table," I continued brazenly, "whether or not they had checked the appropriate administrative boxes."

Henry reached across the table. "Give me your hand."

I did, and for a second, I wondered if he was going to douse me right then with a plastic cup of ice water. With his other hand he gave a pretend slap, the kind formerly administered by nuns with a ruler, but his touch was light and his blue eyes sparkled. "There," he said. "That's all the rebuke you will ever receive from me. Come to the table. If someday, you decide to be baptized, we can discuss it then, but for now, please come to the table."

I started to cry.

The next Sunday, I took communion for the first time. I proceeded toward the altar with the rest of the congregation. When Pastor Henry offered me the bread, he smiled and blessed me by name. I dipped the bread into the chalice of grape juice and put it to my lips, surprised by its sweetness.

I returned to my seat in the pew, by myself that day, but I did not feel lonely. I felt quietly connected to the divine. I was at home with a God who cherished all of His children—not because they had appeased Him, but simply because they belonged.

* * *

I remained wary of the Catholic church, rocked as it had been by sex scandals, patriarchy, and other rituals of misogyny. If I were to catalog my objections to Catholic theology, I would start with the doctrine of original sin. I don't have time for a deity who intentionally flaws his creations but might save them from themselves if they jump high enough through certain denominational hoops. I have no interest in a god who breathes hellfire, but I am putty in the hands of the One who whispers inherent holiness into every child and who sings of the wholeness within people everywhere. I am crazy enough to believe we are all children of the divine, whoever we are and wherever we fall on the map, off the map, on the issues, and on the spectrum, whether we've been baptized, circumcised, whatever, or not.

I wasn't afraid to challenge religious tenets. If truth is true, it will stand up to the questions.

When I registered my theological dissent with Tim, he shrugged. "I'm more of a cafeteria Catholic."

I laughed. "I don't think you're allowed to pick and choose."

"Too bad," he quipped.

Tim often expressed his frustration with the Pope. "He runs the church like a business," he would say. "If they really believed their own bullshit, they wouldn't be afraid of transparency." I appreciated his willingness to challenge the system.

And yet this man had remained faithful through his wife's illness and after her death. When I kneeled at Tim's side in the Catholic church, I felt buoyed by his strength. There was something about holding his hand in the sanctuary. Sitting together in the silence, listening to the liturgy, wishing each other peace. All of this felt sacred. I did not understand all of the holy hoo-hah, but it brought me joy to have our boys—no matter how stinky, groggy, or grouchy they were—collected together in one pew with their morning breath and pillow hair.

And this surprised me: I felt drawn toward the crucifix. The crucifix is bloody and violent, so heartbreakingly unfair that Protestants display the cross without the dead body nailed to it. The crucified Jesus suffered. I was enthralled by Him.

I was raised on a theology that suffering was unreal, and that the key to release was to understand this truth through prayer. When life hurt, and I was sick with dread and sadness, when Danny was bruised and Jason felt abandoned, then the suffering was pretty fucking real. It didn't feel kind or true to say otherwise. Both Dr. Newland and Roger the yogi helped me to practice being present with my suffering; they taught me to approach pain with gentleness and curiosity. Only when I made space for my (and my children's) pain did I move through it with any modicum of kindness or strength.

I did not believe that suffering was a holy emissary, that my pain served as a bit factor in some grand redemption-through-suffering-styled-architecture. But this prophet whose side had been pierced by the spear carried a certain credibility. This intimate Jesus was in the mess of us, and these Catholics did not ignore his suffering. They built hospitals, they sent chaplains, they rolled up collective sleeves. Yes, they prayed. And they baked, they sewed, they marched, they spoke, they wrote checks and letters and songs. There was a divine momentum within the struggle. After all, the crucifixion did not end the story of the man Jesus. Love persisted.

* * *

On our "date night," Tim and I went downtown, where they treated us like movie stars. Maybe because in Los Angeles, one never knows. Or because they liked seeing a couple who spent more time gazing at each other than into their phones. They greeted Tim and me by name and squired us off to a quiet table, as though dodging the paparazzi.

Tim guided me protectively through the restaurant. Still a gentleman.

Once we were seated, the hostess stepped over with two glasses and poured our favorite Pinot Noir. Tim looked at me over his wine glass and said, "I can't believe I got to fall in love with you."

It was unexpected. And too special to let go.

We chatted comfortably, covering politics, pop culture, and promotions. When I needed more work, Tim had helped me update my resumé and prepare for interviews. Tim regaled me with stories from his childhood, like winning a pie-eating contest when he was eight— "two banana cream pies in under two minutes!"—or the time he won "third place in the ping-pong tournament at the Fun Center in the summer of 1978."

Our conversation turned, as it often did, to our collective sons and our shared future. Gregory was focused on his plans for senior year of high school and beyond. Being a teenager was hard enough—navigating the shifting social landscape, the acne, "The Iliad"—and he didn't want to deal with me and two additional younger brothers. I kind of wanted to wring Gregory's neck, but I was pretty sure if I strangled his son, Tim would find me less endearing.

Daniel resented that he wasn't old enough to drive, and he refused to wear his seat belt when I drove him after school, which made me nuts. We spent long minutes sitting in my car in a standoff, me waiting for him to buckle up and him waiting for me to put it in gear. We might have fun baking chocolate chip cookies together, but then he would follow with a comment under his breath or a remark about "the hobbits," as he referred to Danny and Jason.

Danny liked Tim at the edges of our lives, showing up for school open houses or heavy lifting. As long as everyone remained in his or her separate quarters, he was content with the status quo.

Jason was flexible, probably because he was the youngest. He enjoyed Tuesday mornings with the Timmer, and he looked up to both Gregory and Daniel. Other than chronic disorganization and a burgeoning loathing of reading, which troubled me more than it did him, he seemed to be doing well.

All were healthy and passing their classes, some by a greater margin than others. I admired the ease with which Tim navigated boy shenanigans. He never seemed to lose sight of the fact that boys (even teenaged ones) were tenderhearted creatures. "They're not trying to be assholes," he would say, then adding, "It just comes to them naturally."

"I wish we could all be under one roof." I was becoming increasingly impatient.

"They'd still be jerks," he teased.

"There's a reason parents come in pairs."

"I just think it's too soon for Gregory," Tim said.

Waiting was not the answer I wanted. "If we wait for Gregory to graduate from high school, should we wait for Daniel? And Danny, too? What's fair? What if one boomerangs back home before Jason graduates? Will we continue to wait?"

"He's taking the SAT in May. Let's see how he does."

"I'm *tired* of being second in the lineup of priorities! I want to be *first*."

My love reached across the table to hold my hands in his, keeping my gaze. "Oh my Charlotte," he said, smiling, "you're not second.... You're fifth."

I laughed out loud. Like all the best humor, it was funny because it was true. And that was also why it made me sad. "Seriously, what about me?"

He was still holding my hand when he told me, "Charlotte, I'm not going to take a pass on you."

I didn't know what to say.

"I'll make an appointment for us to talk to Father Tomás."

Maybe his priest's blessing would be a step forward.

* * *

Fr. Tomás was the president of St. Francis High School, the Catholic boys' school Tim had attended, Gregory was currently attending, and Daniel planned to attend. I was nervous. My encounter with the priest in my driveway had rendered me a shivering mute in the presence of the stiff white square at the base of the neck, and I was relieved to learn that, as a Franciscan, Fr. Tomás would don a brown robe, not a clerical collar.

On Fr. Tomás's large oak desk were three framed pictures:

1. the Virgin Mary (naturally),
2. his deceased wife (surprise!), and
3. his daughter (who was quite young when her mother died).

His was an unusual backstory among the generally celibate Catholic priests. He had raised his daughter as a single parent, and after she graduated from college, he attended seminary to become a Franciscan priest. The man had lived a life. *This*, I thought, *is a priest who will get it.*

I sat down on a small sofa next to Tim. Tim held my hand and explained to Fr. Tomás that we wanted to be together, which meant blending our families, and we were worried about the boys.

Father listened to our concerns thoughtfully. "You two are blessed to have found each other." He smiled genuinely and said he thought it would be good for the boys if Tim and I were married. "Children need a mother."

I thought this comment missed the point—children needed a father, too—but I bit my tongue.

Then, he settled back in his chair and said, "Tim is a good Catholic." Pause. "There's a two-year course." Pause. "You'll like it."

End of discussion.

I had no intention of taking the two-year course, or even watching a webinar. I didn't want to become Catholic, I just wanted to marry Tim.

On our way out of Fr. Tomás's office, Tim suggested that we talk to Fr. Andrew instead.

* * *

Fr. Andrew had been assigned to a post in Mexico, but Tim finagled a dinner one evening in May when he happened to be traveling through town. In addition to being a priest, Fr. Andrew held a degree in psychology. Maybe his perspective would be different. He arrived at the restaurant wearing khakis and a sweater, and I already felt more at ease.

"You know," Tim said, teasing the priest, "Father is so handsome that the church ladies refer to him as 'Father-What-a-Waste.'"

Fr. Andrew laughed and shook his head good-naturedly.

Tim ordered a bottle of wine from a vineyard with a biblically inspired name, and I found myself relaxing into conversation with this priest.

When our entrees arrived, Fr. Andrew reached for our hands and said a blessing. Then he winked at Tim. "I'll pray, and you pay."

Fr. Andrew listened to us go on about the children, their grief, their healing, their struggles, their amazing and funny selves. We talked about marriage, and I asked whether my not being Catholic would be a divine deal-breaker.

"None of that matters," Fr. Andrew said encouragingly, waving his hand dismissively. "You are honoring the children and being true to yourselves. Everything else will work itself out."

CHAPTER 39

THE TRUTH IN HIS EYES

Now we had *his, his, his, his, his, her, our,* and *our* therapists. Dr. Newland had suggested that Tim and I see a marriage and family therapist to talk about the practical logistics of blending our family, so we added Dr. Asher to our roster. I'm fairly confident that we were the only happy couple Dr. Asher saw.

The statistics were formidable: the divorce rate is even higher for second marriages than it is for first ones. Dr. Asher informed us that it took a good seven years for a family to blend. Nevertheless, he was encouraging. There were strategies to employ. He recommended, for example, that the biological parent be the disciplinarian and the other of us play a cheerleading role. As for timing, he suggested that we get married before Gregory went to college, so he could come home to a family he recognized.

Tim still didn't seem convinced.

* * *

In early June, Tim and I made plans to fly to Vail for a weekend of mountain biking through the aspens. Tim had purchased tickets for an outdoor concert and made dinner reservations. I imagined him pulling a diamond ring from his coat pocket and presenting it to me at a candlelit dinner with a background of stunning mountain views.

And then he canceled. To say I was disappointed would be an understatement.

Tim was worried because Gregory was "acting funky" about his SAT results. Plus, he thought Daniel might be coming down with something. It was hard to tell with that one. Maybe he was sick. Quite possibly he wanted Tim's attention.

I was sick. I wanted Tim's attention. And I was sick of waiting.

"I promise we'll go another time."

I wanted to go cry.

"I had an idea," he said, tentatively. "Since we had already planned to take Friday off, why don't we drive out to Camarillo and go on a baby mountain bike ride while the boys are in school? We can at least salvage an afternoon together."

It wasn't a terrible idea. It would be good for me to practice before we went to Colorado, assuming we did go.

* * *

The hills in Camarillo would be gentler than mountain trails, but I started complaining about the heat as soon as we got out of the car. It didn't help that there was no shade, just packed dirt paths flanked by chaparral and dried grasses. I buckled my helmet, wishing peevishly that we were in the cooler Colorado air.

Tim made riding look easy, and I struggled to keep up. He coaxed me along, promising to stop just beyond the bend, but when I reached that point, he kept going. Just when he looked like he might be about to find a place to rest, we passed a group wearing bright orange vests cleaning up the trail. We kept riding.

I was crabby. I was hungry and winded and wilting in the heat.

As I rounded another bend, I saw a lone oak tree, shading part of the trail. "Finally!" We rode to the tree and got off our bikes. Tim placed his in the dirt just off the trail and leaned mine against the tree. Then he turned his back toward me so I could grab the water bottle out of his backpack. "Can you also grab the Ziploc bag?" he asked, pointing over his shoulder.

I pulled out the plastic bag, expecting snacks, but inside was a book. I handed it to him over his shoulder and reached into his backpack for the water. He turned to face me and handed me a leather diary with an emerald satin bookmark attached to the spine. Our names were inscribed on the front cover, "*Charlotte and Tim.*"

He dropped to one knee.

The ring sparkled at the bottom of the bookmark.

"Will you marry me?"

He was dusty and slimy. I had the worst helmet hair. "*Letmethinkaboutit*…yes!" Tim wrapped me in his arms and kissed me, and I felt light as a breeze.

The ring Tim put on my hand was not the traditional solitaire. It had four small round diamonds held together in the shape of a four-leafed clover. The ring practically told our love story itself, with our four sons at the heart of our union.

"You can exchange it if you don't like it."

"I love it."

"I've had the ring since March. I was going to propose in Vail, but then…the kids…And I didn't have the heart to make you wait any longer."

* * *

Getting engaged in our forties with four kids between us quickly deteriorated into the practical. There was no bottle of champagne, chilled and waiting in the room. No intimate evening together. No luxurious morning after. Instead, we drove back hoping to beat Los Angeles traffic and get to our respective homes before our boys returned home from school. I would spend the evening with Danny and Jason; Tim would spend the evening with Gregory and Daniel. We would first tell our children and then release our happy news to family, friends, and the grapevine.

Jason was excited. "I like the Timmer! I like his kids! I like his house!"

Danny was decidedly not. "I like Tim fine, but why can't we just keep things the way they are?" Gregory and Daniel echoed this sentiment, but in language a bit more emphatic and less G-rated.

As I was tucking Danny into his bed, he asked, "Do I have to call Tim 'Dad'?"

"What would you like to call him?"

"Not Dad. And I am not moving into that dump at Chatham Place!"

It was all I could do not to laugh out loud. The so-called dump was beautiful. But this conversation was not about a house, it was about change.

"I don't even *want* a stepdad."

"That's so interesting," I said, thinking about Danny as an eight-year-old, the too-young-to-be-the-man-of-the-house version. "Right after Daddy died, you wanted a stepfather. I wonder what's changed for you?"

"Before, I didn't know that you could take care of us." He looked at me with his shining blue eyes. "And now I know you can."

* * *

The next morning, Jason proclaimed, "Mommy, I'm not going to change my name when we marry Tim."

"You don't have to."

Then he asked, narrowing his eyes accusingly, "Are you changing yours?"

The ramifications were not insignificant. I liked sharing the same surname with Sam and our children; it unified us as a family. If I had been divorced, I might have readily changed my name to Tim's, but I didn't want Danny and Jason to feel that I was rejecting their father by ditching his name. Going forward, there would be no way for me to have the same surname as Tim and all of our children.

Ultimately, I would decide to avoid the bureaucratic hassle of name-changing. I would simply introduce myself with the last name of whichever boy I was calling the pediatrician for.

* * *

That afternoon, I went over to Tim's house with Danny and Jason in tow. We sat in the living room, all six of us assembled together. Never has an engagement announcement been met with such glum faces. Jason alone might have cheered, were it not for the brooding expressions of the other three.

"You don't have to like it," Tim said. "We only ask that you be kind and respectful."

I reminded them that neither of us was replacing Sam or Debbie. I looked around at them. Four boys was a lot of snips and snails. There would be stinky athletic socks, tons of groceries, and an unfair amount of grief.

Tim continued, "Charlotte and I believe that we are stronger together for all of you."

A moment of silence, while the boys contemplated us with a sense of foreboding.

"When is this going to happen?" one of them asked.

"Soon," Tim said. I didn't intend to postpone the wedding any longer than it took to formulate a guest list and book a venue. Tim had already placed a call to the church for possible dates.

"Where will we live?"

"Here," Tim said. He and I had discussed whether to move to his, my, or a different house to be determined by mutual agreement, but the location of Tim's on its quiet cul-de-sac with the mountain views was irresistible. Gregory and Daniel were relieved; Danny and Jason were nervous. I was already mourning the loss of my designer kitchen.

"When are we moving?"

"After the wedding," I said. Tim and I adopted a conservative approach on this point.

There was another pause as our four sons exchanged looks.

Gregory said, "Okay. I'm going to Connor's. See you later!" It was good to be the oldest and have a driver's license, a set of car keys, and an exit plan.

* * *

We had been worried about how the kids would react, whether they might go spinning into angry crazy places, but our engagement turned a prospect into a certainty. All four boys surrendered to what marriage meant: they were stuck with us—and each other—for better and for worse. Even though they weren't euphoric about the upcoming union, our sons relaxed. They knew Tim and I took marriage seriously. We had lived till death do us part once before, and we were ready to do it again.

It wouldn't be easy. All the boys were nervous about losing the relationship with their surviving biological parent. To them, Tim and I were like the last piece of pie nobody wanted to share.

They would grapple with the question of loyalty. Forming an alliance with a stepparent felt like dishonoring the deceased parent.

And there would be the obvious birth order disorder. Gregory would remain the oldest and Jason the youngest, but both Daniel and Danny would end up in the middle, where nobody wanted to be. Daniel would not want to lose baby status; Danny would not want to lose firstborn status. To add insult to injury, they had *the same name.*

But I felt secure in Tim's commitment to me. He and I would live our way to the answers together.

* * *

I was shelving books with Aunt Nancy before Jason's third-grade class arrived for their weekly library time. "So, all the boys are okay with it?" she asked.

I laughed. "They didn't get to vote."

She looked surprised.

"It's not their decision," I said. "It's mine and Tim's." Jason alone was happy, and even he changed his mind occasionally, which put our approval rating at about 12.5 percent. If we had waited for 100 percent agreement and approval from our children, we might still be waiting.

I could tell she was biting her tongue. Maybe she thought I was acting selfishly or prematurely. And yet, she so desperately wanted me to be okay again. She never said Sam's name out loud. She referred to him as "the boys' father," if at all.

Blending a family would be complicated enough as it was. I didn't have to justify why I believed marrying Tim would benefit our collective sons to anyone outside the boundaries of our nuclear family. Moreover, marriage is a promise between two people, not six. Tim's opinion and mine were the only ones that counted.

That having been said, it was gratifying to have all eight of our parents' approval.

There was a freedom in planning my second wedding. I knew that something would go wrong. Maybe the band would show up at the wrong address, maybe an aunt would show up drunk or not at all, maybe the florist would forget the bridal bouquet. So many details could go sideways, but at the end of the day, I would be married to this wonderful man, and that was the only thing that mattered.

Still, there were logistics. Immediate family—including Tim's, Sam's, Debbie's, and mine—was close to ninety people. When we added our friends, including children—because at this stage our lives all revolved around children—the tally closed in at five hundred.

It was tempting to run off to Las Vegas with Elvis.

But our family had picked us up and dusted us off when life was hard. Our friends had shown up in every imaginable way and at impossible times. It made no sense to exclude them from our celebration. They were how we got here.

Tim suggested the In-N-Out truck.

I balked. "Cheeseburgers? For my wedding? I don't think so."

Tim smiled and shrugged. "Everybody loves it. If we serve something else, they'll swing through the drive-thru on the way home from the wedding anyway. This way, we save them the trouble."

* * *

Tim relied on his faith in times of crisis and celebration—"on my best days and my worst," he always said—and having a robust spiritual framework had stabilized him when the shit hit the fan. Gregory and Daniel—the "big boys," as we started calling them—had grown up with this foundation, and I wanted the "little boys" to have it, too. Shit would surely hit the fan again. I knew that now.

I made it a priority to get Danny and Jason to church every Sunday, and I let them choose whether they wanted to hit the Presbyterian service, with its musical offerings, Pastor Henry, and children's chapel, or the Catholic mass, with its pageantry and Tim. Tim had introduced them to the "dine and dash," meaning that if all the boys behaved during mass, we would slip out the back door after communion and before the litany of announcements and the final procession, and head straight to breakfast. Occasionally, Danny chose the Presbyterian service and Jason the Catholic mass (or vice versa), and on those Sundays, I would go to both churches. To my surprise, I didn't mind the extra pew time. I was recalibrating my relationship with the divine.

I flirted with the idea of being baptized Catholic, as my soon-to-be-husband and stepsons had been. It would be simpler if we were all in the same physical place, but my Protestant-leaning heart couldn't get past the Catholic patriarchy and its politics.

Like Jacob, I wrestled with the angel. I questioned the dichotomy of a good God and a cruel world. I read memoirs of theologians who had deconstructed their faith. I listened to a range of religious speakers. I talked to Genie, who would later forsake her law career in favor of seminary. I started to think of God less as an omnipotent being and more as a benevolent presence—a holiness within the chaos. This God I befriended couldn't necessarily control the ugly mess, but neither did She ignore it. The covenant was not, as I had believed, "I will fix everything" or "Nothing bad will happen to you." The divine promise is: "I will be with you."

* * *

I took the little boys to Bruin Woods again that summer, as I had reserved the vacation in January. By mid-week, we had rekindled our friendships and relaxed into the rhythm of family camp.

Danny found me lounging poolside, and he was visibly upset. "They say I can't use their drum kit tonight. I have to bring my own."

Indeed, not even the mommy advocate could convince the powers that be to let her son use the drum kit conveniently already located on campus. The family talent show started in six hours. If I left immediately—and barring traffic—I could get home, load up the seven-piece drum kit, and return in time.

Not for the first time, I wished that my child had taken up an easily portable musical instrument, like a clarinet or a kazoo, or even an electric guitar like his brother had. I called Tim to vent about the camp's revised drum kit policy.

"I could bring it to you," Tim suggested.

He dashed to my house, loaded up the bass drum, snare, toms, and cymbals, drove up to Lake Arrowhead, and delivered the entire ensemble to the stage. Roadie, stage manager, and fan all in one handsome package.

I fell in love with him all over again.

* * *

Tim took the big boys on the road trip he had been planning since February. They visited several colleges along the way and ended with Lollapalooza in Chicago. I had known I would miss Tim, but I was pleasantly surprised to discover that I missed Gregory and Daniel, too.

I found myself softening in my stance toward them. I was less hurt by their indifference or antagonism. I wanted to know which universities sparked Gregory's interest. I worried about whether Daniel was eating a balanced diet. When Tim reported that Daniel was dancing happily at Lollapalooza, I felt happy. When he said Gregory was nervous about going away to college, I felt anxiety, too.

I had always wanted more children, and here they were.

CHAPTER 40

HEART WORK

It was a balancing act, to live in the moment and honor the path that brought us together. Tim said, "Isn't it so strange? Sometimes you say something so funny, and I think 'I can't wait to tell Deb—she's going to think that's hilarious.'"

It was pretty strange.

***

To heal required learning to live within the contradictions. I had to reconcile my life with Sam's death.

I was devastated by Sam's death, especially by how he died. I would never have chosen for our sons to suffer this sudden, violent, and confusing loss. There was still a part of me that wished I could have protected all of them, including Sam, from the pain they went through. And yet, I loved the life I was building—with Tim and our sons—and none of this would have existed if Sam were alive.

We wouldn't be who we are without having gone through where we've been, like an oak tree withstanding the winds of change. I couldn't explain it, but I didn't regret it. I couldn't imagine a life other than the one I had lived. And I was happy.

I must have known, even on those early dark days of grief, that it was possible for my children to find joy, purpose, and passion in their lives; it was everything I worked for and what I wanted for the people I loved most in the world. It just took me a little longer to realize that joy was possible for me, too.

I didn't delete my past; it was an integral part of me. I still received letters for Sam. Every week, I drove through the intersection where Sam jumped to his death. Sometimes I thought of him with gratitude, occasionally with anger, often with a smile and prayers for peace—for Sam, for our family, for everyone struggling with depression and despair.

None of this negated how crazy head over heels in love I was with my Tim.

I did not replace Sam with Tim, and he did not replace Debbie with me. Tim and I had our own relationship, and we did not love each other less for the journey. The resurrected life expanded to hold the whole of love and loss and pain and joy. On the one hand, I would always love Sam and never quite get over the heartbreak of his suicide, and on the other hand, Tim was a gift and a light in my life. This life was less like puzzle pieces fitting together neatly to form a seamless picture and more like a mosaic created from the pieces of our essential selves. The fragments and shards existed, individually both lovely and heartbreaking. These component pieces of experience and character were integrated into a beautiful whole, held together with patience and love and grit. The work of hearts.

CHAPTER 41

OCTOBER AGAIN (2010)

"Did you ever figure out why?" It was a question I continued to field. But I had exhausted the whys and arrived at this conclusion: *Why?* had ceased to be a productive question. *Why?* would not propel me forward. *Why?* was a question mired in doubt and guilt and failure. *Why?* rooted me in the past, because it was an impossible question to answer. I would never know why.

The relevant question was *What now?*

* * *

It seemed a form of insanity to have planned Sam's third deathaversary baseball game a mere two weeks before the wedding, but it was important for all of our boys that they see us continuing to honor their deceased parents within our reconfigured family.

Zack had made the trek across town with his twins. The boys grabbed their gloves and ran to the field to join Danny and Jason.

"I have to tell you," Zack said with a chuckle, "the other day your nephew was looking at the Calendar section of the *LA Times*, and all of a sudden he said, 'Hey Dad—George Clooney looks like Tim!'"

"George wishes!" I said, laughing.

There is great comfort in the company of cousins, and not just for the children. I no longer referred to Zack as "Sam's cousin." I called him mine.

I looked out at the field, where the kids were playing. Gregory could have balked at participating, but instead he had taken the lead. He was pitching and encouraging all the players with a stream of chatter. Jason took a swing, hit a ground ball, and started running. Gregory scooped up the ball and quickly threw Jason out at first base.

I looked to Tim for his take.

Tim smiled and said, "Gregory would never insult Jason by letting him win. When he wins, he will have earned it."

Our families were coming together.

* * *

Sam's parents did not attend the baseball game, choosing instead to take their grief to the cemetery. I imagined they would shuffle stiffly, hand in hand, along the cement path. My father-in-law would carry an arrangement of flowers. My mother-in-law would hold a rock in her slender and immaculately manicured hand. She would place it lovingly on Sam's gravestone. They would sit on the nearby bench—quietly, pensively—until my father-in-law could no longer stand to sit. Then he would call her, gently, by a pet name and say, "*Vámonos*," and they would make their way back home.

When I visited the cemetery, later that week, I went alone.

I parked at the bottom of the sloping hill and walked up. I couldn't give directions to the spot of Sam's grave, but I knew exactly where it was. The sapling nearby had grown into a lovely tree and provided a wide swath of shade.

I plopped down on the grass next to his gravestone. I didn't say goodbye, exactly; I would always carry Sam with me. And I wasn't really asking for Sam's blessing; I believe Sam had always had my best interests at heart, even when his mind was too muddled to know what that might be. I just wanted to let him know I had forgiven him. Any resentments I clung to only burdened me, and I had let them go. In the process, I had forgiven myself, too.

Years before his death, Sam had told me that if anything ever happened to him, he would want me to get married again. At the time, I wouldn't even entertain the idea. Now, I imagined he would be pleased. He would have liked Tim; they would have cracked each other up if they had met at a party. I knew he would appreciate how Tim treated me, and Tim was exactly the kind of father Sam would have chosen for his sons.

It was a clear blue day, not unlike the crisp fall day on which Sam died, and as I sat, I felt not so much sadness as an expanded sense of possibility.

CHAPTER 42

A FUTURE WITH HOPE

In 2006, I had been sailing happily along in my clichéd white-picket-fence life, with my husband, two kids, a law degree, and our purebred puppy. If someone had told me then that my life in 2010 would be full of joy and love, I would have believed them. I had no reason to think otherwise. If they had predicted that I would run several days a week, and that I would give up my custom kitchen in order to feed twice as many sons, I would have thought they were touched in the head. If they had told me that Sam would die by suicide when our little boys were, in fact, little, that I would accidentally fall head over heels for the town's most eligible widower, and that I would willingly sign up for three mothers-in-law, I would have advised them to put down their glass. I might have suggested that the margarita or blood of Christ—or whatever they were drinking—had gone to their head. I would have backed away slowly. As soon as I was safely out of earshot, I would have called Bess to mock their harebrained idea of God's plan.

Then Sam did die. By his own hand. And a Genius Grant seemed entirely more likely than my ability to get through a single morning without crying the mascara off my face. Which was about the time that a faith-filled, hope-full, fear-less Jane gave me a stone bearing this verse:

"I know the plans I have for you, says the Lord, to give you a future with hope. ~ Jeremiah 29:11 (NIV)."

A future with hope?

It was absurd. It was infuriating. It was offensive. I wanted to throw that stone through a window. I had had a pretty clear idea of what my future would look like, and Sam's suicide was not part of my vision. I stuffed the stone in the back of the drawer.

The thing is, though, that the verse did *not* read, "I know the plans I have for you, says the Lord, *to give you the future you hoped for,*" which is, I confess, often where my prayers start. When things are going as predicted and desired, then a bright future isn't hopeful—it's logical. Hope is really only meaningful when it's bleak and cold and impossibly sad. In the midst of gripping despair and overwhelming fear, hope sounded ludicrous.

But hope showed up in the darkness, even if I didn't recognize her at the time.

Hope whispered, "*I'm here.*" She sent emails in the dark hours while the rest of the world slept, and she offered to share her milk and cookies because she couldn't sleep, either.

Hope showed up unannounced, happened to be in the right place at the right time. She walked toward me along the sidewalk, as if we had planned to meet to help my sons choose ties for their father's funeral.

Hope was contrarian. She uttered the word *forgiveness* while others threatened character assassination, and her gentle voice echoed in quiet moments when I was alone.

Hope was not afraid of my ridicule. She handed me a book, even though I didn't have the focus or the time or the inclination to read. She waited patiently.

Hope was not smug. She never said, "*I told you so.*" She said, "*I'm so glad you're here.*"

Hope watered the dry ground long before the tiny shoots of my new life sprouted up through the dirt, turning their tender leaves toward the sun.

Hope was inflammatory. She handed me a rock with her message, and she was not afraid of my despair and rage.

Hope inundated me with her relentless love.

Hope's tenacious message was that my story wasn't over. Life was yet unfolding love, joy, compassion, gratitude, strength, and family, not in the form that I had expected, but wholly present nonetheless.

I kept the stone in my makeup drawer, next to my lipstick. I had given up wearing mascara, but I still wore lipstick. I saw the stone reminder daily.

And now, I was stepping into the future that my Janes had hoped into existence.

***

The organ and trumpet began "Rigaudon" *maestoso, con moto*, and I proceeded down the aisle, holding an array of white roses and peonies within a border of pale green lambs' ears. I had refused the fashionable strapless wedding gown; it seemed one perilous misstep away from a wardrobe malfunction and not a risk I was willing to take with five hundred guests and four sons in attendance. My dress was a simple design, the silk top tightly ruched to the waist, with a V-neck and an open back. The off-white silk chiffon flowed to the floor with a short train. I didn't wear a veil. Tim and I both knew exactly what we were signing up for this time.

Many speculated that Danny and Jason would walk me down the aisle or that Gregory and Daniel might be Tim's best men. We did not ask this of them. I asked only that they arrive on time wearing their tuxedos. I wanted to give them space for whatever emotions they felt on our wedding day—for Gregory to feel resigned, for Daniel to feel betrayed, for Danny to feel unabashedly unenthusiastic, and for Jason to feel excited or, like my flower goddaughter Claire, grossed out by the kiss. I didn't know how it would feel to watch my surviving parent get remarried, wondering how the new stepparent would change things, burdened by more brothers, fervently wishing—once again—that the calendar could be turned back three years to an altogether different happily ever after. The last thing our boys needed was added pressure to perform if all they wanted to do was take off their too-tight rented cap-toed shoes and throw them against a wall. I did not even request that they smile for the pictures, and one of them did not.

My sweet groom left his post at the altar and met me halfway down the aisle. We tipped our heads together, and his warm hand steadied mine. When we reached the altar, Father Andrew grinned as stupidly as we did.

The priest began the ceremony by acknowledging that Tim and I would not have come to this moment without Debbie and Sam. We had even included them in the program, *In Our Hearts…Debbie Stratz and Sam Maya*. It amused me to think of Debbie and Sam as a sort of odd couple unto themselves, raising a glass in toast to our marital bliss while simultaneously dishing dirt about our quirks.

At one point, I caught Zack's eye. I knew he missed Sam, but he was also genuinely happy for me. He smiled broadly, and I felt buoyed by my cousin's joy.

Not everyone was so generous of heart, but I had betrayed no one, least of all Debbie or Sam. I was dedicating myself to Tim and our four sons, and the opinions of the extended family were not my responsibility. Anyway, their feelings were not about me or my wedding. They were about losing Debbie or Sam. I understood that loss didn't happen once. It happened over and over, in a thousand different ways over the course of a lifetime.

Tim and I knelt and prayed. I tucked my arm under his and thanked the universe for this faithful man. This was a man I trusted to stay at my side.

As we recited our vows, I looked into Tim's eyes, and it hit me once again that this man knew what "in sickness" looked like: the stage-4 diagnosis a death sentence, his high school sweetheart losing weight, vitality, and function, while he faithfully changed her port, her dinner tray, her diaper. That he loved me enough to make this promise over-whelmed me, and the words "in sickness and in health" cracked in my throat. It was not an untested, optimistic, innocent young love that had brought us to this moment. We knew what "for worse" felt like at its worst: one of us would be widowed again.

And then Tim kissed me, and I could breathe. He kissed me again, took my hand, and led me headlong into photographs, family dynamics, and everything else that awaited us on the other side of the church doors.

* * *

When Tim and I arrived at the park for the reception, the clouds cleared and a rainbow appeared. "Like a fairy tale," they said. "Like Sam and Debbie are smiling on you from heaven."

In the Jewish tradition, the couple is married under a chuppah, a ceremonial wedding canopy open on all sides to welcome travelers from any direction. Our wedding reception in the park felt much the same, inviting and jubilant. One Jane showed up straight from her son's football game, the boy still in his jersey and cleats, complete with grass stains, which was exactly the inclusive celebration I had hoped for.

As the line at the In-N-Out truck grew, the children discovered that the King Kone truck was happily handing out ice cream cones—dipped, sprinkled, or plain. Kids ran dizzily around the park with their dessert appetizers.

Much of the afternoon comes to me in snapshots: Jason grinned from ear to ear with stains trailing down his white tuxedo shirt, a combination of a harmless bloody nose and chocolate ice cream. His rented bow tie and jacket were nowhere to be found. Danny rocked on the tire swing with a buddy—just another day in the park, but with slippery, shiny black shoes. Daniel stood at the lawn's edge, talking with a friend.

In a moment captured by our photographer, Gregory and I leaned toward each other. Taller than me, he inclined his head to hear me over the seven-piece band. I remember saying, "I promise I will never try to replace your mother, but I do hope that someday we will have something special of our own." I couldn't tell whether he heard me; he was likely focused on getting to the homecoming dance later that night. He nodded and let me hug him.

Debbie's parents embraced me warmly. Ted and Joan had chosen to love me long before I stepped tentatively into their lives. When I married their son-in-law, that made me—ipso facto—their daughter. They never treated me any other way.

Sam's mother held me and said, "Charlotte!" She always pronounced my name with a hard "ch" sound, like chocolate. "Sammy would be so, so proud. Of you, of Tim, and of all of the boys. And I am so happy." This moment has always struck me as a testament to her character. Truly, she was my mother-in-love.

When Sam and I had married twenty years previously, his mother had put her hands on my waist and said with delight, "It's going to be hard to fit into this dress after the babies come!" The memory made me smile. I was the same size then as I had been when I graduated from college. Same as when I got pregnant with Danny and after his first birthday. Same again with Jason. After Sam died, I lost my emotional and physical equilibrium, but by the time I married Tim, I had found my balance and arrived back at my normal weight.

The band leader started to sing, "Come Rain or Come Shine." Love took my hand, and we danced.

Tim and I did not plan a honeymoon trip. It was too soon to leave our boys. But we did run off to Ojai for our wedding night. Bess of the 365 days and nights of emails handed us cheeseburgers through the limousine window, and the driver whisked us away.

"I don't know how I got so lucky," I said to my groom.

"I don't know that you did." Tim laughed, knowing that it wouldn't be a quick trip from "I do" to happily ever after.

CHAPTER 43

MOSTLY GLITCHY WITH A
CHANCE OF GRACE

T he limousine brought us back to reality early Sunday afternoon. I picked up Danny, Jason, and Parker, and together we arrived at "the dump at Chatham Place." Danny wasn't thrilled about moving at all, and Jason didn't like having to share a room. Gregory and Daniel were unhappy about having to share their house. And Tim's elderly cats were decidedly aggrieved by the introduction of the dog who, despite the age betrayed by his whitening muzzle, wagged jauntily, exploring the house and yard.

Dinner at home with all six of us under one roof might have felt mythical, if not for the woebegone faces. The dining room table was so narrow that the kids bumped into each other's knees underneath, earning it the moniker "the too skinny table." It was singularly untenable for a family of six.

I had set up new twin beds in the room for the little boys, but it didn't feel like home. Danny and Jason had their pajamas and toothbrushes, clothes for the next day, and their backpacks for school. It would have felt as decadent as a sleepover on a school night, if only they'd be returning home the next day. Instead, all four boys, both cats, and the dog looked at us suspiciously, as if they were waiting for Tim and me to blink so they could start marking their territories.

That night I retreated into the master bedroom, my boy-free refuge, and curled up in Tim's bed. As hard as it was, I would rather be building this life with Tim than my own without him.

Monday morning started early with a kiss and coffee in bed. It was divine.

Then began the onslaught of breakfast preferences, lunch logistics, personal hygiene debates, and managing carpools to three different campuses.

With all four boys ensconced at their respective schools, Team Jane made a dozen trips between my old house and the new one. We raced the clock, moving clothes and toys and books. If my friends hadn't known where the skeletons were in the closets before, they surely did now. They moved those brittle bones right across town in a minivan.

The Janes moved with efficiency and good cheer, just as if they were orchestrating a PTA fundraiser, organizing closets, drawers, shelves. They barely paused for lunch, finishing the little boys' room and starting on the kitchen. One Jane looked both baffled and amused when she said, "It looks like somebody just dumped a box of kitchen utensils into this drawer." And it did.

It would not be easy to transform the testosterone zone into a home.

There wasn't a single linen cabinet in the house, no coat closet, not even a medicine chest. Nothing was organized. The kitchen featured the smallest oven I had ever seen, a broken dishwasher, and no pantry.

The laundry room was a diminutive, windowless afterthought. Only a narrow stacking washer and dryer fit inside. It was as if the contractor had forgotten that people would live in the house, kids who spill, teenagers who sweat, and adults who appreciate clean towels. A single set of sheets would fill the tub of the washing machine. The mound of laundry accumulated in front of the machine was so high that if the washing machine had been a Venus flytrap, it could have simply closed its mouth on a collection of polo shirts and started agitating.

The dryer had two settings: nuclear and worthless.

I would spend my first week in the house with the constant hum of the washer and dryer as my soundtrack.

Around 2 p.m., Susan said, "We have time for one more trip. This time for your things. It should feel like home for you, too."

"Okay. Could you grab Sam's watches, too? So they don't get lost in the move."

I had been focused on helping Danny and Jason transition from the only house they had ever known, but I had grown up in that house, too. It was the house I came home to after college and then law school, the house Sam and I bought from my parents, the house I brought my babies home to. It was hard to let go.

Tim encouraged me to move out slowly. "You don't have to do this all at once. We have time," he said.

Susan packed up a few days' worth of my clothing, the leather box, and the green and brown leopard print ottoman from my recently decorated living room. It was unabashedly girly, and the colors matched Tim's décor perfectly, almost as though Susan had planned it.

* * *

One item that was taken off my to-do-list was my job as an attorney. The day he learned I was engaged, the partner I worked for told me that he had hired a full-time lawyer to take my part-time place. While I thought it was patently unfair that he had not offered me the full-time position, it wasn't worth investing the emotional energy to fight it. Instead, I considered it a maternity leave for my blended family.

* * *

Whenever asked how many children I had, I responded "four sons." I didn't hesitate. All four were mine. Even when one crashed the car or failed an exam.

It sometimes felt like I was playing house. I had imagined our new family, and now we would live our way into it. I set my expectations low. I didn't need our rearranged family life to be great. I just needed it not to suck, but the learning curve was steep. Tim had the advantage of both experience and the fact that the little boys, ages nine and eleven, were amenable to his involvement. He described my jumping into step-parenting as "walking into the buzz saw that is teenagers." I had leap-frogged from elementary-aged children to fourteen-and-eighteen year-olds, whose job was to push away from me.

Teenagers were hard—really hard—surly and selfish, defiant and obnoxious. They were also sweet, insightful, and vulnerable. I began to see more of these qualities in Gregory and Daniel as we spent more time together. When I heard stories about them as babies and toddlers, I wished I had known them then, too. Debbie had been denied the experience of raising her little ones into teenagers, and I didn't take it lightly that I held this position in Gregory's and Daniel's lives. As the adult in the room, my job was to become more patient with my children, more understanding of them, more creative because of them, more flexible for them, and more generous with them—not the other way around.

Gregory watched me like a hawk around his brother, scrutinizing our interactions. He knew Daniel was a pill, knew he pushed every envelope, resisted authority of any kind. Daniel was still so wounded by his mother's death, so angry, and all I could do was be his personal chauffeur or bake apple pies for pi day at school. Once in a while, as Daniel and I were debating the merits of algebra or seat belts or leafy greens, Gregory would smile approvingly and turn away.

"Stay in there with Daniel," one of Debbie's friends encouraged me. "He's a handful, but he's got a giant heart."

The fact that Tim and I had both been widowed made some aspects of blending a family easier than it was for our divorced counterparts. Tim quipped: "I'm not unhappy that the handsome Cuban isn't show-ing up on my doorstep and taking my kids every other weekend." Since we didn't share custody with anyone else, Tim and I could present a unified front for our sons, and we did our best to reinforce the same standards for all of them. Tim and I didn't formally adopt each other's children, but we did draft a joint estate plan that included all four boys equally. Not that there was much left after all the therapy.

With any luck, the legacy they remember will be love.

* * *

I missed my custom kitchen. Tim's kitchen had beautiful light, two functioning burners, limited counterspace, an oddly inaccessible refrigerator, and no pantry. It was perfect for setting out the catering and gazing out the window but not ideal for cooking dinner family style. As I stood pouting in the kitchen, Tim wrapped his arms around me. "Let's order takeout and look out the window!"

I would learn to do that more often, but still, cooking for a family of six and adjusting the quantities to accommodate teenage appetites was something of a culture shock. I spent so much time grocery shopping that I felt like I should pay rent at Trader Joe's.

I didn't rearrange much of the décor. Some things I could not have moved if I had wanted to, like the porcelain Lladró nativity scene Debbie had glued to a shelf in the living room; the wise men and barn animals revere the holy family year-round at the dump. But I did place an order for a simple round table that would comfortably seat six. And I installed shades on all the bedroom windows. In an unprecedented show of unity, none of the boys complained about this change.

* * *

Danny seemed to be adjusting, but he struggled to fall asleep in his new room. He didn't drift off until after midnight, and he was hard to rouse in the morning. My dear husband, I was learning, was also something of an insomniac. He kept a rosary at his bedside, and when he couldn't sleep, he prayed. In the morning, I would discover the string of wooden beads nestled in the sheets. When I mentioned to him that Danny was having trouble sleeping, Tim gave Danny a rosary of his own. Tim explained how praying the rosary relaxed him back to sleep, and that night, Danny fell asleep peacefully. For years afterward, Danny woke up each morning with the rosary beads still wrapped around his hand.

* * *

Daniel was red-faced when I picked him up from school one afternoon. "Some of the guys at school were telling 'Your Mama' jokes," he fumed. "*Fuck them!*"

I understood immediately: "Your Mama" jokes aren't that funny when your mama is dead.

"They can't say that shit about my mom," he said.

"Do you think they really meant your mom?"

The guys might not have even known Daniel's mother had died. But that didn't matter. The boy was enraged, which probably hurt less than the pang of missing a mother he lost so young.

I was grateful for a few miles in the car together. A rogue tear rolled down his cheek, and he wiped it away with the back of his hand. We sat together in the driveway for a moment. When we got into the house, he let me hug him.

"Maybe it would be funnier if they were 'your step-mama' jokes?"

Daniel smiled slyly.

"Tell me about your mom." We sat down at the too skinny table with freshly baked peanut butter cookies and milk and started to talk. He seemed to know intuitively that I wouldn't leave him to unravel in this space alone.

"She swore a lot. And drank too much Diet Coke." He felt betrayed by not having been told how gravely ill she was. "I thought she was going to get better," he said. "They told me she was going to be okay."

I was humbled by the fact that he shared his vulnerable heart.

Two days later he yelled at me through tears, "You stole *my mother's* socks!"

"Excuse me?"

"I found *pink socks* in your laundry!"

First of all, yelling does not equal kindness or respect. Second, you went through my dirty laundry? I didn't say these thoughts out loud. This outburst was never about laundry. He desperately wanted to hold onto his mother, if only by her pink ankle socks.

He kept the socks, and I made a mental note to add running socks in a shade other than pink to my shopping list. Such was the stepmother two-step: a mama joke forward and two pink socks back.

* * *

One night, as I was settling Jason to bed, he blurted, "Mommy, you don't even *wish Daddy was back* anymore!" He hurled the accusation at me and waited.

I looked at him for a moment before responding. I had promised him honest answers to hard questions. "You're right," I said gently. "I don't."

My son's brown eyes filled with tears, and I explained, "Daddy is never coming back. And it doesn't make sense to me to wish for something I cannot have. If I did, I would miss out on the love that is here for me now."

Undeterred, he yelled, "You don't even *MISS* Daddy anymore!" He pointed his finger at me, and angry tears rolled down his cheeks.

"*That*," I said, "is not true. I miss him every single day." I paused, and he softened. "I especially miss Daddy when you're sad or when you do something awesome or just whenever. And I hope—with all my heart—that he can see you, because he would be very proud."

There was a time when my head simmered constantly with thoughts of Sam. Over time, the swirl subsided, but still a thought of Sam floated through—a wisp, a breath, a memory. I don't think I will ever live a day in my life when I do not think about Sam and wonder.

* * *

It was mid-December. I had the Christmas CDs playing, and I was preparing a family favorite turkey meatloaf with späetzle and garlic green beans, when Daniel returned from Christmas shopping with an aunt. I heard the door slam. He stomped into the kitchen. The enraged teenager was practically steaming.

"How dare you!" He pointed a quivering finger inches from my face.

I set the chef's knife down—the recommended course of action when faced with an enraged teenager—and turned toward him.

He shouted, "You told my great-grandma that she would never see her family for Christmas again!"

I did the extended family calculation in my head. Somebody was upset that we would miss their Christmas Eve party this year.

"Daniel, I never said that."

"Are you calling my great-grandma a liar?"

I was instantly aggravated—not at Daniel—at the aunt and great-grandmother who had set his fuse and waited for him to blow. Shaking with indignation, I turned my attention to the trembling heart in front of me.

"Sweetheart, we'll see your great-grandma for Christmas breakfast."

"But you told her she would never see us again!"

Daniel and I stayed in impasse for several long minutes.

I was doing my level best to accommodate all the grandparents—Christmas Eve with my parents, Christmas breakfast with Debbie's, and Christmas dinner with Tim's. Thank goodness Sam's parents were Jewish so we had one night of Hanukkah.

Meanwhile, Tim and his father were in the next room, hearing every piercing word. I knew Tim would want to rescue me and that he would be furious with Daniel, but we had discussed with Dr. Asher that Tim needed to allow me to work through such tensions myself. I took a breath.

"Daniel, you know me. Does that even sound like something I would say?"

He stared at me. "No," he admitted, and his tears started to fall, "but she told me you did."

I started crying, too, and I shook my head. "I promise you I never said that."

The boy was torn. He wanted to believe his aunt and great-grandmother, and he wanted his mommy and all her holiday traditions back. At the same time, he wanted to trust me and be an integral part of our blended family. Above all, he wanted not to have to choose.

The heart grows. I knew this to be true. Love was not a zero-sum game. I wanted Daniel to know—not just intellectually, but deep in his being—that there was love enough for all of us.

"Why would she say that?" he asked.

"I don't know, sweetheart. Maybe she's just afraid of losing you."

I opened my arms and we hugged. He was nearly my height, quickly becoming a man with broad shoulders, and yet floppy like a puppy. We stood embracing each other until we both steadied.

His holiday spirit restored, he dashed downstairs to his room and called out, "When will dinner be ready? It smells delicious!"

Only then did Tim and his father come into the kitchen. The look on my father-in-law's face was a combination of rage and helplessness; he seemed shocked that anyone would heap more friction on a pair who had already been through so much. His was a private witness to the inner work of blending our family. Rarely at a loss for words, Karl pulled me into a tight hug, silently showing his support.

* * *

The depressing truth about therapy is that it doesn't change any of the assholes around you; you can only change your assholey self. In that regard, it is not unlike prayer.

I showed up faithfully on Tuesday not having showered after yoga, not even wearing lipstick. I was juggling my life as a wife and mother to four kids, two cats, and a dog, but I could not say whether I'd brushed my hair.

Dr. Newland was pleased. "That's good," she said. "You're focused on what's important and not on what other people might think of you."

"Mascara would be easier," I quipped.

"Would you be willing to try an exercise in trust?"

I looked at her quizzically.

"You're carrying so much. I wonder what it might feel like for you to release it."

I lay on the carpeted floor as she tucked props beneath every part of me—a narrow pillow under my neck and a bigger one beneath my knees, a light blanket under the small of my back, folded cloths under my wrists and ankles—bearing the weight of my entire body. By the time she was done propping me up, every muscle in my body relaxed. I was completely safe, and the relief was so profound, so exquisite, that I dared not move. I closed my eyes, and the tears flowed, soaking the pillow under my head.

I surrendered. I had this sense that whatever forces of gravity pressed against me, I could trust life itself to hold me securely.

After I don't know how long, Dr. Newland put her hand on my shoulder, indicating our session was drawing to a close. With my eyes still closed, I said, "If I didn't have a pedicure appointment this afternoon, you might never coax me out of this office."

I heard a smile in her voice when she said, "Whenever you're ready."

* * *

Time alone in the car with Daniel was fraught. He still refused to wear his seat belt. When Tim implemented a fifty-dollar fine for seatbelt infractions, I quickly made one hundred dollars, ensuring the child's safety, but it didn't improve my relationship with Daniel. He complained about my driving, my opinions, my dog. My offenses were numerous. The tug and pull in our relationship was exhausting. It felt like he was testing to make sure that I wouldn't leave. I could practically hear his subconscious saying, "How big of a jerk do I have to be to make her go away? Dangit! She's still here!"

Part of the challenge, of course, was that nothing I did would ever compare to what Debbie did or would have done in Daniel's imagination. The dead mother was the deified mother. Perfect was pretty tough competition.

I added a picture of his younger self to his contact in my phone, so that I would see the little boy inside the man-child when he called. I changed his ring tone, so when my phone quacked, I remembered to pause, smile, and bring love to my listening.

I drove the high school freshman to and from school, to Office Depot to get another purple pen for his science class, to friends' homes for school projects or parties. I packed his lunches and found his lost textbooks. Against school policy, I dropped his calculator off at school when he had a math test he had forgotten about. The school wanted to teach him responsibility; I wanted to show that he could count on me.

One afternoon, he told me that he had tried out for the school play. The next day, I was the first to hear that he had gotten the part.

When the round dining room table arrived, Daniel was beside himself with indignation. I heard him wailing to Tim from behind closed doors, "She's ruining everything!"

My offense: I had moved the too skinny table to the edge of the room, where I arranged a display of family photos featuring all of us, including Sam and Debbie. And I had installed the she's-ruining-everything table in the dining room, where the six of us would be able to eat dinner without knocking knees and elbows.

Stepparenting teenagers was a bit like handing my cardiologist a pizza cutter for my open-heart surgery. There seemed no end to the hemorrhaging or the hurt feelings. Every evening, I curled up in Tim's arms. He held me while I cried and listened to me vent. He said something silly to make me smile, and I giggled through my tears. He did not let me go. We chatted late into the evening and made love in the quiet hours.

And when the sun rose on a new day, we began again.

* * *

The day after Mother's Day, Gregory stayed home sick. When I checked on him, he was curled up in his bed, eyes swollen and rimmed red. I was reluctant to check for a fever; the last time I had touched his forehead, he shook me off so violently that even his friends were embarrassed by his reaction. I suspected, however, that even if I were to test his temperature, I would find that what ailed him could not be measured by mercury. It broke my heart.

I didn't know what it was to lose a parent. My mother still made me my favorite comfort food when I was sick, and my father continued to torment me with his unconditional optimism.

"Can I do anything for you?" I asked him.

He shrugged.

One of the lessons I had kept from those painful, longing years before I had sons to call mine was that children were a gift from Life more than a creation of my own. To be a mother in Gregory's life was a privilege. "How about some soup?"

He nodded and attempted a smile.

I went to the kitchen to make a chicken broth with egg drop and noodles, my go-to for my sick children.

* * *

There was a tradition at St. Francis High School that each of the seniors brought his mother a rose during the Baccalaureate Mass, the night before graduation. The 160 or so graduates searched the packed church, each looking for his mother. When Gregory found Tim and me, he keyed on his father. He didn't make eye contact with me. He handed the rose to Tim and embraced him for an extended moment. He gave me a perfunctory hug and returned to his seat with his class.

When Tim handed me the rose, it felt like a consolation prize.

I knew it was painful for Gregory to graduate without his mother, and I was not his mom. But I was still hurt. I had hoped that after having been married to Tim for six months, Greg might be softening towards me. It didn't feel like he had.

* * *

The summer evaporated into day trips to the beach, action films, and more video games than summer reading. As far as I was concerned, the Xbox was a time-vortex, sunshine-deficient, brain-stealing addiction. The boys emerged from their play sessions glassy-eyed, malnourished, and grouchy. If I could have taken a sledgehammer to it and throw the offending electronics over the balcony without aggravating the already tenuous fraternal harmony, I would have. Until—

The night before Gregory was set to go away to college, all four boys were playing *Super Smash Bros.* They sat shoulder to shoulder on the sofa, controllers in hand, laughing and joking and playing together. It made me insanely happy.

The boys were starting to act like brothers: they fought, they had fun, they got jealous, and they protected each other. They would surreptitiously compliment each other, and they stepped on each other's last nerve. They shared a common ground that none of them wanted or would have wished on anyone else; they understood that about each other. They were all so different, and they were living the idea that there was love for all of them in our family.

* * *

And now we had a freshman in college. I had been catapulted from elementary back-to-school nights into Parent Weekend at a university. Tim and I left the menagerie at home with a grandparent and flew to the Midwest for some quality time with our oldest son. I had missed Gregory—his sense of humor, his cleverness—and it was fun to meet his roommates and take him out shopping and to dinner.

Before heading to the airport on Sunday, Tim and I took Gregory to mass and then brunch. When we dropped him back at his dorm, I gave him a hug and said, "Bye, I love you." Like I always do.

He replied, "Bye, I love you."

It was the first time he had said those words to me, and even though, by the widening of his brown eyes, I knew it was accidental, that he only said it out of homesickness or habit, I was thrilled that he let his guard down enough to let the "I love you" fly out of his mouth. It was too late for him to take back. Those three words hung suspended in the air like the thought bubble above a cartoon character, and I snatched them into my heart. I felt like a kid on Easter morning who had discovered a chocolate bunny and stuffed bites of chocolate in her mouth as she ran away, foil still sparkling in her teeth.

CHAPTER 44

OCTOBER AGAIN (2011)

F our years had passed since Sam died, the length of an entire presidential term, which might seem interminable or fleeting, depending. The time since Sam's death felt both. Between 2007 and 2011, Jason lost all his baby teeth and Danny grew over a foot; in some ways they were entirely different people than the ones their father had known. They hadn't forgotten Sam. None of us had. We carried him with us every day. Grief, like children, does not confine itself to convenient timetables.

When I asked Danny and Jason whether they wanted to host a fourth baseball game, they said no. They had grown embarrassed about their father's suicide and didn't want to call attention to his absence. They no longer needed the event to feel the community's support. They found companionship in their lifelong friends and also enjoyed making new friends, who assumed Tim was their father and called him "Mr. Maya." Tim never corrected them. Neither did Danny or Jason.

Instead of playing baseball, Tim, Daniel, Danny, Jason, and I went out for dinner on Sam's deathaversary. Over cheeseburgers and shoestring French fries, the boys traded stories of Sam and Debbie, while I marveled at the bonds forming at our shared table.

CHAPTER 45

CHASING AFTER GHOSTS
AND DREAMS

One of the gifts of a second marriage was perspective. Things that might have bugged me the first time around didn't bother me at all. Tim was constitutionally incapable of telling the difference between a teaspoon, a soup spoon, and a serving spoon. He tossed them all indiscriminately into the silverware drawer. He did, however, empty the clean dishes from the dishwasher and wash all the pans by hand.

He snored as convincingly as the bear impersonators from the long-ago Cub Scout camping night. But he was breathing and very much alive.

Tim danced me around the kitchen when he arrived home to the smell of brisket and grilled onions. "You are my favorite wife."

"How rude!" I laughed, but it made me happy to hear him say it. "I have the advantage that I'm alive."

"That helps," he admitted, kissing me, "but it's not the only reason."

The only thing Tim and I argued about consistently was which one of us would die first. Neither one of us thought we could survive being widowed again.

* * *

I had come to enjoy running. Running didn't intrinsically solve my problems, but it was empowering. There was an alchemy in the act of putting one foot in front of the other. Movement was success. Inertia was not holding me back. On a good day, I reached that meditative space where I was simply rhythm and motion and power.

I did eventually run that half marathon in honor of Sam, some four years after my first try. Bess and I trained together—same running schedule, opposite coasts. Tim took care of all things kid-related when the long Saturday training runs knocked me out for the rest of the day.

On a foggy June morning in Ventura, Tim, Bess, and I crossed the finish line. I couldn't have done it without them. As the African proverb goes: *If you want to run fast, go alone; if you want to run far, go together.*

I'm glad I did it. And I hope I never feel the need to run that far again.

* * *

My little black dog suffered from the congenital heart murmur that commonly afflicted his breed. Our vet was optimistic, assuring me that Cavaliers live into their teens. Parker's heart and lungs were working harder to accomplish less; he was taking three different heart medications. He still loved to play fetch, but he quickly tired, holding onto his Frisbee and skirting past me and back into the house.

Even so, Parker's tail wagged. I didn't look to his head for confirmation that he was well, I looked to his tail. Between his declining health and hearing loss, his eyes and ears didn't necessarily respond immediately. But his tail always did.

* * *

The Bruin Woods summer vacation decision had started to become awkward. Should Danny, Jason, and I continue this tradition separately? Include Tim and Gregory and Daniel in family camp? Start over with something new? It was still too hard to let go.

That summer, the scales tipped in favor of Bruin Woods. Gregory was already back at college, and Daniel's high school started midway through the week, so the plan was for him to stay home with Tim. While I was packing up the car, it occurred to me that Daniel could join us for the first part of the week. I thought it might be fun to share our favorite summer vacation with him. That is, if he would want to.

I floated the idea out to Tim, assuring him that Daniel's summer reading would happen in Lake Arrowhead. He assured me that it wouldn't have happened regardless.

I found Daniel in his room with his summer reading book closed and his computer open. I asked, "What would you think about coming with us to Bruin Woods for a few days?" and braced myself for rejection.

"Really?" He appeared intrigued. "But my mom was a Trojan…" The cross-town rivalry between USC and UCLA remains a vibrant one. We were a house with divided loyalties.

I smiled. "To be honest, there are some Trojans in the Bruin mix." One had even planted a tree on the Lake Arrowhead property to honor Sam's memory.

He jumped up. "What do I need to bring?"

"Jeans, sweatshirt, swimsuit…And your summer reading!"

That afternoon, I drove up to family camp with Daniel, Danny, and Jason. Tim stayed home with Parker and the disgruntled cats.

Daniel loved his introduction to Bruin Woods, notwithstanding the obligatory Trojan-bashing, and then I drove him back home for the first day of his junior year of high school.

About forty miles into our drive, he said, in typically obscure teenage parlance, "You're not my mom, but…you're my mom. You know what I mean?"

I did.

I was not his mother, but I did mother him.

CHAPTER 46

OCTOBER AGAIN AND AGAIN (2012–2016)

E very October 20 came around like my own personal and peculiar lunar new year. Time passed more quickly as the years since Sam's death increased, and still the annual observance brought moments for reflection and comfort food.

***

People didn't seem to get that even though we appeared to be a functioning nuclear family—and in many ways were—we were also six people who still grieved. Children, in particular, revisit their grief at each developmental stage. We kept pictures of Sam and Debbie all over our home, not just glued in albums hidden from view but displayed on shelves and in framed portraits on the living room walls. We didn't draw mustaches or devil horns on their photos (not since Danny was nine, that is, when he had defaced all of Sam's pictures in one album). I thought it was healthy to acknowledge how we arrived here together, but there was no real end to the tears.

We had conversations about Sam and Debbie frequently, in the car, at the she's-ruining-everything table, while watching their favorite sports on ESPN (hers basketball, his baseball), and most often, at bedtime. We honored Sam's and Debbie's lives. We grappled with their deaths. We moved along in our lives, continuing to find love and joy and passion. We were all healing, and we would continue to do so. But we did not ever forget.

* * *

I wouldn't say that my decision to be baptized Catholic was particularly inspired. It certainly wasn't that the Catholics were theologically "right," either in theory or in practice. It was about finding my way together with Tim. I found strength and comfort by worshipping with him at my side, and I was tired of being excluded from the Catholic table. The parish priest made it easy. He put me on a four-month fast-track, and I was baptized at the Easter Vigil service. "Touched by the Holy Spit," as my goddaughter described it, which sounded accurate, as tender and intimate, if disgusting, as a Mother-God's sacramental fixing of Her child's hair.

The following year, Danny decided that he wanted to be baptized as well, primarily because the rest of our family had been, and Jason jumped right in with his brother. Again, the parish priest expedited the process. At that baptism, the big boys brought forward the water for the priest to baptize the little boys. It was a beautiful moment of acceptance—Gregory, Daniel, Danny, and Jason coming together as brothers, the six of us becoming one as a family.

From a theological standpoint, I didn't feel much better from the "in crowd" looking out at those still excluded—for whatever reason—from communion, from leadership, and from heaven's approval. In my heart, I remained something of a religious fruit salad, finding inspiration from the kindest, most insightful and irreverent theologians, whether or not they were Catholic or even Christian. I was inspired by those absorbed in doing heaven's work on earth, not because they gave a shit about any afterlife but because they were passionate about loving humanity.

Most often, I quoted Anne Lamott's sage and succinct religious tenet: "Don't be an asshole." Unfortunately, more than one of my sons attributed this particular quote to me personally in a theology assignment at their Catholic high school. All I could say in my defense was that at least the child was listening to me.

I grew more comfortable with the divine paradoxes: that God is loving but shit happens, that life is eternal but people we love and cannot live without will die, that our imperfections bring us that much closer to wholeness. Our experiences as human beings include the range from love and joy to complete mess, and I believe that the divine is with us in all these places. If we can find forgiveness—for those who have hurt us, and for our own glitchy selves—then the journey will be ever so much lighter.

Eventually, we would attend an Episcopal church whose rector welcomed everyone with this introduction: "Whoever you are and wherever you are on your journey of faith, there is a place for you at Christ's table." This invitation rang true to me. Pull up another chair—or two or ten—and grab a plate. There was love enough for more. It's like our Cuban-Jewish-Swiss-Christian   Science-Italian-Catholic-Midwestern-Agnostic Thanksgiving Dinner table. It's going to be delicious and loud and lovely, if a bit unorthodox, and we are going to laugh until we snort Pinot Noir from our noses, an exhibition of this theology of extravagant and inclusive love.

* * *

I was standing in the kitchen one afternoon when I heard Daniel burst through the front door after school. He called out excitedly, "Hey, Mom!" as a preface to the news that he had gotten a part with a solo in the spring musical. He hugged me, grabbed a cookie off the counter, and dashed down the stairs to his room.

I was stunned. He had never called me Mom; he always called me Charlotte—or worse.

I had baked my way through a lot of flour and sugar and eggs to reach this moment. This child who had provoked me and tested me and stretched the limits of my patience and humor had just humbled me. *He called me "Mom."*

It was all I could do not to dissolve into happy tears. He had grown a Charlotte-shaped space in his heart.

Ironically, this would make his transition away to college doubly painful. Over the course of Daniel's high school career, I had created ads for the theater programs of the musicals in which he performed, as well as his senior ad for the yearbook. I attended every one of his parent-teacher conferences, sometimes with Tim and occasionally alone. I defended him and encouraged him and threatened him and challenged him and grounded him and celebrated him.

When Daniel was a junior, I introduced myself to his religion teacher by saying "I'm Daniel's wicked stepmother." She looked horrified and blurted out, "No you're not. You're gorgeous!" I laughed, and she added protectively, "He only says good things about you." By then he was one of my most ardent fans.

There were many mornings during the course of Daniel's high school career when I stood at the sink, with my heart in my meditation bowl, open to receiving whatever the boy would bring me that day. His pain and grief had transformed me into a more patient and compassionate mother. Some days his raw emotions reduced me to ranting, and other days his gentleness and contagious joy softened my own sharp edges. We had practiced acceptance and forgiveness and found our way to bridge the distance between us.

I loved him with my whole heart, and it was time to let him go.

* * *

"I can't remember what his voice sounds like," Jason mused one night.

It felt like he was losing his father again.

"I don't really talk to my friends about Daddy's death," he said, matter-of-factly. "They don't get it."

It made me sad that he couldn't confide in his friends. They were good young people, but they were inexperienced in grief. In the realm of mental health, it is essential to stay present in each other's distress, in our joy, in our confusion and anger and gratitude, all of it. Not that this is easy, even for adults. I had learned to create space for hard feelings and to hold them gently and with awareness. Jason, too, seemed to know intuitively what he needed.

"They're never going to feel like I did," Jason continued. "And maybe the right thing for me isn't the right thing for them. There are some things that are only a 'me' thing because it's too big to explain, and if it wasn't a 'me' thing then there would be a word for it or something. And everybody has their own 'me' things." Which, if I understood him correctly, translates as: *Everybody is responsible for their own healing.*

* * *

Anxiety took hold well before sunrise on a January morning in 2015. Tim had gotten up with Parker. The little black dog's breathing was ragged, but he perked up when he saw me trudging sleepily up the stairs. At one point he dashed—like an exuberant puppy—down the stairs to steal cat food. Minutes later, he practically flew onto my favorite reading chair. It would have felt as though he had faked the episode so he could steal several pleasures simultaneously if not for the wet-sounding cough. He eventually settled down for a belabored nap. I left a voicemail for the vet.

After the sun rose, I woke up Danny and Jason to get them off to high school and junior high. I felt certain that our vet would adjust the canine heart medications, and all would be well. I had just enough time for a run before his clinic opened. I put on my headphones and laced up my shoes.

I usually ran with music, often clicking "random" and letting it surprise me. That morning's playlist seemed eerily choreographed. Every song featured themes of death and goodbyes. I began to worry in earnest. After two miles, tears started to well in my eyes, and I thought, *Not today. Don't let it be today. Not until after the boys have graduated from high school. They have suffered enough. And I will need this dog to comfort me through my empty nest.*

Several songs later, I returned to my front door, turned the key, and looked over to the little black dog's usual waiting-for-her-to-come-

back-home spot in front of the air conditioning vent. His tail was perfectly, horribly still.

"Nooo!"

No part of him wiggled or wagged. Not when the house alarm beeped.
Not when I called his name. Not when I kneeled to touch his head.

"Parker! No. No. No. No. No."

His lifeless body was still warm. He had had his fatal puppy heart
attack when I was out on my run.

I heard my own wailing, rising from a deep well of pain.

"Don't leave me!"

I howled in that distinctly bereaved pitch, which, if it could, would
bring back the deceased.

It's too soon.

I sobbed uncontrollably, and suddenly the weeping was no longer
only about Parker. It was as if that moment resonated in a specific key,
unleashing all my previous griefs with one triggering note. I had never
had the freedom to express this deep-rooted grief, never spontaneously
wailed after Sam's death. I had kept my composure for the police and
in front of my children. Now I howled, releasing an anguish so raw and
pure it felt like every cell was exhaling pain and gasping for hope. There
was no balm for such pain except to experience it.

I crumbled to the floor with Parker and cried until my heart and
lungs ached. Sweat, tears, and snot dripped together into a wholly grief-
stricken mess. I was not a pretty picture.

I found it oddly cathartic to be alone—just me, my little black dog,
and my grief.

When I eventually called Tim, he returned home and joined me on
the kitchen floor.

The worst part was not the silent tail or the still heart or the unmov-
ing ears or the blue-tongued evidence of his heart failure. It wasn't even
his final piddle on the floor. The worst part was the slow hours waiting
to tell our sons. Their first puppy. A faithful friend. Always up for a
game of fetch. Or a cozy nap. Or stealing a snack. The little black dog
with his soft ears and gentle heart carried their sorrow and lifted their

spirits at their lowest points. Danny and Jason had had Parker in their lives longer than they had had Sam.

Ours may not be a culture comfortable with death and grieving, but ours is a home where broken hearts are seen, heard, and nurtured. When Danny and Jason came home from school, I strained under the weight of their grief. We sat together silently, tears running down our faces. We stroked the cold spaniel ears. We held his hushed tail, the first dead body that Danny and Jason had ever seen or touched. His furry little body was so cold, but it wasn't creepy or morbid. It was just sad. There was a sense in which the little black dog simply left while we weren't looking, leaving his body behind to let us know that he had gone. As if he had timed his death to protect us from the pain of his final moments.

The conversation turned to their father and his suicide. Sometimes we go for weeks or months without discussing Sam's death, but invariably, something happens, and we pick up a thread. None of us had seen Sam after he died. It was a question that, not surprisingly, the boys brought up as they faced death once again. Both Danny and Jason seemed to forgive me a little for choosing not to let them see Sam after he left us that October afternoon. Their father was so much more than that one terrible day, and I hadn't wanted Sam's bloody brokenness to be imprinted on the boys as their last memory of Daddy. It would have been impossible to unsee.

In this regard, the little black dog had given us his final gift—a gentle, tender death. The end of his life was not tragic or traumatic. It was just his time to go.

It was hard to believe that the little dog who was all heart could have died of heart failure. We sat next to him, tenderly stroking his cold ears. His heart no longer failed him, and his love did not fail us.

We were, of course, heartbroken.

* * *

My little black shadow followed me silently for weeks. His toenails were not clicking on the hardwood floor, paws shuffling after me. He was not scratching at the door to be let out. Or in. Again. He was not barking for a cookie. He was no longer wheezing. I heard clearly the echoes of what I desperately missed—the thump, thump, thump of his tail wagging against the side of his crate every morning.

I could hardly focus in the midst of the noise Parker was not making.

He was the best fetcher I had ever had. And those therapeutic spaniel ears had comforted me through long, dark nights. I missed his wiggly waggly self. Parker was no longer love in a dog shape. He was, simply, love.

I had forgotten how distracting an absence can be.

I heard his heart murmuring in the gentle fall of raindrops on the roof, mimicked by the thump, thump, thump of his feathered tail. The winter storm settled like a depression, and I surrendered to grief. Grief is a normal sadness, the protestations of a love that cries for more long after the object of its affection is gone. A heart broken. It was a simple grief, uncomplicated by guilt or rage or fear. I had just wanted more time.

* * *

In the spring, Gregory called me for an assist with a college psychology project. I dropped everything when the boys called me, maybe even faster for Gregory and Daniel, which sometimes made me feel like a better stepmother than mother.

The assignment was to interview someone about their marriage. Technically, he wasn't supposed to ask his parents, but he justified it because: 1) I wasn't his biological mother, and 2) he had procrastinated on this project and was running short on options. As for me, I wasn't going to blow the whistle on him because: 1) our relationship was more important than any schoolwork, and 2) he called me!

The conversation would be taped, so when he started the recording, he acted as though I was a family friend. A few minutes in, he asked, "What was the biggest impediment to you and your husband getting married?"

You were, I thought, and the irony of it made me smile. Gregory's apathy was harder than Daniel's animosity. I had wanted desperately not to push Gregory away, which was a particular challenge when pushing away was the appropriate developmental milestone for his then-teen-aged self. "Well," I began, "when you are a single parent with two kids, dating a single parent with two kids, the logistics are just really compli-cated. It's hard to find time together. There were activities and events and school projects and unscheduled emotional meltdowns and illnesses and, especially with four boys, multiple trips to the emergency room."

After about an hour, he concluded the interview and turned off the recording. We chatted another minute, but before hanging up, he said, "Just for the record, Charlotte, I am really glad you married my father."

* * *

I missed his call that Mother's Day. Gregory didn't often leave voice-mails, but that day he did. I pressed play. "Hi Charlotte—it's Greg. Your son." And then he laughed, realizing there was no chance I didn't know who he was. "I just called to wish you a happy Mother's Day…"

Those two words, "Your son." I was elated.

I pressed play again.

* * *

"Hey, Mom?" Jason's eyes sparkled.

I loved these moments when an insight captured his attention, and he wanted to share his epiphany.

"Isn't it funny how to us, Daddy will always be Daddy? We used to call you Mommy, and now you're Mom. But Daddy never grew up to be Dad. He will always stay Daddy."

* * *

The junior year theology project was to make a personal cross, and Danny had a specific design in mind. The vertical piece of the cross would feature a picture of the building that Sam jumped from. Danny had not previously visited "Daddy's jumping spot" in person. As usual, he reached these milestones in his own time. Now he was ready.

I drove him to the intersection. Danny faced into his grief with wisdom. It was easier to view this landmark through a photographer's lens. Camera in hand, he could distance himself, just enough, to be in this space without feeling overwhelmed by its significance. He took several photographs, crossing the street to find the right perspective. It wasn't a particularly beautiful piece of architecture—storefront on the street level, with four levels of parking structure above—but the sky was blue with bright white clouds, and the adjacent tree was tall and leafy. We then printed an oversized photograph, which Danny wrapped around an eighteen-inch length of a two-by-four.

On the left of the horizontal bar of the cross, Danny placed an old family picture of Sam, me, himself, and Jason. On the right side, he affixed a family picture of Tim, Debbie, Gregory, and Daniel, encircling that photograph with a wide blue ribbon.

He attached a written explanation: *"My dad died when I was 8 years old. He died by suicide. A few years later, my mom remarried to a man whose wife had died around the same time as my dad. She died of colon cancer. I made this cross in honor of the two of them. The vertical portion is an image of the building my father jumped off of, and the horizontal portion is a sideways blue ribbon, because the blue ribbons are the colon cancer awareness symbols.*

"The scripture passage I chose is from Matthew 28:20. It says, 'And behold, I am with you always, until the end of time.' Jesus said this to the disciples after he was resurrected from the dead. I think that this applies not only to Jesus, but also to all who have died. Even though they are no longer physically in this world, they are always in our hearts and memories. Also, in reference to Jesus' resurrection, there is new life that can come from death. Without these deaths, my mom and stepdad would not have met, and my new family with them would not have formed. It is a way for us to find the good in even the most tragic of circumstances."

This from the boy who had, for years, refused to say "dead" or "dad."

* * *

Over dinner one night in 2016, Jason blurted, "Everyone says that Daddy was such a great guy, but I think he's a loser. What kind of jackass abandons his wife and two little kids? Be a *real* man!"

His anger was understandable. He had been abandoned by a man he could no longer remember.

Sam had fathered Jason for six years. Now Tim had been fathering Jason for nearly nine. Tim had coached his basketball teams and taught him how to mow the lawn. Tim stayed in the game with patience, heart, and humor through Jason's teenage stinkiness, tuition payments, data overages, bent sheet metal, and increasing auto insurance premiums. And always through his grief. He loved Jason. It was impossible for Jason to believe that Tim would ever willingly leave him, but Sam had.

Several years before, when the parents of one of Jason's friends had been engaged in a particularly venomous divorce, leaving the child a bit at sea in their wake, Jason eyeballed Tim and me. "Are you *sure* you're not going to get a divorce?" Tim didn't skip a beat. "If your mother is ever crazy enough to leave me, I am going to spend every last dime I have getting custody of you and your brother, and when I do, we'll sit around in our underwear, eating pizza and watching football." In other words, *I'm not going anywhere.*

As a young man, Jason no longer saw his father as a hero. He was disappointed in Sam's weakness. I had hoped that the wisdom of his childhood would soften the edges of Jason's pain and quiet the tumult of his sorrow, but his adolescent rage grew.

"You say his mind was sick, Mom, but I don't think so. He knew enough to apologize in his note."

I didn't have an answer for that.

It was hard to watch my child suffer. I wanted to protect him. I wanted to help him. I wanted to share my insight and my resources, but I also wanted to trust him to build his own resilience. The elephant in the room, of course, was Sam's suicide. How did I balance Jason's need for me to release him with my abject terror at the thought of his following in Sam's footsteps?

How far do I let him fall?

Jason had always been an insightful and intuitive child, funny and social, but halfway through high school, he still struggled academically. He talked constantly in class, often landing himself preferential seating in the front row (or worse, in the Dean of Discipline's office). He'd had the tests: high IQ, highly ADHD, far-sighted. He saw letters in color. I wondered whether he might have dyslexia, but he didn't want to go through any more testing. He didn't even want to wear his reading glasses.

I didn't care about his grades. It was his adamance that terrified me. The shadow of Sam's suicide in these moments froze my own ability to be calm enough to let the child fail. Jason was accomplished and diligent and faithful and kind and well-positioned for success, but he was still a teenage male and therefore at increased risk for dangerous behavior and substance abuse. Suicide rates are rising in this country, especially among young men. According to Centers for Disease Control and Prevention, suicide rates among adults ages thirty-five to sixty-four are also increasing. I am not likely to stop fretting about this issue for the foreseeable future.

We will always carry Sam's suicide with us—not because it defines Sam or us—but because Sam is part of who we are. Because we loved him then. Because we love him still.

CHAPTER 47

HAPPILY EVEN AFTER (2017)

"I waited twenty-five years for you," Tim tells me endearingly.
Every time he says so it makes me smile. I feel as though we are still new and, at the same time, that we have belonged to each other for as long as I can remember.

* * *

When I married Tim, I plunked boxes of toys, memorabilia, and housewares from my house into his already crowded garage. We left camping gear, sports equipment, decorations, and family treasures in a perilously disorganized pile, because we were up to our eyeballs in parenting young boys. Every time I was looking for *that one thing* I knew I had somewhere—the embarrassing photograph from junior high, my grandmother's costume jewelry, the St. Patrick's Day leprechaun—I rifled through boxes and bags to find it. Every time, I thought *I could get rid of half this stuff and nobody would miss it*, but instead of wasting quality time in the bedraggled garage, I baked cookies with the kids or took them to the movies or sipped a beer with my husband on the patio, and the dust bunnies seemed to crank out a few more Christmas ornaments while I wasn't looking.

It was embarrassing how much we were holding onto. Even more embarrassing was how much it cost. We had our garage full plus a large storage unit. Tim would say, "The storage costs about one therapy session a month." And since Danny and I were the only ones still seeing therapists, this calculation seemed reasonable; it was easier to pay the storage fee than to dig into the emotional grenades lurking in those bankers boxes. Our garage was a figurative and literal minefield. Financial records and vinyl ones were stacked precariously around bicycles, coolers, and the lawnmower. But the boys' projects and photos stopped us in our tracks, and we held on dearly to anything with a connection to their deceased parent, even ticket stubs or signatures on a yellowed card. We couldn't replace those, and there would be no more to come.

I didn't want to keep it all, but I didn't want to risk getting rid of something of Debbie's that held special significance to the boys or to Tim. I worried about dishonoring Sam by clearing out everything. Without his stuff, would I remember?

All these pieces—check stubs, knickknacks, Sam's law school diploma—had linked me to him in ways I had already forgotten we were connected. Letting go of the last of Sam's belongings felt like cutting the ties between Sam and his children in ways they might not be able to retrieve. Would I be able to answer the question, *What was Daddy's favorite novel?*, for example, if I'd donated it to the library? Without the stuff, would they ever have that moment when they stumbled across something that jogged their memory of a moment with their father? Like his handwriting on the old-fashioned bank books from the kiddie accounts he had set up for them? Memory is such a slippery, unreliable thing, and the stuff carried its own credibility. It was tangible. It had happened. He was here.

After a few years, the storage cost doubled, and it became harder to justify each month's avoidance. I could have driven myself crazy imbuing every object with special meaning, but eventually I was ready.

Tim and I sifted and sorted, filling trash bags and boxes, some bound for charity and others to the shredder. I gradually got rid of Sam's shoes, hats, suits, books, and files, keeping only his ties and the teddy bears that Jane crafted from Sam's favorite t-shirts. I packed up photographs to keep for scrapbooks and let most everything else go. All we really ever have is our time together.

But by the time Jason and Danny were just shy of a driver's license and the right to vote, I couldn't find Sam's watches. I was furious with myself. I could picture the light brown leather box that I had tucked away so carefully for their sixteenth and eighteenth birthdays, and I scoured the garage and every closet in the house. No luck.

I was beside myself. I had lost the last little pieces of Sam himself.

* * *

When the postcard arrived from Bruin Woods, alerting me that it was time to secure our summer spot, I left it on the kitchen counter instead of immediately sending it back with a deposit check. Danny and Jason had gone to family camp for eleven summers, and Daniel four, but I wanted all six of us to do something together that we hadn't done before. I wanted to take our family on our first international trip. After a few weeks, I dropped the postcard into the trash. I felt a tug of sadness and then a fluttered excitement at the prospect of something new.

That summer, we picked up our rental car from Heathrow and drove out to the English countryside. We toured Blenheim Palace, Iffley Road Track, and Oxford, where we had a little incident hardly worth mentioning involving irretrievable keys in the boot of the rental and a spot of rain. Without a car, we walked six miles along a highway to reach breakfast and scrapped our plans to visit Stonehenge. We spent the rest of the week in London proper and were inordinately grateful for the Underground and ubiquitous cafés. We climbed to the top of St. Paul's Cathedral and explored the Tower of London. We meandered through Harrods and Hyde Park. We played board games every night.

We returned to the dump at Chatham Place happy and exhausted, with a renewed appreciation for history and Shakespeare, a taste for tea and champagne and affection for each other. We vowed never to rent a car abroad again.

The thing that was so beautiful about the entire trip was that we didn't feel like a blended family, we were simply a family. A family with a new puppy, two cats, and two Daniels. A family with eight grandparents and four parents…if you count the dead ones, which we do.

* * *

Tim and I were in the garage, pillaging through boxes of holiday decorations, when I heard him inhale sharply.

"Are you okay?" I asked.

He was peering into an open box, and I felt a fluttering of fear. *What bomb did he find?* An old anniversary card? A funeral program? A favorite photograph?

Tim turned to me with tears in his eyes, and handed me a small, light-brown, leather box. "Is this…?"

I didn't even need to open it to know what it contained. I lifted the lid, and the watches were tucked safely together inside, just as I had left them, one for each of Sam's sons. Tim and I were both in tears as he wrapped me in a hug.

"I told you we would find them," he said.

* * *

I gave the watches to Danny and Jason on a regular summer day without fanfare. They were home, and I happened to think about it. "Oh, hey…I found your father's watches. Do you want to see them?"

They looked to each other first, and then at me. It struck me that both Danny and Jason were taller than the man whose watches I was offering. For a long time, Danny was too angry to want anything that belonged to his father; then Jason was. Now they seemed receptive to the connection. It was time.

Not that their process will end any day soon. Like the hands traveling around the face of a clock, they will continue to revisit their father's suicide. Every funeral hour will contain a hint of their father's death. There might be a moment when they trip over the words "till death do us part," knowing how painful that future day will be, but choosing love anyway. Sam's death will provide the barometer for measuring all their future losses. They might wonder, the year they turn forty-one, at how young that age seems and contemplate how much more they want to accomplish. They may pause again, at forty-two, realizing that they are older than their father ever got to be and feel a renewed sadness at all that their father missed. A beautiful, clear blue fall October afternoon might—for no apparent reason—fill them with a sense of longing. They will think about their daddy if, one day, they look into the innocent young eyes of their own six-or-eight-year-old children. It is my hope that, when they do, they understand deep in their marrow that there is no way they would choose to exit that scene. I hope that they will think of their father with a renewed compassion and come to believe, as I do, that only a significant and fatal illness would have taken their daddy away.

It was time, too, for me to let go of my iron grip on their healing, time to hand my sons the reins to their relationship with their deceased daddy. I could not control their process, much as I would have liked to. When I reread Joan Didion's memoir some ten years after the first time, I was struck by how much of the story revolved around how gravely ill her daughter was and how helpless she was to protect her child in the wake of her husband's death. No wonder I'd had such a visceral reaction. It had tapped into my worst fears.

At the end of the day, Danny and Jason would need to navigate their own journeys. As Dr. Newland told me time and again, "In any relationship, you are only one hundred percent responsible for your fifty percent. You don't get to control theirs." My fifty percent was downward-dogging, meditating, cursing, mental-healthing, mothering, pedicuring, remembering, researching, running, and snacking my way toward healing. I lived my life; my sons would get to live theirs. Still, I hope I showed them that it's possible to feel rage and not be consumed by it. I hope I taught them that it's possible to fail and to be loved regardless. I hope I taught them that it's never too late to start again.

We sat together on the sofa, and I opened the box.

Jason blurted, "I want the black one!"

Danny smiled because he had been hoping for the silver one.

Jason squirreled his away into his room, where he kept a special box with a few pictures of Sam under his bed.

Danny tried on his and then noodled with the different dials. He had already downloaded the instruction manual, figuring out whether it was a wind-up or whether it needed a new battery. It had been so long, I couldn't remember, but he would discover the answer for himself.

CHAPTER 48

FALLING IN SOUTHERN CALIFORNIA

It might have been a perfectly ordinary Saturday if only Sam had taken a nap. Then again, it might not have. I wonder now what might have spilled out if he had allowed his tears to fall. I know I will never know.

What my friend Kirk failed to mention, what he let me figure out for myself, was that the grief sandbag will never empty completely. I will always carry it with me. There will be times when I feel its full weight again—like when the boys graduate, or pull the same stupid teenage shenanigans as their father, or walk with his slightly lopsided gait, or when a desperate friend calls me because her son is suicidal. In these moments, the pain of Sam's death crushes me. There are seasons when it is light, an angel songbird on my shoulder, but there is never a time when it is absent and altogether quiet.

Sam may have thought that he was erasing himself from our lives, simple as a keystroke, but in fact, he had placed his life on the shoulders of all of us who loved him, an invisible appendage we carry, sometimes slowly or with a limp. He did not grant us a new life, or even a fresh start, as he might have imagined in his diminished state, but as we become stronger, more skilled, we come to appreciate that the weight of his death need not suppress the lives that are still ours to live.

After the tectonic plates shift, it's wholly unrealistic to think I could live without fear. But there is a sense in which death creates an urgency in life, an increased intention to live with passion and joy and depth. I have learned to live with the fear, to embrace the life I have knowing that it might hurt, to let my children soar knowing that they might fall, to be touched by the beauty of a landscape knowing that it could go up in flames. To allow myself to love open-heartedly, and if the unimaginable comes to pass, even then, to allow it to open a place of greater compassion, patience, and trust. I will not let fear take the wheel, but I might let her ride shotgun, as long as she whispers and wears her seat belt and keeps a vigilant eye on the edges of the road and the journey ahead. I am still learning to live in the mystery.

I know too well that love and prayers are insufficient to ensure the outcome I most desire, and also that love simply is, though often in ways that I cannot predict. The "Good News," such as it is, is that the story isn't over yet. I hold fear in one hand and hope in the other, and I let light and strength draw me forward into the unknown.

When I look at the picture of Jason I took on that fall day in October, his sweet six-year-old self looks adorable and innocent in his garish soccer uniform. The memory, though colored with sadness, makes me smile. But most of what I see when I look at that photograph lies beyond its borders. At that moment, Danny was playing at the edge of the soccer field, and Sam was across town climbing up the stairwell of a parking structure. I see, too, a man I did not know fighting for his young wife's life and two more sons I would one day call mine. I hold the photograph in my hand, and I see so much more life—and so much more love—than I could ever have imagined.

ACKNOWLEDGMENTS

T his book took me twelve years to live and a decade to write. I am grateful to so many people whose lives have touched mine and whose literary influence has shaped *Sushi Tuesdays* into the book I had hoped it would be.

Many thanks to my agent, April Eberhardt, who had faith in me and championed this memoir from the beginning and through every step.

Heartfelt gratitude to Karin Gutman who built the narrative scaffolding to hold up the story and whose writing community provided a safe place to write.

It has been a joy to work with the team at Post Hill Press, led by the incomparable Debby Englander, especially Heather King and Melissa Smith, who were patient with my questions and carefully shepherded *Sushi Tuesdays* to completion. Special thanks to Nikki Terry for her thoughtful website design, to Merri Weir for being my Twitter partner, and to my publicist Kim Dower for her work to connect readers with *Sushi Tuesdays*.

Words would not have been wrestled to the page without my writing partner, Joanie Raney, her keen eye and thoughtful questions. She is several Janes-worth of friends, a faithful hiking buddy, fellow book group junkie, parental sounding board, and my least complicated friend.

I'm indebted to early readers of the manuscript: to Genie Baumann, lifetime winner of the funny contest and fellow recovering attorney, who read, reviewed, and rah-rah'ed the manuscript too many times to count; to Katherine Tasheff, whose memory, photography, emails, sass, snark, and brutal honesty I depend on (Did I mention I love you?); to Kirk Oden, companion on the journey and purveyor of bacon, dark chocolate, and celebratory convictions; to Chanel Brenner, for her poet's eye view; and to Alec McCabe, whose journalistic lens provided feedback well above my paygrade.

I am grateful to dear friends: Christine & Stuart, whose friendship and culinary skills made and make my weekends so much better; Katie B., whose friendship and faith has been a gift in my life since we were kids; Caren C., who chose paint colors for my walls, my outfits for special occasions, and the love of my life; Jay & Connie, who have held me in their arms and prayers as long as I can remember; my "big sister" Milly M., for teaching me how to show up in a crisis; John & Catlan, John & Louise, and Christopher B., for generations of friendship; and Anne D. for extended emotional support hikes.

Thank you to Ginny and the She-Wolves: Denise, Jenny, Maria, Rashmi, Susan, and Susie; for patience and laughter through the miles, the injuries, the tears, and the personal bests.

Thank you to the club nobody wants to be in: Elise, Lori, and Suzanne; for the gentle welcome and the pomegranate martinis.

Thank you to my book groups, my small group, my Bruin Woods buddies, my yoga instructors: Valerie A., Bettina A., Monica B., Ann B., Rosalyn J., Ellen K., Mary P., Joan R., Kathy S., Rachel L., Mary D., Nancy Y., Katie B., Katy C., Diane D.B., Rora M., Jenny S., Kim & Natalie B., Carol E., Andree F., Lori G., Carol E., Loa B., Krissy H., and Roger N.

Thank you to the Janes by so many names: Chen A., Angela B., Caroline B., Joe B., Martha M., Tom B., Claire C., Ernesto D., Robin D., Cynthia H., Lisa H., Madeleine H., Tiffany H., Cynthia J., Joyce L., Alison M., Kyle M., Kim M., Lori M., Bryn O., Ilana P., Jane P., Pam R.-L., Belinda R., Karen R., Marti S., Jon T., Krissy Z, Katie & Chad, Laura & Tom, Dick & Cindy, Jack & Suzie, Melinda & Rob, and Lauryn & Tim.

Thank you to Tim's Janes: Janet B., Ed C., Greg C., Dyon T., Taline K., Molly M., Gloria N., Coach Pop, Karen S., Mark S., Marcy W.,

Bill & Suko, Steve & Kim, Herb & Beth, Wes & Marissa, Peter & Christine, Alison & Mike, Lauren & Luis, Stephen & Jeannette, Andrea & Camy, Tom & Gabi, Cathy & Jim, Lisa & Lew, George & Lynn, Curtis & Stella, Sandy & Mark, Barbara & Tom, Paul & Annie, John & Annie, Julie & Marty, Kathleen & Mark, and Alan & Lin.

Note bene: Thankfully, *his* and *her* Janes are now all *ours*.

I so appreciate my family's prayer warriors and therapists: Fr. Chris, Pastor Gary, Fr. Matt, Rev. Mike, Fr. Tony, Dr. Sara D., Dr. Jane E., Dr. Ken H., Dr. Matt J., Dr. Debra K., Dr. Karen S., Patricia S., and Rev. Alice Z., who named this book a decade ago. With special thanks to Sister Carolyn and the spiritual reflection sisterhood, especially Pat B.

I have the most incredible family without whom none of this would be possible. I am especially grateful for my parents Rosemary and Paul, and my sister Mary and brother-in-law John; Tim's parents Connie and Karl, and his sister Karla; my brothercousin Zack, whose unconditional love for my children and me continues to sustain us; my sistercousins Fanny and Nyla, who lift me up and keep me laughing; my sistercousin Heather, for encouraging me to dream out loud; my Cuban family, Gaston & Regina, José & Silvia, Mimi & Jimmy, Robbie & Melissa, Grace, and Blue, for their continued love and connection; Ted & Joan, for their leadership and open hearts, and my sisters Janet and Sandy.

I remain grateful to Sam for his life, his love, and his legacy. And to Sam's first responders, Good Samaritans, and the Pasadena Police Department; thank you for doing the worst part of your job well.

I am grateful to Debbie for her life and her loves. She knew that her husband and children would continue to find love, and it is my honor to love them.

When I started putting the suicide survivor's journey into words, I didn't know where the writing might lead or who might connect with it, but I decided that if sharing my heart made a difference in one person's life, then it would be worth it. I am grateful to every reader of *Sushi Tuesdays*. You are my One.

My children and children-in-love: Jason, Danny, Daniel & Emily, and Gregory & Amber, and my granddaughter Maeve; you all are my reasons.

And my husband Tim: thank you for everything; you are my heart's beat.

ABOUT THE AUTHOR

Author photo by:
Karen Ray karenrayphotography.com

Charlotte Maya writes about suicide loss, resilience, and hope on her blog, SushiTuesdays.com. Widowed at thirty-nine, when her children were six and eight, Charlotte's writing explores the intersections of grief, parenting, and self-care—particularly within the context of suicide. Her work has been highlighted in *Hippocampus Magazine* and on The Mighty, and she has been featured on the A2A Alliance and the *Your Next Chapter* podcast with Angela Raspass. Charlotte lives in Southern California with her family and enjoys hiking in the local foothills, as well as downward-dogging with her so-called hunting dog. She received her B.A. from Rice University and her J.D. from UCLA.